the
daniel
cure

the
daniel
cure

The Daniel Fast Way to Vibrant Health

SUSAN GREGORY
& Richard J. Bloomer, PhD

ZONDERVAN®

ZONDERVAN

The Daniel Cure
Copyright © 2013 by Susan Gregory and Richard J. Bloomer

This title is also available as a Zondervan ebook. Visit www.zondervan.com/ebooks.

This title is also available in a Zondervan audio edition. Visit www.zondervan.fm.

Requests for information should be addressed to:

Zondervan, *Grand Rapids, Michigan 49530*

Library of Congress Cataloging-in-Publication Data

Gregory, Susan, 1950 –
    The Daniel cure : the Daniel fast way to vibrant health / Susan Gregory and Richard J. Bloomer.
        pages cm
    Includes bibliographical references and index.
    ISBN 978-0-310-33565-8 (hardcover)
       1. Diet therapy. 2. Fasting – Religious aspects – Christianity. 3. Nutrition. 4. Reducing diets – Recipes. I. Bloomer, Richard J. II. Title.
    RM216.G82   2013
    615.8'54 – dc23   2013020504

Published in association with the literary agency of Ann Spangler and Company, 1420 Pontiac Road S.E., Grand Rapids, MI 49506.

Cover photography: iStockphoto®
Interior photography: iStockphoto®
Interior design: Beth Shagene

Printed in the United States of America

13 14 15 16 17 18 19 20 /DCI/ 23 22 21 20 19 18 17 16 15 14 13 12 11 10 9 8 7 6 5 4 3 2 1

We dedicate this book to those who shared their experiences with us so that we could in turn share with others. We thank the men and women who committed themselves to the Daniel Fast clinical studies, to the thousands of people who have shared their fasting stories on our digital platforms, and to those whom we have personally met over the years. Thank you for your dedication, generosity, and sincerity.

contents

PART 5

twenty-one-day devotional

PART 6

conclusion and resources

acknowledgments

SUSAN GREGORY

I am humbled and thankful to have the opportunity to teach and support so many men and women around the world as they seek a deeper relationship with God through prayer and fasting. I always enjoy hearing the stories as they enter into this holy discipline.

To Anna Andrews: I appreciate so much the support you provide to me and to the thousands of people who come to us for prayers, information, and encouragement.

To my support team: Thank you for your generous help whenever I need assistance, answers, or wise solutions that keep my work strong and viable in this ever-changing environment.

To my family: I give thanks for your love, encouragement, and understanding as I take leave with my computer and write, and write, and write some more.

To my coauthor, Rick Bloomer: Thank you for following God's urging to start the Daniel Fast clinical studies, for leading and inspiring your excellent research team, and for your commitment to truth and excellence.

To Ann Spangler: Only God knew so many years ago when we met in Israel that we would be linked together as co-laborers for the cause of Christ as author and literary agent. I so appreciate your professionalism, wise counsel, and friendship.

To Sandra Vander Zicht and Tom Dean from Zondervan: Thank you for your commitment to healthy living and for championing this work and leading it to the pages on which it now resides.

To God: Thank you for your love, grace, and care as you allow me to minister to others and lead them to know Christ and his limitless love and sound ways.

RICHARD ("RICK") J. BLOOMER

First and foremost, I am grateful to my Lord: Thank you Father for leading me to the place in my life where I possess the knowledge, experience, and ability to coauthor this book, and for providing me with the motivation and desire to get this information on paper in an attempt to help others. What a blessing it is to be a part of your master plan.

To my wife, Chrissy: Thank you for your continued support—including carving out time for me to focus on my writing. Your interest and encouragement have been instrumental to my success. In particular, your growing walk with the Lord has motivated me to further pursue my own relationship with him. Indeed, a godly woman is the best gift a husband could ever ask for.

To my two children, Evan and Madison: Thank you for allowing Dad to spend time writing this book when I typically would be spending the time playing with you, for keeping the noise in the house to a manageable level while I worked at home, for calling me downstairs to dinner all those nights, and for giving me the love that every father desires.

To our family friend Pam Custer: Thank you for turning Chrissy on to the Daniel Fast. Without your prompting, Chrissy and I might never have done the fast, my team might never have done the related research, and I might never have coauthored this book.

To all of my research assistants over the years: Thank you for the countless hours spent in the lab in support of our research endeavors. *Your* efforts have allowed *my* efforts to look that much better.

To Susan Gregory: Thank you for keeping me on track with my writing and for having the passion to guide so many into a growing relationship with the Lord.

To Sandy Vander Zicht at Zondervan: Thank you for sharing your editorial wisdom and expertise. A true master at your craft, you have helped shape this book into its final form, and we are fortunate to have your guiding eye directing our text.

To all of the other experts at Zondervan, including the editorial staff, as well as Tom Dean and the marketing staff: Thank you for having the vision and passion for making this book a reality and seeing it through to its final form.

introduction

WE ARE IN A CRISIS. AS A NATION, WE ARE IN A REAL MESS WHEN IT COMES to our health and well-being—spiritually, emotionally, and physically. Spiritually, many people are alienated from God or refuse to accept Jesus as Lord. Emotionally, many of us struggle with issues such as ongoing depression, relational wounds, or self-defeating behaviors. But it is perhaps the physical aspect of this crisis that is most striking. The sad truth is that the vast majority of us fail to adequately care for ourselves. Some are dangerously unhealthy due to a lack of knowledge about how to live a healthy lifestyle. Others know what to do but can't seem to let go of the sweet, salty, or fatty foods that threaten their health. The overwhelmingly poor state of our physical health is so pervasive, many actually consider it *normal* to have a lifestyle characterized by inadequate sleep, lack of physical activity, and unhealthy eating habits.

This health crisis has led to an epidemic rise in *lifestyle* diseases—those that can be prevented or controlled in most circumstances by personal choices—such as obesity, type 2 diabetes, and cardiovascular disease. The rapid increase in lifestyle diseases is prevalent across populations, regardless of race, gender, socioeconomic status, and religious affiliation (or lack thereof). And these conditions have a direct or indirect impact on *all* of us. First, we are impacted economically by the rising costs of health care and medical insurance. Second and more importantly, we are impacted physically by an impaired quality of life. Even if you don't suffer from one of these diseases personally, it's likely someone you care about does. Or perhaps you are living a life free of disease but recognize that your lifestyle choices are not conducive to optimal health. You recognize the need to make changes. In this book, we offer a surprisingly simple solution—one we hope you will consider.

PERSONAL ENCOUNTERS WITH THE DANIEL FAST

In 2007, my coauthor Susan Gregory followed a divine prompting to blog about the Daniel Fast, a plant-based partial fast inspired by the prophet Daniel. To date, her blog (*www.daniel-fast.com*) has received more than 9 million visits. With so many people interested in learning more, Susan has had the privilege of guiding fasts for tens of thousands of individuals, many of whom have come to know Christ through their experience. Now known as "The Daniel Fast Blogger," Susan is the author of the best-selling book *The Daniel Fast: Feed Your Soul, Strengthen Your Spirit, and Renew Your Body* and continues to coach many who want to explore the spiritual benefits of fasting.

I (Rick) first encountered the Daniel Fast a year later, but in a different way. In the fall of 2007 my wife, Chrissy, was pregnant with our second child, and the twenty-week ultrasound revealed that our soon-to-be-born daughter had spina bifida. From the time of Madison's diagnosis until her birth approximately eighteen weeks later, we learned all we could about the condition. Within her first three days of life, she had two surgeries. The first repaired the spinal defect — an open "sac" on her back that had to be closed to prevent infection and additional damage to her spinal cord. The second placed a flexible tube, called a ventriculo-peritoneal shunt, in the left ventricle of her brain. The shunt allowed cerebrospinal fluid to drain into the abdomen, avoiding a buildup of excess fluid and pressure in the brain — a common condition in children and adults with spina bifida.

When Madison was six months old, the shunt stopped working properly and needed to be replaced. She underwent surgery and in the days that followed developed an infection that required hospitalization. She received intravenous antibiotics and after three days was released. On returning home, Chrissy began a twenty-one-day Daniel Fast. She had learned about the fast from a family friend. Her purpose was simple — to pray for our daughter's health. About a week later, Chrissy took Madison out of the bathtub one night and noticed a one-inch bulge on the side of her neck. We knew from experience and from all of our reading and study what an infected shunt looked like — and this was it.

We quickly called the neurosurgeon, who told us to get to the hospital right away. It was about 7:00 p.m. We put Madison down to sleep in our bedroom while we hurriedly packed and made arrangements for someone to come to the house and stay with our two-year-old son, Evan. At one point, Chrissy looked up from packing her suitcase and said, "How will I ever comply with this fast in the hospital?" We knew from the fourteen days we'd spent in the hospital following Madison's birth that hospital food was not remotely Daniel Fast compliant. The last thing Chrissy needed was one more complication. She had enough stress caring for a severely ill child. But after thinking about it, Chrissy felt a strong need to continue the fast. She had made the commitment to dedicate herself to the Lord during her twenty-one-day fast, and she would stick to it. Along with clothing and a toothbrush, she packed rice cakes, natural peanut butter, and fruit.

Within an hour, our friend arrived who was to care for Evan, and we were ready to leave. Chrissy went into our bedroom to wake Madison and suddenly called me. I thought something must be wrong and expected the worst. But when I looked at Madison, I saw that the bulge from her shunt was no longer protruding on her neck. No swelling, no discoloration—perfectly and beautifully normal! We called the neurosurgeon, and she suggested we continue to observe Madison's condition and see how things looked in the morning.

Well, in the morning, Madison looked great, and—praise be to God—she has not had one major health problem since that night, now more than five years ago. In fact, she started walking on her own in the fall of 2010, running and jumping in the summer of 2011, and taking ballet lessons in the fall of 2012! God is powerful and miracles *do* happen every day.

Some people might consider the issue with the shunt and Chrissy's resolve to keep her fast a mere coincidence, but we know better. Madison's healing was the awesome and mighty hand of God at work, abundantly blessing our family! And this is just one of the miracles our family has experienced through fasting.

CLINICAL STUDIES OF THE DANIEL FAST

This initial experience prompted both Chrissy and me to begin 2009 with a Daniel Fast. After completing my first fast, I was impressed not only with how it impacted my spiritual growth but also with the health benefits I experienced. In fact, I was so intrigued that I decided to design a clinical study to investigate the health-specific effects. Not everyone has the option of launching a scientific study, but it was relatively easy for me. As a professor and director of the Cardiorespiratory/Metabolic Lab at the University of Memphis, my ongoing research is focused largely on the cardiovascular and metabolic impact of using nutrition to manage and treat disease. My research team and I conducted the first clinical investigation of the Daniel Fast in the fall of 2009.

Our initial results were more than impressive, demonstrating favorable effects on a variety of health-specific outcomes, including reductions in blood pressure, cholesterol, and markers of systemic inflammation,* as well as an increase in antioxidant capacity† and molecular compounds important for blood vessel health and blood flow. Since that initial work, we have conducted several additional studies, all demonstrating positive outcomes and supporting our initial findings.‡

During my research I became aware of Susan's work with the Daniel Fast, and I contacted her in 2010 to share our research results. We were both excited about each other's work, and even in that first conversation we discussed the possibility of coauthoring a book. You are now reading that book. Indeed, God has an interesting way of drawing people together to bring about his plans.

HOW THIS BOOK WILL HELP YOU

In this book, we provide spiritual, educational, and health-specific reasons to consider an initial twenty-one-day Daniel Fast. We also offer evidence showing how the Daniel Fast provides health-enhancing effects and why these effects are important—with emphasis on obesity, type 2 diabetes, cardiovascular disease, and inflammation. We provide tools and tips to help you through the process of adopting a modification of the Daniel Fast as a sustainable lifestyle that we call the Daniel Cure. We give you information on nutrition essentials, a variety of Daniel Fast recipes, and options for modifying the traditional Daniel Fast approach to fit your lifestyle. Finally we provide, as the overarching theme of the book, biblically based guidance to assist you in your quest.

This book is about much more than just information—it's about understanding that information and putting into practice what you have learned. We encourage you to engage the Daniel Cure in four steps.

1. Carefully and prayerfully read the chapters in part 1, "About the Daniel Cure," to understand the true power of fasting and prayer. Seriously consider how this plan can favorably impact your life and the lives of those you interact with.

---

*Inflammation is God's creative way of helping the body protect itself. With any injury or infection, the body causes inflammation to promote healing. However, long-term inflammation can be a problem. See chapter 8 for more information.

†Antioxidant capacity is the total of all antioxidants working together to help fight off free radicals, to neutralize their damaging effects. In general, a higher antioxidant capacity is preferred.

‡For more information about our research, read "The Science behind the Daniel Fast" on page 281.

2. Absorb the information presented in part 2, "Taking Control of Your Health," as well as in the appendixes to assess the current state of your health. What are you doing well? What could you be doing differently? Are there family members or friends who might embark on a lifestyle change with you? Starting this plan with someone (your spouse or other close family member or a friend) may be of great benefit to you. Consider the evidence and then think about how altering your food intake in accordance with the Daniel Cure guidelines may have a profound impact on your overall health and quality of life.
3. Study the material in part 3, "Getting Started," to understand how you can make the Daniel Cure work in your life. This includes a vitally important planning stage that will help you to start and finish strong.
4. Review part 4, "Meal Planning and Recipes," to generate ideas for meals and snacks to include in your weekly food plan. Add these to the healthy foods and meals you regularly consume now to generate a realistic and health-enhancing meal plan that you can adhere to.

Once you are familiar with the information, we encourage you to begin your plan with a traditional twenty-one-day Daniel Fast. During your fast, consider using the twenty-one devotions in part 5 to help you meditate on God's Word and listen for his guidance. You may want to keep a journal to reflect on your spiritual growth, on God's direction in your life, and on what you are learning about your relationship with food. The twenty-one-day fast is a powerful launching pad for a new way of healthy eating because it helps you to break from old habits while providing both spiritual guidance and nutritional principles to sustain your lifestyle journey. Your basic nutrition knowledge will improve as you read food labels, a necessity so that you know what you are consuming. And you'll have a better understanding of recipes and food pairings and find out which foods you enjoy most. During the twenty-one-day fast, you can adjust your plan according to your preferences, using the information in part 3 as your guide.

Although our work with the twenty-one-day Daniel Fast provided the impetus for this book, what you now have in your hands is much more than a short-term plan. We encourage you to consider adopting this plan (or a modification) for *life*.

AN INVITATION TO A LIFESTYLE

We invite you to accept this life-changing plan — the Daniel Cure. Our goal is to provide insight and guidance to lead you through a meaningful experience of a twenty-one-day Daniel Fast and to open the way for you to adopt a whole new approach to food based on its principles. That's ultimately what the Daniel Cure is—a lifestyle. Why would we encourage you to make such a significant decision? Because we believe it can change your life—in body, soul, and spirit.

Will this be easy? Probably not. But it is doable. Each year, thousands of people successfully adopt a new and healthy lifestyle of optimal nutrition. Simply follow the guidelines presented in this book and seek the Lord's help every day. Even if you've tried many other plans in the past and failed, we invite you to try again. This time is different. This time you will succeed. This time you have a plan that is realistic, a plan that is focused not simply on cutting calories and losing weight but on a physical and spiritual renewal. This time you have God as your guide and as your daily companion. Come to him and embrace his grace for your journey. He will meet you right where you are.

about
the daniel cure

CHAPTER 1

are you ready
to feel better?

"I'VE STRUGGLED WITH WEIGHT ISSUES ALL MY LIFE," SAID PATTY, A SOFT-spoken woman in her mid-forties. "I'm one of those who have tried every diet available, but nothing ever worked for me. That's why I was so surprised when I started losing weight on the Daniel Fast. It was so easy for me. Plus, my cholesterol counts got into a healthy range ... and I felt better than I've felt in years!"

Patty is like many men and women who start out using the Daniel Fast primarily for spiritual reasons but experience significant improvement in their physical health as well. Within a few days, most people sense an increase in their energy level. Many who have been suffering with joint pain can move more freely with little or no pain. Many with elevated cholesterol and blood pressure note a dramatic decrease — one that places their values within the "normal range." Those with diabetes can regulate their blood-sugar levels using food rather than increased medication. It might seem hard to believe that a plan that is so simple could have such dramatic benefits — and that positive changes start to happen within days! But this is a common experience for Daniel Fast participants.

So, how might something like this happen for you? Here's one possibility. Imagine that you feel chronically sluggish and most days you have a hard time pulling yourself out of bed. You start the Daniel Fast, a biblically based partial fast that restricts some foods. For the first time in your life, you eat a variety of meatless meals and drink only water. Within a few days, you begin to feel better. In fact, you feel years younger and have more energy than you've had in a very long time.

Or imagine that you're diagnosed with high cholesterol. The doctor could prescribe medication to lower your cholesterol. Or you could treat your high cholesterol with a healthy food plan and possibly no medication. This appeals to you. Not only would your cholesterol levels improve but you could experience other health benefits, including weight loss and an increase in energy. You'd also reduce significantly your risk for a variety of lifestyle diseases. You might even feel more balanced emotionally and stronger spiritually. These are all possible simply by giving your body the food it was designed to use.

That's why so many, after using the Daniel Fast for a mere twenty-one days, describe their experience as life-changing. Although the fast is fairly simple, the results are amazing. Even those of us who routinely practice the Daniel Fast and teach about it continue to be impressed by the results people experience —which is why we don't want you to limit yourself to just twenty-one days of feeling better.

After you complete the Daniel Fast, you can build on the momentum of that experience by making permanent changes in the way you eat and how you care for your body. We call this lifestyle approach the Daniel Cure—a plan with the potential to heal many common and serious ailments. Think of the fast as a jumpstart and the Daniel Cure as a simple and sustainable way to practice healthy living. This is a principles-based approach for eating that you can customize to meet your needs and preferences. Treat this approach as your personalized health-care system—one with widespread physical and supernatural benefits. With this uncomplicated eating plan, you can toss out all your diet books and step into a powerful way of living as you take charge of your health with nutritious eating. All along, the One who created you— spirit, soul, and body—is your guide. Every step of the way, God is directing, motivating, and encouraging you as you open your heart and your health to his care. (See "Be Ready" on page 6.)

WHY YOU MIGHT NOT FEEL SO GREAT

Human beings have an exceptional capacity to keep trying to improve. We try to fix who we are and how we live our lives. Take a stroll through a bookstore and notice the shelves of self-help books on just about every topic imaginable. We all want a rewarding and fulfilling existence. We want to get better. We want to move to the next level. And as followers of Christ, we want love, joy, peace, and health in good measure—pressed down, shaken together, and running over! But there seems to be a huge gap between the reality of our everyday lives and our dreams for what we want. Our wishing and hoping and thinking and praying doesn't seem to be getting us the results we desire.

Spiritual and Emotional Malnutrition

The sad truth is that millions of people exist in a state of severe spiritual and emotional hunger. Some experts even describe it as a kind of malnutrition. Men, women, and children who are hungry for love and significance feel a painful emptiness, and many will battle this pain throughout their lives.

What do hungry people do? They eat. People who are spiritually and emotionally malnourished often feed themselves with the temporary "nourishment" of self-defeating behaviors—overspending, substance abuse, sexual immorality, excessive use of social media and video games or other digital entertainment. And then there's food—overeating, poor eating, eating disorders, and more. Of course, these things never satisfy the hunger for what these spiritually and emotionally hungry men, women, and children really need. In the words of the old country-western song, these hungry hearts are "lookin' for love in all the wrong places."

The love that they're looking for is found only in God. Until we feast on God's love and grace, the peace that surpasses all understanding (see Philippians 4:7) will elude us. We will continue our fruitless search and will remain unsatisfied.

As you reflect on how people in general respond to spiritual and emotional hunger, what comes to mind about your own life? Take a few minutes to reflect on this important issue.

- Are there any behavior patterns you tend to rely on for temporary nourishment?
- In what area of your life are you most aware of feeling spiritually hungry? Emotionally hungry?
- On a scale of 1 – 10 (with 1 being severely malnourished and 10 being well nourished), what number would you say best describes your spiritual life right now? How about your emotional life?

Lifestyle Conditions

Four terms summarize the painful truth about the typical North American lifestyle: stressed, sleep deprived, sedentary, and malnourished.

- *Stressed.* We're busier, more distracted, and more stressed than ever.
- *Sleep deprived.* Chronic lack of adequate rest is so pervasive that the Centers for Disease Control and Prevention (CDC) now considers sleep deprivation a public health epidemic.[1]

- *Sedentary.* According to the United States Bureau of Labor Statistics, the average American adult sits in front of a television screen for almost three hours every day.[2]
- *Malnourished.* Did you know it's possible to be simultaneously overweight and malnourished? That's what happens to the person who eats too many "empty" calories—foods high in sugar and fat but low in nutrients.

And what do all of these lifestyle trends add up to? Staggering consequences —physically, financially, and emotionally. It's estimated that 42 percent of the US population will be obese by 2030[3] and that the incidence of chronic disease will continue to skyrocket. According to CDC reports, there is a direct correlation between being clinically overweight, or obese, and the increased risk for the following conditions:

- heart disease
- hypertension (high blood pressure)
- dyslipidemia (high "bad" cholesterol and/or triglycerides, low "good" cholesterol)
- stroke
- type 2 diabetes
- cancers (endometrial, breast, and colon)

BE READY

As a child of God, you are well equipped with everything you need for a godly life (see 2 Peter 1:3). This includes areas that involve daily struggle. And for many of us, overeating and choosing unhealthy food options *are* daily struggles. If you find yourself lacking the discipline to be successful in this area of your life, consider claiming victory over this challenge in the name of Jesus.

You may feel that struggles such as resisting a piece of cake or staying on your dietary plan somehow don't rise to the level of God's concern. However, Scripture invites us to "pray in the Spirit on *all occasions* with all kinds of prayers and requests. With this in mind, be alert and always keep on praying for all the Lord's people" (Ephe-

sians 6:18, emphasis added). This includes *you* and the specific things you may be struggling with, regardless of how big or how small. Pray often for the Lord to give you strength, to give you discernment, to give you discipline, patience, peace, and then joy as you follow through on the dietary plans that you set for yourself. Remember that this new lifestyle approach of optimal eating will lead you into the healthy state of body and mind that you desire for yourself and that God desires for you.

It is vitally important to know your plans and limits before entering any situation. For example, if you make a commitment to adhere to the Daniel Fast for twenty-one days, you want that promise to be foremost in your mind. Know

- liver and gallbladder disease
- sleep apnea and respiratory problems
- osteoarthritis
- gynecological problems (abnormal menses, infertility)

In addition to compromising health and quality of life, these health problems exact a huge financial toll. The Bipartisan Policy Center's Nutrition and Physical Activity Initiative (NPAI) puts it this way:

> In short, obesity is the most urgent public health problem in America today. It is a primary reason why life expectancy in large parts of the United States is already several years lower than in other advanced countries around the world. For millions of Americans, it means many more years — even decades — of sharply reduced quality of life. More broadly, the costs of obesity and chronic disease have become a major drag on our economy. Escalating health care costs are the main driver of our spiraling national debt, and obesity-related illness comprises an increasingly large share of our massive health costs. The obesity crisis is therefore not just a health crisis, but a major contributor to our fiscal crisis.

The center's recent comprehensive study cites widespread obesity as the leading offender:

what foods are allowed and what foods are not allowed. Anticipate any challenges you might face and what you'll do in all situations — at home, at work, in social outings. When you prepare yourself, you will rarely need to make tough decisions. Why? Because you will have already made your decision before the difficult situation presents itself — you already "rehearsed" the event in your mind.

For example, let's say you attend a catered lunch meeting while on the Daniel Fast. The food consists of fruit and vegetable platters, hummus, a cheese platter, sandwiches, cake, a variety of sweetened beverages, and bottled water. Without discipline and without prior planning, you might walk into the room with your coworkers, follow their lead, and grab a sandwich, an assortment of cheese, a piece of cake, and a sweet tea — choices that likely will make you feel like a failure after the meeting. However, if you head into the meeting with a plan to consume only Daniel Fast food, you might opt for some fresh vegetables and hummus, fresh fruit for dessert, and water as your beverage. You eat as much as you want and are fully satisfied. Perfect.

Set boundaries for yourself up front, before the situation presents itself. Limit your choices — most people do better with fewer rather than more choices. This works with eating and health-specific goals and it works in most other areas of life. Come to the Lord in daily prayer — he will protect you, guide you, and lead you to victory!

Fully two-thirds of Americans are overweight or obese. One-third of American children are overweight or obese. And among children under the age of six, nearly one in five is overweight or obese. Obese people are far more likely to develop chronic diseases like diabetes, hypertension, asthma, heart disease and cancer. Obese children are more likely to have one or more risk factors for cardiovascular disease, to be pre-diabetic (i.e., at high risk for developing diabetes), and to suffer from bone and joint problems, sleep apnea, and social and psychological problems such as stigmatization and poor self-esteem. They are also very likely to become obese adults. In short, obesity is the most urgent public health problem in America today.[4]

More difficult to measure is the cost of the effect obesity has on emotional well-being and overall quality of life. It's no secret that obesity is often associated with poor self-esteem, depression, and social isolation. Individuals who are obese may lack the energy to meet workplace demands or even the routine pleasures of family life, such as playing with young children or enjoying physical intimacy with a spouse.

As you think about your own physical health, what comes to mind about the way you care for your body? Ask yourself:

- Are there any eating patterns you know are not good for your health?
- On a scale of 1–10 (with 1 being very unhealthy and 10 being very healthy), what number would you say best describes your lifestyle choices right now? What about the condition of your overall health?
- What hopes do you have for your lifestyle and overall health?

HOW YOU CAN BEGIN TO FEEL BETTER

These lifestyle concerns are not just for the nameless masses, but are ones we all need to take seriously. The increasing rates of heart disease and type 2 diabetes are not empty threats. Strokes and cancer diagnoses are not reserved solely for *other* people. These are very real perils facing every man and woman who routinely makes risky lifestyle choices—including everything from not getting enough sleep or exercise to substance abuse and poor eating habits. But here's the almost-too-good-to-be-true news: You don't have to be one of the statistics. No matter where you are, you can take steps toward greater health and vitality. If you want to be healthier, if you want to have more energy, if you want to experience the life God created you for, please hear this: *You can.* Yes, it will require making lifestyle changes, but the rewards are more than worth it.

As you take that first step on a new path—the Daniel Cure—your journey begins with a twenty-one-day Daniel Fast. This partial fast was inspired by the prophet Daniel. For three weeks, you'll eat a variety of plant-based foods, cleansing your body of additives, preservatives, flavorings, processed foods, caffeine, and alcohol. Although the types of foods you'll eat are restricted, the quantity is not. You can eat as much food as you wish. But food should not be the focus of your fast. Rather, as you begin to learn the principles of healthy eating, your focus is on God. Each day, through prayer and Bible study, you develop your relationship with him and seek his guidance and motivation.

After the twenty-one-day Daniel Fast, you can use the Daniel Cure principles (see chapter 10) to develop a personalized healthy eating plan that is realistic and sustainable for you. This customized plan is your ticket off the road that leads to deteriorating health and chronic diseases. And the ticket is free ... the only "cost" being your willingness to say, "Yes, God, I want to be healthy."

The Daniel Cure principles are based on both the irrevocable truth of God's Word and the rich resources of contemporary science. As you learn more about healthy eating and the stunning and intricate ways the human body works, our hope is that you will gain a greater appreciation for your body and for your Creator. And we trust you will see that one of the best ways to honor the Lord and the life he gave you is to take very good care of yourself — spirit, soul, and body.

We hope you decide to accept the invitation to take full responsibility for caring for the body God has entrusted to your care.* And we pray you will gain a deeper and more profound understanding about the spiritual being you are — a one-of-a-kind masterpiece created by the most awesome Artist of all. He created you so you could be a holy instrument and a sacred temple — a dwelling place for the most high God.

I (Susan) can promise you that the rewards of the Daniel Fast far outweigh the challenges. And this is no empty or theoretical promise. Since 2007, I have taught people all over the world about the Daniel Fast and interacted with tens of thousands who have used the fast to seek God. I've witnessed the positive changes they experience through fasting, including stunning answers to prayer. I've read the joyful notes from those who have been surprised at the amazing health benefits they experienced in just twenty-one days of eating "clean" plant-based meals. And everything I have learned from people about

---

*As with any new health program, before you embark on the Daniel Cure lifestyle plan, we recommend you schedule a physical examination by your primary-care physician. Discuss your interest in adopting this lifestyle plan, starting with a twenty-one-day Daniel Fast. Make certain you receive approval before you begin, in particular if you have health problems and/or use medications. Do not avoid this important appointment.

the impact of the Daniel Fast on health has now been scientifically documented and affirmed in multiple clinical trials conducted by Rick and his team. (See "The Science behind the Daniel Fast" on page 281.) The Daniel Fast will change you. That's a promise.

This book is designed to help you reclaim the ancient tradition of prayer and fasting. You'll make wise decisions based on scientific research and take steps to truly care for your body—the wonderful gift God has entrusted to you alone.

▇▇▇▇▇▇▇▇ TURN YOUR THOUGHTS INTO ACTIONS ▇▇▇▇▇▇▇▇

1 Think about your spiritual life using metaphors of food, such as nutrition, hunger, and starved. What three to five words, images, or phrases would you use to describe your spiritual life? You might consider your spiritual "diet," degree of nourishment or malnourishment, and the intensity of your hunger for God. For example, *I feed myself only once a week when I go to church. I am spiritually malnourished. I'm not sure I even feel hungry for God right now.*

2 In what ways do you hope the Daniel Fast might help you to experience greater physical health and vitality? Write down three to five changes you hope to experience. For example, *I hope to have more energy to play with my toddler. I want to reduce my risk factors for developing diabetes. I want to lose weight.*

3 Identify a spiritual activity you would like to include as part of your daily life. For example, you might want to have a daily prayer time, or daily Bible reading and study, or a quiet time with the Lord to simply listen for his direction in your life. Think about a discipline you can adopt and start doing it today. Set it up as an appointment with your Creator and keep it just as you would an appointment with a doctor or a friend.

the power and mystery of fasting

"I had never asked God to help me with my eating habits before," admitted Mary, a mother of two and a participant in one of the Daniel Fast clinical studies. "On previous diets, I felt like everything was up to me. But with the Daniel Fast, God is so intricately involved that it's added a different and powerful dimension. The way I eat and take care of myself has totally changed. I am amazed to be where I am today with my health and my weight. And I know I can continue this way of living. In fact, now I have family members and friends asking me to help them. I'm turning into a Daniel Fast evangelist!"

We know that God wants us to lead healthy lives. We also know he is eager and ready to help us as we commit to this goal. Too often when we go on a diet to lose weight, we rely on our willpower to keep us on track. But willpower often fails and we eventually quit. However, using the Daniel Fast with health as our priority and God as our guide is far different than going on a diet — it's a spiritual experience designed to bring about lasting change.

BIBLICAL FASTING

Biblical fasting is always about abstaining from food — not refraining from activities such as using Facebook or watching television. Biblical fasting means refraining from all food or certain foods for a spiritual purpose for a limited period of time. The Hebrew word for "fast" is *tsôwm* (twoom), which means "to cover the mouth." The Greek word for fast is *nēstĕuō* (nace-tyoo-o), which means "to abstain from food."

A fast is a highly focused period of time when we examine our lives and seek to align ourselves with the ways of God. We do this by separating ourselves from our typical patterns and routines and entering a spiritual experience for a given time. (See "Fasting 101" below.) Fasting is a spiritual discipline and the practice has tenets that we want to follow so we can be assured a successful experience.

Fasting Is Temporary

Fasting is temporary, which means it's doable. Even lifelong meat lovers can practice the Daniel Fast and go without meat for just twenty-one days. Setting aside a specific and limited amount of time for fasting sharpens our focus on God. We then can enter more deeply into his truths. As we open our hearts to the Holy Spirit and purpose ourselves to learn from him, our Father is able to minister to us as his precious children.

Fasting Is a Mystery

The spiritual power we experience through fasting is a mystery. In the Bible, the term "mystery" refers specifically to insights and truths we understand only when God reveals them directly to our spirit. When we fast, we fully surrender

---

FASTING 101

What Types of Fasts Are There?

There are three main types of fasts:

1. Absolute or complete fast, in which you consume no food or water.
2. Normal fast, in which you consume only water.
3. Partial fast, in which you consume some foods and beverages and not others. The Daniel Fast is a partial fast.

The type of fast you choose is not as important as the purpose — to draw near to the Lord during a time of focused prayer.

When Should I Fast?

A fast can be for an occasion, such as Lent, or set by leaders of a church (for example, a churchwide fast). Most important is choosing the dates to fast by what you believe the Lord is calling you to do. Seek God's guidance as you consider the timeframe for your fast.

How Often Should I Fast?

There is no single answer. For many, a time of fasting is a way to satisfy in part a longing for the spiritual realm we call home. If you feel the Lord is calling you to fast one week per year, fine. If he's calling you to fast one day a week throughout the year, that's also fine.

How Long Should I Fast?

The length of your fast depends entirely on what you feel the Lord has called you to do. You might wake up one day and, during a quiet time of prayer, hear the Lord speaking to you. You decide at that moment to fast the entire day until the next morning. Or you might plan a longer fast and decide to fast for three days, ten days, twenty-one days, or forty days. You might even be led to fast one day a week for a period of time, or one meal per day for a period of time. Your actions should simply be guided by the Lord.

ourselves to God—spirit, soul, and body. We submit our will to God, follow a set of guidelines about food, and open our hearts to this mystery. God miraculously uses our submission to strengthen us, empower us, fill us, and change us. We get a taste of what Jesus meant when he said, "You are in me, and I am in you" (John 14:20). When we fast we focus more of our attention on God through prayer and study. One can pray without fasting ... but you cannot fast authentically without praying.

Without this spiritual dimension, a twenty-one-day partial fast like the Daniel Fast would be no different than a typical diet. But since this is first a spiritual experience—made to draw us closer to God—we aren't dieting. Instead, we are placing ourselves into holy submission.

On a diet, we might occasionally cheat or fail to keep the promises we made to ourselves. But a fast is different. Because when we fast, we are partnering with God for a spiritual outcome. We are expecting him to impact our lives, so we maintain our commitment to him. Here's another difference: When God's Spirit empowers our spirit, we experience his support and become steadfast in our commitment. Suddenly we have the power and the desire to say no to things not allowed on the fast. Our motivation to succeed becomes so much stronger than the temptation to drink a can of soda or eat a slice of pizza. This new-found discipline is part of the powerful mystery of fasting.

Fasting Feeds Us

For many, the demands of everyday life are so packed with activities, responsibilities, and to-do lists that feeling overwhelmed is normal. With so many pressures, few have time to feed their soul. The result is spiritual and emotional starvation—a deep inner hunger for peace, rest, and security. And this hunger is pervasive. At every age, in every walk of life, too many of us are starving for the nourishment that only God can provide.

When we fast, we come to the Lord's table and feast on his love, care, and wisdom. We change our behavior. We slow our pace. We focus intently on spiritual matters and enjoy what our souls are truly hungry for—Jesus, the Bread of Life.

Unfortunately, too many of us try to satisfy our hunger with the spiritual equivalent of "fast food"—self-defeating behaviors, relationships that have more to do with feeding carnal hunger than the longing of the soul. Author and pastor John Piper writes, "Do you have a hunger for God? If we don't feel strong desires for the manifestation of the glory of God, it is not because we have drunk deeply and are satisfied. It is because we have nibbled so long at the table of the world. Our soul is stuffed with small things, and there is no room for the great. If we are full of what the world offers, then perhaps a fast might express, or even increase, our soul's appetite for God. Between the dangers of self-denial and self-indulgence is the path of pleasant pain called fasting."[5]

Truly, the call deep within us beckons not for physical food or pleasures. What our souls are truly hungry for is the Bread of Life—the Lord—who said, "People do not live by bread alone" (Matthew 4:4 NLT). And Jesus responds to our hunger with this invitation: "Come to me, all you who are weary and burdened, and I will give you rest. Take my yoke upon you and learn from me, for I am gentle and humble in heart, and you will find rest for your souls" (Matthew 11:28–29).

Fasting Invites Us to Rest and Reflect

Our Lord knows us better than we know ourselves. He knows what we need, just like he knew what the disciples needed when they were weary: "Then the apostles gathered to Jesus and told Him all things, both what they had done and what they had taught. And He said to them, 'Come aside by yourselves to a deserted place and rest a while.' For there were many coming and going, and they did not even have time to eat. So they departed to a deserted place in the boat by themselves" (Mark 6:30–32 NKJV).

Fasting is a way to come away for restful one-on-one time with the Lord. It's a kind of spiritual retreat built into the fabric of everyday life. In addition to limiting food, fasting invites us to limit or simplify our schedules. Instead of trying to squeeze in time with God between getting kids into bed and watching the latest reality show, we prioritize our time with God. For a while, we say no to some things so that we can devote ourselves entirely to saying yes to the Lord. When we fast, we rest at the feet of Rabbi Jesus and learn from him. We embrace the promises from God's Word rather than the circumstances of the world. This is the kind of rest our souls long for.

Within the resting place of fasting, we have time and space to reflect on our lives. In God's loving presence, we "give careful thought to [our] ways" (Haggai 1:7) and invite the Lord to show us where our ways are not aligned with his ways. We acknowledge our weaknesses and confess our failures. Then we ask the Lord for forgiveness, strength, and guidance as we begin to make changes. These could be significant changes in the way we eat and how we treat our bodies.

When we fast, we make the choice to become soft clay in the hands of the Master Potter. We present all of who we are—spirit, soul, and body—to all of who he is. We invite the wise and loving hands of our Creator to mold us and shape us so we can bring even more glory to him. And through the spiritual discipline of prayer and fasting, we come into more consistent alignment with God and his purpose for our lives.

A JOURNEY TOWARD A LIFESTYLE OF HEALTH

Your desire to be healthy is a hope God can fulfill—and it starts when you begin a twenty-one-day period of prayer and fasting. This initial three-week experience is an excellent launch pad for choosing the Daniel Cure lifestyle. Of course, it's important for you to understand that you may be presented with some challenges along the way, as discussed in "The Physical and Spiritual

THE PHYSICAL AND SPIRITUAL CHALLENGES OF FASTING

Most of us understand the physical challenge of a fast—especially an absolute fast (no food or water) or normal fast (no food). There can be a physical discomfort as well as a psychological strain when fasting since many people are addicted to food and food components, such as caffeine. However, beyond the physical challenges, it is crucially important for you to understand that you may come under attack from the enemy (Satan). A fast is indeed spiritual warfare.

When some people hear the term "spiritual warfare," they think of something otherworldly, not quite real. But spiritual warfare *is* real. Because the ultimate purpose of your fast is to deepen your relationship with the Lord, it is a threat to the enemy. The last thing Satan wants is for us to grow in our relationship with our heavenly Father. Therefore, you should expect attacks from the enemy while you are fasting. These may occur at work or during recreation or even while you are praying. You will need to stand firm. The apostle Paul taught believers in Ephesus how they could stand against temptation:

> Be strong in the Lord and in his mighty power. Put on the full armor of God, so that you can take your stand against the devil's schemes. For our struggle is not against flesh and blood, but against the rulers, against the authorities, against the powers of this dark world and against the spiritual forces of evil in the heavenly realms. Therefore put on the full armor of God, so that when the day of evil comes, you may be able to stand your ground, and after you have done everything, to stand. Stand firm then, with the belt of truth buckled around your waist, with the breastplate of righteousness in place, and with your feet fitted with the readiness that comes from the gospel of peace. In addition to all this, take up the shield of faith, with which you can extinguish all the flaming arrows of the evil one. Take the helmet of salvation and the sword of the Spirit, which is the word of God.
>
> — EPHESIANS 6:10-17

You can do it. As a child of God, you have been equipped to rule. Remember, God is living in you and he has already defeated the enemy. Claim victory over Satan in the mighty name of Jesus, our Savior and Risen Lord.

Challenges of Fasting" on page 15. The key to a successful fast is to prepare ahead of time so that you're ready for challenges when they come.

The Daniel Fast is a partial fast, which means some foods are eaten and others are restricted. We'll cover the guidelines of what to eat in the next chapter. But for now, as we focus on unlocking the power of fasting—and how that impacts your health—it is important to understand that when you're on the Daniel Fast, you will eat only healthy foods grown from seed and drink only water—all items that are good for your body.

You also can learn more of what God teaches about your priceless value and about his unchanging desire for you to be healthy. You can learn more about the amazing way your body was designed and how it works to serve you so you can bring glory to its Creator. Your relationship with God will grow deeper and become stronger and more secure.

And as you feed your body only foods that it was designed to receive, your internal organs and systems will start to heal and rebuild to restore your health. Within a few days, as you connect with the Lord, you'll experience a marked difference in your spirit. You'll sense greater peace, joy, and calm as you allow the Lord to direct your steps. Your body will be filled with more energy. You will experience a sense of well-being and vitality. And this is just the start! As you continue on your twenty-one-day partial fast, you'll feel better and better with each passing day.

When you complete the fast, your body will feel cleansed and restored. Our hope is that you not only feel better physically but that you can also more fully embrace this biblical description of you: "For we are God's handiwork, created in Christ Jesus to do good works, which God prepared in advance for us to do" (Ephesians 2:10). And it is our prayer that you will then take the next step into the Daniel Cure and adopt a healthy and sustainable lifestyle—one that is both satisfying to you and brings glory to God.

Changing something as central as our eating habits is a challenge. But the Daniel Fast prepares and guides us so we can make this significant change. Plus, God will continue to help us as we submit our will to his will, put our trust in him, and allow his Spirit to guide and encourage us. This is when we truly can experience the Master's promise, "What is impossible [for people] is possible with God" (Luke 18:27).

■ TURN YOUR THOUGHTS INTO ACTIONS ■

1 Have you ever asked God for his help in your quest for improved health? Why or why not?

2 Tell God exactly what you desire for your own health. How do you see yourself in mind and body to best serve him?

3 Make an initial commitment today to follow a twenty-one-day Daniel Fast. You can determine the exact start date later. For now, just make the commitment. Then read the remainder of this book, develop your plan of action, and get started.

what is
the daniel fast?

THE DANIEL FAST IS A BIBLICALLY BASED, PARTIAL FAST INSPIRED BY THE prophet Daniel. This method of fasting involves eating only plant-based foods and drinking only water. It eliminates all additives, preservatives, flavorings, processed foods, sweeteners, solid fats, deep-fried foods, leavening, stimulants, and alcohol, what we call clean eating. (See "What Is Clean Eating?" on page 20.) Although the kinds of foods are restricted, the quantity is not. You can eat as much food as you want, keeping in mind that this is a fast.

THE BIBLICAL STORY BEHIND THE DANIEL FAST

The Daniel Fast is based on the fasting experiences of the Old Testament prophet Daniel.* Daniel found himself in Babylonian captivity with his three companions, Hananiah, Mishael, and Azariah (renamed by the Babylonians as Shadrach, Meshach, and Abed-Nego and who were thrown into the fiery furnace). Even though he was a captive, Daniel wanted to honor God and follow the dietary practices of the law of Moses. When offered the meat and wine of King Nebuchadnezzar, Daniel made this request: "Then said Daniel to Melzar, whom the prince of the eunuchs had set over Daniel, Hananiah, Mishael, and Azariah, Prove thy servants, I beseech thee, ten days; and let them give us pulse to eat, and water to drink. Then let our countenances be looked upon before thee, and the countenance of the children that eat of the portion of the king's meat: and as thou seest, deal with thy servants" (Daniel 1:11 – 13 KJV).

Pulse is food grown from seed. From this reference we derive the principle

---

* *The Daniel Fast: Feed Your Soul, Strengthen Your Spirit, and Renew Your Body* (Wheaton, IL: Tyndale, 2010) provides additional teaching about this method of fasting. You'll also find more information on *www.daniel-fast.com*.

of eating no animal products on the Daniel Fast and drinking only water. The fast is restricted to fruits, vegetables, whole grains, legumes, nuts, and seeds. Healthy oils, herbs, and spices are also allowed.

Daniel 10 describes another time Daniel fasted. The prophet was mourning over the seventy-year occupation of Israel by the Babylonians. He sought God's wisdom and entered into a time of prayer and fasting. "In those days I Daniel was mourning three full weeks. I ate no pleasant bread, neither came flesh nor wine in my mouth, neither did I anoint myself at all, till three whole weeks were fulfilled" (Daniel 10:2–3 KJV).

Another translation says the prophet ate no "pleasant food." This passage is the basis for eliminating breads and desserts, sweeteners, stimulants (such as caffeine), deep-fried foods, and alcohol. Jewish fasting principles also eliminate leavening and food substitutes that try to work around these restrictions in an attempt to satisfy physical cravings.

It's important to note that the Daniel Fast guidelines are not about trying to eat as Daniel ate. Instead, they are principles derived from the restrictions Daniel followed that establish the boundaries for a spiritual fasting experience. Like all Christian fasts, the primary purpose of the Daniel Fast is to separate yourself from everyday life for a period of time. During this set-apart time, you devote yourself entirely to the Lord. You open your heart to him and seek his fellowship, direction, assistance, and intervention for specific purposes.

DANIEL-FAST FOOD GUIDELINES

The foods allowed on the Daniel Fast are rich in nutrients, flavors, and colors. You can create a variety of appetizing and wholesome meals and snacks. (See part 4, "Meal Planning and Recipes" on page 143.) As you prepare and enjoy your meals, you can have the confidence that you are providing your body exactly what it needs for cleansing and optimal health. As you prepare for your fast, here are some food guidelines to keep in mind.

Foods Allowed on the Daniel Fast

On the Daniel Fast, you may consume all fruits, vegetables, whole grains, legumes, nuts, seeds, quality oils, herbs, and seasonings. The only beverage on the Daniel Fast is water. (For more information about water and fluids, see chapter 11). Juice may be used as an ingredient in recipes and meal-replacement shakes, but not as a beverage. Additions to your water such as lemon slices, mint leaves, or cucumber slices are allowed as long as you can still call the beverage water. (See "The Health Benefits of Water" on page 29.)

Foods Not Allowed on the Daniel Fast

Foods restricted on the Daniel Fast include all animal products, dairy products, added sweeteners, deep-fried foods, processed and refined foods, artificial flavorings, chemicals, and preservatives. Also not allowed are alcohol, caffeine, coffee, tea, leavening (baking powder, yeast, etc.), or solid fats (margarine and shortening). Some people ask why natural sweeteners (such as honey or stevia) aren't allowed, noting that they are in fact "natural" and the Daniel Fast is all about consuming natural foods. Just because Daniel Fast foods are all natural, not all natural foods are allowed on the fast. For additional Daniel Fast guidelines, visit *www.DanielCure.com/guidelines*.

No Food Substitutes

Lines can get a little blurry when it comes to food substitutes. Although some food substitutes are healthy alternatives when not fasting (for example, applesauce for oil or butter; flax meal for eggs), you should avoid using food substi-

WHAT IS CLEAN EATING?

From a health standpoint, the Daniel Fast is a plant-based, whole-food, non-refined, clean-eating plan with a few additional restrictions. In simple terms, *clean* eating means food in its natural form, without adulteration. No chemicals, additives, preservatives, flavorings, colorings, or added sugar or fat. You'll find most clean foods around the perimeter of the grocery store, not in the store aisles.

The terms "whole foods" or "non-refined foods" indicate foods in their natural form. In contrast, "refined foods" or "processed foods" are reengineered by the food industry and, in the process, typically depleted of some or all natural vitamins, minerals, and fiber.

White flour is an example of a refined food. It is the result of highly processed and finely ground wheat flour, typically bleached, from which most of the bran and wheat germ have been removed. Removing the bran removes fiber, one of the most significant ingredients that has huge health benefits. Fiber is essential for lowering cholesterol and maintaining regularity. The bran is rich in essential fatty acids, starch, protein, vitamins, and dietary minerals, making it a nutritional powerhouse. Removing the wheat germ also removes a high concentration of many other nutrients, including fiber, iron, magnesium, manganese, protein, omega-3 fatty acids, phosphorus, potassium, selenium, vitamin E, zinc, complex carbohydrates, calcium, and B vitamins (including folate, niacin, thiamine, and vitamin B_6). In processing, removing the bran and the wheat germ depletes the flour of much of its nutritional value.

This is just one example of how food processing impacts the nutrient content in the foods we eat. Which is partly why processed foods — especially white bread, pasta, cake, crackers, cookies, pretzels, and similar food items — are not allowed on the Daniel Fast. The best foods are clean, wholesome foods — those created to nourish, heal, and satisfy our bodies and our appetites.

tutes in an effort to diminish the restrictions of the spiritual-fasting experience. For example, bacon is not allowed on the traditional Daniel Fast, yet there is "vegan bacon" made of ingredients that may be consistent with the fasting guidelines. The same is true for some egg replacements. The individual ingredients may be allowed, but the purpose of the food is to provide a substitute for the real thing.

The significant element in fasting is that foods are restricted. This immediately puts our self-will—sometimes referred to as the "flesh" part of human nature—in conflict with the guidelines. Fasting includes profound lessons about things like submission, self-control, and walking according to the Spirit. However, when we substitute foods on the traditional fast so that the restrictions are watered down or eliminated, then we assert our self-will to pacify the flesh and bypass the discipline essential for spiritual growth. Rather than stretching and growing, we choose to stay immature, doing what we want to do. The apostle Paul taught the Corinthians about this condition: "And I, brethren, could not speak to you as to spiritual people but as to carnal, as to babes in Christ. I fed you with milk and not with solid food; for until now you were not able to receive it, and even now you are still not able; for you are still carnal" (1 Corinthians 3:1–3 NKJV).

To hold true to the Daniel Fast guidelines, food substitutes are discouraged. As you consider what you will and will not eat on the fast, examine your heart. There are times when I (Susan) am not totally sure about a food, so I will ask the Holy Spirit to be my guide. There is no way we can bamboozle the Holy Spirit, and so when we come to him in good faith, we receive the direction we need.

No Processed Foods

Food processing transforms raw or whole foods into food in other forms. Raw potatoes are processed into things like potato chips, frozen hash browns, and instant mashed-potato flakes. In the process, healthy nutrients are often removed. To make these foods shelf stable and appetizing, food manufacturers add things like salt, sweeteners, artificial flavorings, and other chemicals, ingredients that can promote disease over time.* This is contrary to the Daniel Fast guidelines.

---

*Salt is one ingredient that is added in large quantities to processed foods. For example, it is estimated that up to 75 percent of the sodium in the average American diet comes from salt added to processed food (or to restaurant foods). Even if you are limiting the salt added via the salt shaker, you may be consuming high amounts of sodium without even knowing it.

Eliminating processed foods means avoiding foods that have been reengineered. For example, white rice has had the hull and the germ removed. White flour is milled to remove the most valuable food elements in the wheat grain so that only the starchy white part of the grain remains. Enriched flour sounds good, but it's actually flour to which small quantities of nutrients have been added in an attempt to make up for the fact that vital nutrients have been stripped during processing. Our objective with eating according to the Daniel Fast guidelines is to always consume food in its most natural form, free of processing and full of nutrients. (See "What Is Clean Eating?" on page 20.)

The restrictions on the Daniel Fast require us to pay more attention to the foods we eat, and that's a good thing. In fact, one of the biggest "aha" moments that people experience on the Daniel Fast is when they learn what's in packaged and canned foods by reading the ingredients lists on food labels. We often

IS THE DANIEL FAST THE SAME AS A STRICT VEGETARIAN DIET?

No. The Daniel Fast is much more than a strict vegetarian diet. Vegetarian diets involve removal of some or all animal products from the diet. A strict vegetarian diet removes all animal products. The most stringent of all is the vegan diet. It eliminates all animal products from the diet and from life in general (no leather, no furs, etc.). Variations of the vegetarian diet include:

- **Lacto-ovo** vegetarian: prohibits the intake of beef, poultry, pork, fish, and shellfish but allows consumption of eggs and dairy products.
- **Lacto** vegetarian: prohibits the same things as lacto-ovo vegetarian but also prohibits intake of eggs; consumption of dairy products is allowed.
- **Ovo** vegetarian: prohibits the same things as lacto-ovo vegetarian but also prohibits intake of dairy products; consumption of eggs is allowed.
- **Pesco** or **pesce** vegetarian (sometimes referred to as Pescetarian): allows consumption of fish.
- **Pollo** vegetarian (sometimes referred to as Pollotarian): allows consumption of poultry.

There are various other combinations of these plans, but this list gives you an idea of what a vegetarian plan might include.

Strict vegetarian/vegan plan followers consume no animal products, not even honey. In many ways, this plan is similar to the Daniel Fast. However, these diets *do not* prohibit processed foods, refined carbohydrates, bread with yeast, sweeteners, additives, preservatives, flavorings, coloring, caffeine, or alcohol — all items that are not allowed on the Daniel Fast. Because of these differences, we believe that the Daniel Fast is a healthier plan than a traditional vegetarian or vegan diet.

Eliminating processed foods, desserts, additives, and preservatives — clean eating — has significant health benefits. Following a traditional vegetarian or vegan diet, which does allow for non-animal products that are nevertheless unhealthy, may not yield the same results as the Daniel Fast.

hear comments like, "I never realized all the added sugar, salt, and chemicals that are in packaged foods!" And once they know what they're eating, they often make changes that become permanent. "There are a lot of foods I can't eat anymore," said Patty, a participant in one of the Daniel Fast studies. "Now that I know what's in them, there is no way I can put them in my mouth. I can't believe I didn't know about all the additives in packaged food!"

THE NUTRITIONAL BENEFITS OF DANIEL FAST FOODS

The popularity of the Daniel Fast didn't originate as a healthy eating plan. Its sole purpose was to function as a spiritual discipline to allow individuals to experience the power of prayer. However, the foods we eat on the Daniel Fast are natural, whole, and packed with the nutrients and elements our bodies need for optimum health. In our view, this plan is far superior to most other nutrition programs targeting enhanced health. (See "Is the Daniel Fast the Same as a Strict Vegetarian Diet?" on page 22.) Let's take a closer look at the nutritional benefits of Daniel Fast foods.

Nutrient Dense

The core of the Daniel Fast eating plan is whole foods grown from seed. These foods contain essential vitamins, minerals, fiber, and other valuable agents necessary for your body's good health. For example, phytochemicals — compounds found only in plants — have antioxidant-and immune-stimulating properties. Many scientific studies report that phytochemicals provide protection to the cells in your body, resulting in improved health. To have the good health you desire, it's essential to eat a variety of fruits and vegetables.

Most of the foods on the Daniel Fast, especially the fruits and vegetables, are naturally low in calories and in dietary fat. They are considered nutrient dense, which means they have a high ratio of nutritional value per calorie — especially in contrast with processed foods, which are typically nutrient poor. For example, one ounce of potato chips (about fifteen chips) has 160 calories. To accumulate 160 calories in raw spinach, you would need to eat more than twenty-two cups of the dark-green leaves, which, by the way, are packed with vitamins and other nutrients. Potato chips are high in fat and lack almost all nutrients. Spinach, however, has no fat, is a good source of niacin and zinc, and is a very good source of dietary fiber, protein, vitamin A, vitamin C, vitamin E, vitamin K, thiamin, riboflavin, vitamin B_6, folate, calcium, iron, magnesium, phosphorus, potassium, copper, and manganese.

Low Fat and Low Cholesterol

Because the Daniel Fast is plant based, very little saturated fat or cholesterol enters your system. Except for a few plant-based oils, most saturated fat and cholesterol come from animal products, including (higher-fat varieties of) meat, poultry, and dairy. So during your fast, you are feeding your body primarily foods that have little to no saturated fat or cholesterol — the two nutrients that collectively can contribute to elevated blood cholesterol and hardening of the arteries (arteriosclerosis), which can lead to serious problems such as heart attack, stroke, and even death.

High Fiber

The extra good news is that many foods grown from seed contain an abundance of fiber. Fiber is actually poorly digested by your body. Normally, we don't think of poor digestion as a good thing, but with fiber, it is a good thing. Because fiber is not fully digested, it works its way through the gastrointestinal tract and acts like a sponge to soak up undesirable substances, such as cholesterol, and helps them to be eliminated from your system. Without adequate fiber, blood cholesterol could remain high and increase the likelihood of blood vessel disease, potentially leading to heart attack and stroke.

Low Glycemic Index

The foods you eat on the Daniel Fast are mostly low on the glycemic index (GI). This benefit is particularly important if you want to lose weight, reduce body fat, or lower your blood sugar levels. If you're not familiar with this important analysis factor, here is the clinical definition:

> The glycemic index (GI) is a ranking of carbohydrates on a scale from 0 to 100 according to the extent to which they raise blood sugar levels after eating. Foods with a high GI are those which are rapidly digested and absorbed and result in marked fluctuations in blood sugar levels. Low-GI foods, by virtue of their slow digestion and absorption, produce gradual rises in blood sugar and insulin levels, and have proven benefits for health. Low GI diets have been shown to improve both glucose and lipid levels in people with diabetes (type 1 and type 2). They have benefits for weight control because they help control appetite and delay hunger. Low GI diets also reduce insulin levels and insulin resistance.[6]

In other words, you should avoid processed foods with a high GI in favor of natural foods with a low GI. If you are following the Daniel Fast, this will be a given, because processed food is not allowed. But let's say you're not adhering to a Daniel Fast regimen and you're simply trying to make healthy food choices. For example, you might be preparing to make a sandwich and have the choice between a white-flour pita (GI equal to 70) and a whole-wheat tortilla (GI equal to 35). Choose the whole-wheat tortilla for healthy eating. It should yield a much lower blood glucose and insulin response than the white-flour tortilla and will better support your healthy lifestyle.*

The premise is quite simple. When you eat a meal of foods with a low GI, they are digested more slowly than foods with a high GI. Because of this slower digestion, the low GI foods don't produce a spike in your body's blood sugar. This is important because a spike in blood sugar triggers the release of insulin—a hormone that regulates blood sugar levels. Over time, the excessive blood sugar and insulin secretion may lead to metabolic disorders such as type 2 diabetes. This is one reason why men and women with type 2 diabetes are very often able to control the disease when they adopt the Daniel Fast plan. (For more information about diabetes and nutrition, see chapters 6 and 11.)

High-Quality Carbohydrates (Complex versus Simple)

Carbohydrates are divided into two categories, based on their chemical structure—complex and simple. In general, the more complex the structure of the carbohydrate, the longer it takes your body to digest and absorb the food. Vegetables, whole grains, and beans are all complex carbohydrates. These should be eaten in abundance when following the Daniel Fast.

In contrast, the simpler the structure of the carbohydrate, the quicker your body can digest and absorb the food.† Fruits are technically classified as simple carbohydrates (they contain a sugar called fructose) but are very healthy foods. They can be eaten in abundance. However, most other foods containing simple carbohydrates (such as soft drinks, candy, cookies, and cakes) are deemed unhealthy and should be eliminated when following the Daniel Fast.

Why is this important? First, because complex carbohydrate foods are

---

* It should be noted that while the GI of individual foods is important, the overall *quantity* of food consumed is also important. The combination of these two factors is something referred to as the "glycemic load." In addition, foods are usually eaten in combination, and the GI of individual foods will be altered when they are combined with other foods. Individuals may respond differently to the same food, in terms of blood glucose and insulin response. To be safe, include as many low GI foods in your eating plan as you can and eat small and frequent meals. One exception: high GI foods may be consumed following strenuous exercise in an attempt to replace depleted carbohydrate stores.

† While this relates to our discussion of the GI, not all simple carbohydrates have a high GI and not all complex carbohydrates have a low GI.

typically much more nutrient dense than simple carbohydrate foods (with fruit being the one exception). Second, because, as in the example of the white-flour pita and the whole-wheat tortilla, the faster your body digests and absorbs the foods you eat, the greater chance that your blood sugar will spike, leading to excess production of insulin. Over time, chronically elevated insulin leads to problems with your body's ability to make use of sugar in the bloodstream and supply it to body tissues, leading to elevated blood sugar and the potential for or eventual diagnosis of type 2 diabetes.

Your body's metabolism is designed to work in harmony with your body's needs and the food you consume. When you were an active child, your body required a lot of energy. Perhaps your school lunch included a cheese sandwich and an apple. You ate it and your blood sugar rose slightly. This signaled your pancreas to secrete the hormone insulin, which acts as a sugar controller. Insulin was released and said, "Okay, sugar, let me guide you out of the bloodstream and into the muscle cells where you can be used for energy." Your cells were pleased to be offered this sweet food and opened their gates to receive it. Your blood sugar fell to ideal levels as the sugar was absorbed by the cells and then either burned through your activity or stored in muscle cells for later use. You felt great and all was well and good.

But fast-forward to your adult life. What happens when you over-consume calories, especially simple carbohydrates? And what happens now that you are inactive during most of the day, unlike when you were a child? If you are over-consuming carbohydrates, your body must work overtime to produce more insulin to help control the increase in blood sugar. If you do this regularly, the body eventually becomes less sensitive to the insulin that is produced. In simple terms, insulin just doesn't work as well anymore. The result is elevated blood sugar with no place to go. So fat cells assist and start storing some of the excess sugar.

When this happens over and over again — as is the case for most people who are overweight or obese — muscle cells are more likely to say no to the insulin when it comes knocking. This describes a common condition known as "insulin resistance." The pancreas is a diligent little organ and wants to do a good job for you. So when excess sugar continues to enter the bloodstream, it pours out more and more insulin, even though the muscle cells have almost closed their doors. This sets off a host of problems that may eventually lead to type 2 diabetes — and other related conditions such as heart disease. Your body that was wonderfully designed to serve you now has high insulin, high blood sugar, and lots of belly fat. Not the picture of health you want for yourself.

In fact, your body is now on the road to potential and serious life-threatening diseases.

No Added Sweeteners

One of the restrictions on the Daniel Fast is added sweeteners of any kind. That includes granulated sugars, honey, syrups, and all the other sweeteners flooding the market these days—including sweeteners with no calories. So your body gets a twenty-one-day break from the overabundance of sugar entering your bloodstream. Your pancreas now excretes a reasonable amount of insulin and, in time, your muscle cells wake up, start to listen again, and soon open their doors to receive the sugar to create the energy you need.

THE DANIEL FAST VERSUS TRADITIONAL DIET PLANS

We've been asked, "Why does the Daniel Fast work for me when so many other diet plans have failed?" There probably are many answers to this question, but we'll offer three observations. First, the Daniel Fast typically requires a swift education in nutrition. In order to adhere to the Daniel Fast guidelines, it's essential to carefully read the list of ingredients on food labels. This increased awareness of what's really in the foods they're eating often causes people to make healthier food choices — both during and after the fast. This is why we encourage you to make a twenty-one-day Daniel Fast the first step in your lifestyle approach to the Daniel Cure. In addition to teaching you more about food and nutrition, it will allow you to focus on the Lord and seek his guidance as you begin your journey into a healthful lifestyle.

Second, the Daniel Fast is all about eating the right foods — foods that are nutrient dense rather than calorie dense; foods that are rich in vitamins and minerals, as well as fiber; foods that satiate you. In contrast, many diet plans are mostly about cutting calories. The Daniel Fast does not place a restriction on *how much* you can eat. Rather, it places a restriction on *what types of foods* you are eating. Many people who have spent years suffering through diet programs in which they were forced to count calories and deprive themselves of needed dietary energy enjoy the "freedom" of the Daniel Fast plan. They feel satisfied. And this is important for sticking with the plan long term. In fact, in our studies, people adhering to the Daniel Fast for six months reported significantly better compliance (about 80 percent) than people following diets such as Atkins and Ornish (about 35 percent) and Zone and Weight Watchers (about 40 percent). That's important to know.

Third, there are no restrictions on how macronutrients (protein, carbohydrate, and fat) are combined with one another or at what particular time food must be eaten. Within the guidelines, you simply eat what you want, when you want, and as much as you want. These freedoms typically result in the consumption of an abundance of healthy, nutrient-dense, fiber-rich food that offers a satisfying feeling of fullness. This very often includes consuming fewer calories than normal, leading to weight loss and body fat loss over time, as well as improvements in other health-related outcomes.

This is often why men and women on the Daniel Fast describe feeling as if they have received a surge of energy. Their bodies have been reset and are now working as they should. Many other parts of your body will start to operate in a life-giving way rather than being weak and overworked. Plus, now that your muscle cells are open for the business of burning glucose for energy, you rid the excess sugar calories from your diet and start losing weight. That's why we frequently hear comments like this one: "I've never been able to lose weight, but on the Daniel Fast I lost twelve pounds in just twenty-one days."

A DOABLE FAST

One of the significant benefits of the Daniel Fast is that it's doable and flexible. (See "The Daniel Fast versus Traditional Diet Plans" on page 27.) People who would have too hard of a time staying on a water-only or juice-only fast for an extended period of time find that the Daniel Fast is achievable. Within the Daniel Fast guidelines, meals can be as simple or as creative as you like. You might opt for an easy rice and bean combo or perhaps you know your way around the kitchen and decide to experiment with a few new culinary creations each week. You might also consider using meal-replacement shakes as discussed in chapter 13. Whatever you decide, your nutrition plan can be complete, satisfying, and relatively easy to follow.

If you have special health needs, the Daniel Fast is also adaptable. For example, we guide pregnant or nursing mothers to add lean chicken, beef, or fish along with low-fat dairy to their meals to make sure they are consuming enough protein to nourish the precious life they are supporting. The same goes for those with celiac disease or other health issues. Simply maintain the core of the Daniel Fast and, in consultation with your doctor, make slight adjustments to meet your special needs.

The Daniel Fast is the perfect launch to your journey on a lifestyle of health. The fasting experience provides the boundaries we need to enter into a time of submission and discipline, along with the spiritual power and support we receive from the Lord. As we study God's Word and seek his wisdom about our health and our life in Christ, our minds are renewed and our resolve strengthened. Meanwhile, our body experiences a cleansing and resetting that dissolves cravings, awakens our taste buds, and positions us for the life of health we desire.

THE HEALTH BENEFITS OF WATER

Water is essential to your good health. Maintaining adequate hydration leads to many health benefits. For example, your body needs water to regulate your temperature, protect and lubricate your joints, moisturize the air that enters your lungs, protect your internal organs, aid in the transport of nutrients and oxygen into your cells, help your organs absorb nutrients, and maintain normal metabolic function.

Water is the primary component of your body and makes up the majority of your tissues. For example, muscles are composed of approximately 70 percent water; your brain is approximately 80 percent water; your blood is approximately 80 percent water; and your bones are approximately 20 percent water. Every cell in your body needs water to function properly. That's why the body can go without food for a number of days but begins to break down within three days of no water. The next time you drink a glass of water, think of the good care you are providing for the many physical components of your body!

Water also has great benefits for weight loss. When your body is dehydrated, it sends a signal to your brain to "consume." However, instead of drinking fluids, we often interpret this signal as the need to eat—and consume unnecessary calories. Staying hydrated helps to eliminate this problem.

Water also fills your stomach, providing a temporary feeling of fullness. A common and scientifically validated tip to lose unwanted pounds is to drink a large (16-ounce) glass of water before each meal, as well as a glass of water with your meal. This zero-calorie beverage helps to fill you up and can help to reduce food intake, resulting in a loss of weight over time.

Water also plays a crucial role in disease prevention. Such was the case in a clinical study conducted at the Center for Human Nutrition at the University of Sheffield, England. Researchers found that women who are adequately hydrated reduce their risk of breast cancer by 79 percent. Another study at the Fred Hutchinson Cancer Research Center in Seattle found that women who drink more than five glasses of water a day (about 1½ quarts) have a 45 percent reduced risk of colon cancer compared with women who drink two or fewer glasses of water a day (one pint or less). Impressive results considering the ease with which we can all increase our daily water intake.

■ TURN YOUR THOUGHTS INTO ACTIONS ■

1 Do you have apprehensions about fasting? Or are you excited and eager to experience this spiritual discipline? Perhaps you have a mix of feelings. Take a few minutes and identify your thoughts about fasting. If you have apprehensions, what can you do to overcome them so when you do begin your fast, you will be armed and ready?

2 Make a commitment to review over the next week every food label for the packaged foods you purchase for yourself and your family. See "Making Sense of Ingredients on Food Labels" on page 138. This exercise should open your eyes to the plethora of unhealthy ingredients contained in many packaged foods.

3 Pick one day this coming week and consume only water as your beverage. Aim for one gallon over the course of the day. Then reflect on how you felt. If the results were positive, consider water as your beverage of choice from that point forward.

taking control of your health

CHAPTER 4

your body matters

I'll admit it. Sometimes I (Susan) wish my legs were longer. And there are a few other things I'd change about my body if I could. Maybe you can relate. It seems most of us struggle with dissatisfaction about our bodies and our appearance. But have you considered how God thinks about you and your body? Like David in the Old Testament, have you ever marveled at how God created you—and thanked him for such a gift? In considering his body, David skipped right over dissatisfaction and went straight to praise: "For you created my inmost being; you knit me together in my mother's womb. I praise you because I am fearfully and wonderfully made; your works are wonderful, I know that full well" (Psalm 139:13–14).

No matter how you feel about your body right now, we hope you will open yourself to the truth of David's words, which is the truth about how God created you—wonderfully and with purpose. If more of us were like David and could see ourselves the way God sees us, our spontaneous response would be praise rather than dissatisfaction or disappointment or self-loathing. We would feel better about the way God created us, and we would take better care of ourselves.

As you enter this part of the Daniel Cure, we suggest you set aside any poor body images you might have. For the moment at least, hush the negative inner voices that keep telling you you're too fat, or too short, or too plain looking. Instead, as much as possible, take a step back and try to see yourself the way God sees you—the way your Creator sees you. Remember, it is God who "saw all that he had made," and declared that indeed "it was very good" (Genesis 1:31).

THE HUMAN BODY IS GOD'S MASTERPIECE

To better understand the masterpiece God made when he created the human body, allow us to take you on a mini-tour of just one of the amazing systems that keeps your body alive — the vascular system, composed of your blood vessels. Beneath your skin is an intricately designed and masterfully created symphony of biological instruments. These hollow tubes transport liquid life throughout your entire body. If you were to set all your blood vessels end to end, they would wrap around the earth more than twice!

You have three main types of blood vessels: arteries, veins, and capillaries.* All of these vessels work in concert with your heart and lungs to comprise the cardiovascular and cardiorespiratory systems. Arteries and veins are large vessels composed of smooth muscle, elastic tissue, fibrous tissue, and a thin layer of cells called endothelium that lines the interior surface of the blood vessels. As the heart beats and forcefully ejects blood, the blood passes directly into the arteries. The pulmonary circulation system first plays its essential role. The pulmonary arteries carry oxygen-depleted blood from the right side of the heart to the lungs to receive oxygen, and oxygen-rich blood is carried to the left side of the heart. This oxygen-rich blood is then pumped by the left side of the heart into the aorta — the largest artery in the body — for transport throughout the body. Veins, which do not contain as much muscle as arteries, carry oxygen-depleted blood back to the heart from body tissues.

Capillaries are very small vessels, smaller than a hair, and consist entirely of endothelium, which regulates blood flow into and out of tissues. This occurs through a rather complex series of events involving smooth muscle and two specialized chemicals: endothelin, which causes vessels to constrict, and nitric oxide, which causes the vessels to open.

Arteries and veins generally run parallel throughout the body and are connected through a web-like network of capillaries embedded in tissue. The strong left-ventricle muscle of the heart pumps blood into the aorta, which then passes it along into arteries of decreasing size, finally arriving at the capillaries. This is where tissues, such as your muscles, extract the precise amount of oxygen from the blood that they need to perform a given task. For example, your muscles need less oxygen while you're at rest, much more when you're active. As your blood passes through tissues, it loses oxygen and gains waste products such as carbon dioxide. Moving into your veins, this "venous," or

---

*Included in the category of arteries are the much smaller arterioles; included in the category of veins are the much smaller venules.

deoxygenated, blood returns to the right side of the heart, where it is pumped once more to the lungs, drops off carbon dioxide for removal from the body (which happens when you exhale), and is saturated with oxygen (when you inhale) before it returns to the left side of the heart to start the journey all over again. A single round trip takes about a minute.

This amazing process occurs continuously throughout life, with average-size adults pumping approximately five liters of blood throughout their bodies every minute of every day. And that's in a resting state. With vigorous exercise, the heart has to work faster and the volume of blood can increase to between twenty and forty liters of blood per minute. So that's about 1,900 gallons of blood per day while at rest, and about 300 gallons during a sixty-minute, moderate-intensity workout. The heart is an impressive pump.

Your body's vascular system is just one of the many components of this mighty machine God created and entrusted to you. Every part of your body is

I'VE EXPERIENCED REPEATED DIET FAILURE. WHY SHOULD THINGS BE DIFFERENT NOW?

If you've had disappointing experiences with previous diets, you might be wondering, "Why would the Daniel Cure plan work for me?" Well, beyond the distinctions between this eating plan (which makes no restrictions on the amount of food consumed) and the poorly designed plans so often followed, the most important reason is this: In the past, you may have tried to do things on your own—through your own power and your own ability. With the Daniel Cure, we encourage you to come to the Lord and ask for his guidance and strength as you embark on this journey. Allow God to become your personal trainer!

For many of us today, food has almost become an idol and takes priority in life. To overcome this attachment to food, we need the Lord's help. In fact, we all need God's help in everything we do, no matter how big or how small—this includes adopting a lifestyle approach to healthy eating. Just like all good earthly parents, our heavenly Father is here for us whenever we call, always wanting to be with us and to assist us. In response, we consistently demonstrate our love for God by being obedient to his Word (see John 14:15).

You might say, "Well, I don't even believe in God. How does all of this apply to me?" Quite simply, it doesn't. But it could. God loves you and he desires to have a personal and intimate relationship with you. It is our prayer that you will come to accept Jesus as your personal Lord and Savior. It's not difficult, and it doesn't require any special preparation. If you feel the tug of the Holy Spirit on your heart right now, simply surrender to him. Admit that you are a sinner. Ask for his forgiveness. Declare your repentance (a changing of your ways). Commit your life to following Christ from this day forward. Give yourself to him and allow him to live inside you, directing your path and shining his light for all to see. It's the most important decision you will ever make.

intricately designed to work together so you can maintain good health every minute of every day. That's the way God engineered the human body—as a stunning, amazing, powerful, and purposeful masterpiece!

In the coming chapters we'll explore more about the body—and we'll look at what happens when this amazing work of art is neglected or abused. Our hope is that you will be so captivated by God's awesome gift to you that a new desire will rise up within you to give your body the very best care, complete with a new lifestyle aimed at optimizing your health.

YOU ARE MORE THAN A BODY

The body is a masterpiece, but it is just one part of the amazing composition that makes us human beings created in God's image. Consider what these words from the apostle Paul reveal about how God created us: "Now may the God of peace Himself sanctify you completely; and may your whole *spirit, soul,* and *body* be preserved blameless at the coming of our Lord Jesus Christ" (1 Thessalonians 5:23 NKJV, emphasis added).

So what does this mean? I sometimes explain Paul's statement this way: "You are a spirit. You have a soul. You live in a body." Let's take a closer look at each one.

You Are a Spirit

God created human beings in his image, and God is a Spirit (see John 4:24; 2 Corinthians 3:17). It is the spirit within you that connects with the Spirit of God. When you accepted Christ into your life, your spirit was reborn: "Flesh gives birth to flesh, but the Spirit gives birth to spirit" (John 3:6) And as a new creature in Christ, "you were washed, you were sanctified, you were justified in the name of the Lord Jesus Christ and by the Spirit of our God" (1 Corinthians 6:11). Born-again believers have a living spirit that is in Christ: "But whoever is united with the Lord is one with him in spirit" (1 Corinthians 6:17).

You Have a Soul

Your soul encompasses your will, intellect, emotions, and personality. The Greek word for soul is *psyche,* and it is most often translated as "life." This part of our human nature is not immediately transformed when we are born again. If you were stubborn before you gave your life to Christ, you will still be stubborn after you give your life to Christ. However, as you submit yourself to the Spirit of God and learn from him, you will be transformed. The apostle Paul wrote, "Do not conform to the pattern of this world, but be *transformed by the renewing of your mind*. Then you will be able to test and approve what God's will is — his good, pleasing and perfect will" (Romans 12:2, emphasis added).

Our faith journey includes growing in the love and knowledge of Christ so we can be transformed. Then we become more in line and consistent with who we are in Christ.

You Live in a Body

The body is the physical container for the soul and spirit. God's Word clearly establishes that caring for the body is critical to our well-being and our life with God. The apostle Paul affirmed this when he wrote, "Do you not know that your bodies are temples of the Holy Spirit, who is in you, whom you have received from God? You are not your own; you were bought at a price. Therefore honor God with your bodies" (1 Corinthians 6:19 – 20).

Spirit, soul, and body encompass the totality of the human experience. God designed all three parts of us to work together in harmony and health. As children of God, we are called to be the best we can be and bring glory to our Creator. And God miraculously equips us to do this: "His divine power has given us everything we need for a godly life through our knowledge of him who called us by his own glory and goodness. Through these he has given us his very great and precious promises, so that through them you may participate in the divine nature, having escaped the corruption in the world caused by evil desires" (2 Peter 1:3 – 4).

When we accept our new life in Christ and our godly nature, we want to submit to the Lord and follow his ways. We submit our will to his will and we develop the deep and abiding trust children have for their Father.

FREE WILL AND TRUST

When God created human beings, he gave us free will — the freedom to make our own choices. Why? In part because God created us in his image and he has free will. One of the significant choices free will enables us to make has to do with trust — especially when we face difficulties and temptations. Three stories in the Bible demonstrate what our choices reveal about whom or what we trust most.

- *Adam and Eve.* God gave Adam and Eve everything they needed, denying them only one thing: "Of every tree of the garden you may freely eat; but of the tree of the knowledge of good and evil you shall not eat, for in the day that you eat of it you shall surely die" (Genesis 2:16 – 17

NKJV). Nevertheless, when they were tempted, they listened to the deceiving words of the serpent. Adam and Eve had free will and chose to trust the enemy rather than God.

- *The Israelites in the Exodus.* God delivered his people from slavery in Egypt and told them he would give them the Promised Land (see Deuteronomy 1:8). But in spite of God's demonstrated goodness and faithfulness, the people allowed their difficult circumstances to overwhelm their trust. They repeatedly doubted God, tested him, disobeyed him, and ultimately chose to worship an idol instead of him (see Acts 7:39–43). As a result, God caused them to wander for forty years and an entire generation died in the wilderness, never reaching the Promised Land. The Israelites had free will and chose to trust an idol rather than God.

- *Jesus in the Garden of Gethsemane.* On the night he was betrayed, Jesus was "overwhelmed with sorrow to the point of death" (Matthew 26:38). Knowing he would soon be arrested and crucified, he went with his disciples to the Garden of Gethsemane to pray. With his face to the ground, he cried out, "My Father, if it is possible, may this cup be taken from me. Yet not as I will, but as you will" (Matthew 26:39). Even in the face of death, he submitted himself to God. Jesus had free will and he chose to trust God.

God created you with a free will. Just like Adam and Eve, the Israelites, and Jesus, you have full control to choose what you will do and what you won't do. Will you trust God and follow his ways? Will you align your thoughts, emotions, personality, and actions with the way, the truth, and the life of Jesus?

Just as God didn't impose his will on Adam and Eve in the garden, or on the Israelites in the wilderness, or on Jesus at Gethsemane, God doesn't impose his will on us. We have free will, and with free will comes the responsibility to choose. The root word in responsibility is "respond." We can choose how we respond to the temptations and difficult circumstances we face. However, it's important to note that having choices does not mean we have control of the outcome once we make a choice.

Think about it. If Adam and Eve could have foreseen the consequences of eating the forbidden fruit, perhaps they would have chosen differently. But it's also true that their decision wasn't based on the consequences—God had told them they would die. That's a pretty steep consequence. Ultimately, their choice was motivated by a lack of trust in God. They did not trust that God knew what was best for them. They didn't believe God when he warned them.

This remains true for us today! Too often, our choices demonstrate a lack of trust that God knows what is best for us. And yet we know that trust is what God calls us to do. He truly does know what is best for us, and he wants us to have the blessed life that Jesus died to give us. As children of his, as heirs to his kingdom, he's given us promises, power, and authority. And he's given us the free choice to be like Adam and Eve who placed their trust in the enemy, like the Israelites who placed their trust in idols, or like Jesus who placed his trust in God. The choice is ours — who is the one we will trust?

YOUR BODY IS GOD'S TEMPLE

As followers of Jesus, most of us are familiar with this teaching from the apostle Paul: "Do you not know that you are the temple of God and that the Spirit of God dwells in you?" (1 Corinthians 3:16 NKJV). To better understand what it really means that we are the dwelling place for God, it's helpful to know something about the tabernacle, which was the first structure God designed to fulfill his desire to dwell with his people.

The tabernacle was a portable sanctuary where the Israelites worshiped God during their forty years in the wilderness. God so wanted to be with his people that he gave Moses precise instructions about the purpose, construction, and furnishings for the tabernacle (see Exodus 25:40). When the tabernacle was completed, God took up residence there: "Then the cloud covered the tabernacle of meeting, and the glory of the LORD filled the tabernacle" (Exodus 40:34 NKJV).

God appointed Moses' brother Aaron as the first high priest and caretaker of his dwelling place. As high priest, Aaron was the only one who could enter the Holy of Holies — the inner sanctuary — and he could enter only once a year on the Day of Atonement (Exodus 30:10; Hebrews 9:6 – 7).

Aaron took his assignment very seriously and fulfilled his duties with the utmost care and precision. After all, this was a holy place, the very dwelling place of God, the Most High.

Take a moment to imagine yourself in Aaron's place. Picture yourself getting dressed in the priestly vestments, using meticulous care because you know you will soon step into God's dwelling place on earth. As you enter the outer court and approach the altar, you know that the Lord is very near, residing behind the curtain, above the mercy seat in the Holy of Holies, the most sacred place of all.

Can you picture it?

If you are a follower of Christ, this most sacred place of all — the place where God dwells — is *you*. Your body is the holy of holies. Now read what the Scriptures have to say about you: "Do you not know that your body is the temple of the Holy Spirit who is in you, whom you have from God, and you are not your own? For you were bought at a price; therefore glorify God in your body and in your spirit, which are God's" (1 Corinthians 6:19–20 NKJV).

How does this truth impact you? Do you really believe it — that God lives *in you*?

Does your body matter? Yes! Your body matters because it was God who made it — just for you! And it matters because you are not your own. Jesus Christ, the only Son of God, offered himself as the sacrifice for your redemption (see Hebrews 9:11–15). You are a masterpiece of God's design, a priceless treasure in the eyes of the Creator who made and redeemed you for his holy service. Plus, your body is the home of the living God.

If we fail to grasp this truth — that we are God's holy temple — we will continue to mistreat our bodies. Can you imagine Aaron tossing garbage into the Holy of Holies? Or allowing the curtains surrounding the outer court to be defiled with graffiti? Unthinkable! Yet when it comes to physical health, many Christians treat their bodies more like a garbage dump than the temple of the Most High. Instead of eating with great care, they fill their stomachs with the poorest quality foods — foods empty of nutrients and loaded with calories, sugar, fat, and chemicals. And consider this sad fact: Most dog food has a higher nutritional value than the diet consumed by the average American. The same is true for rodent chow fed to lab rats. This is insane!

As a result of our poor dietary choices, we are a nation afflicted with a host

CREATE AND MAINTAIN A HEALTH FILE FOR YOU AND YOUR FAMILY MEMBERS

It's often easier and more interesting to track your health when you know your starting point. We suggest that you maintain a simple health file for you and for each member of your family. The file should include the most important physical measures, which are typically part of routine physical exams. This includes your body weight, waist and hip circumference, resting heart rate, blood pressure, blood cholesterol, and blood sugar. You might also include other measures that you or your physician feel are important. Doing so will allow you to review your results regularly (annually) and quickly. You can then work with your physician and other health-care professionals to determine what, if any, course of action is needed to improve your results. For your convenience, we have created a template health file that you can download and use. You can find it on our site at *www.DanielCure.com*, as well as in the appendix "The Daniel Cure Health File" on page 274.

of preventable diseases, including obesity, type 2 diabetes, and cardiovascular disease. Many of us walk around tired and suffer from poor quality of sleep. Most men, women, and children don't move their bodies enough. We are discouraged, stressed, and maintain a generally poor outlook on life. As a result of all the poor choices, you could say that many of us are "existing" rather than "living." With the Daniel Cure approach, you can take control of your life. (See "I've Experienced Repeated Diet Failure. Why Should Things Be Different Now?" on page 35.)

As children of God and heirs to the mighty throne, we don't have to settle for just existing. We can clean the temple in which God dwells and rededicate ourselves to caring for it. In the name of Jesus, we can boldly proclaim, "I can do all this through him who gives me strength" (Philippians 4:13). Take a stand for the glorious and healthy life God wants you to have. Accept God's invitation to take responsibility for your choices. Focus your efforts on improving your health through the Daniel Fast and the Daniel Cure lifestyle principles. A healthier life of service and vitality awaits.

Let's get started.

■■■■■■■■ TURN YOUR THOUGHTS INTO ACTIONS ■■■■■■■■

1 Take a few minutes to reflect on the goodness of your body—the fine detail God put into creating you. Write down four to six things you are grateful for. Then express your thanks to God for the masterpiece that you are. Thank him that you are fearfully and wonderfully made. Be specific. For example, "Father, I thank you that you give me the breath to run three miles each day. I thank you for my strong heart and the way it pumps life-giving blood to all my body parts. I thank you that my stomach works just as you designed it to operate. I thank you that you designed my body to be strong and capable of helping others."

2 Assess your health by establishing a baseline. Make an appointment for a routine physical and follow the guidelines in "Create and Maintain a Health File for You and Your Family Members" on page 40.

CHAPTER 5

losing weight and preventing obesity

A RECENT NEWS REPORT HIGHLIGHTED THE STORY OF AN AMERICAN MAN who, while traveling throughout Africa on a mission trip, was asked, "Is it really true that people in America actually pay money to *lose* weight?" The man who asked had little food to eat. He would consider himself blessed to sit down to one good meal a day or to provide the same for his family.

Of course, the answer to the man's question is a sad but emphatic yes. Weight-loss products along with related elective procedures and services amount to a multi-billion-dollar-per-year business in the United States. All of this expense, yet we are still grossly overweight. In fact, many people are clinically obese. Poor food choices are fueling an obesity epidemic in our nation and in other nations around the world.

This crisis is costly. A recent study from the group Campaign to End Obesity now estimates obesity-related costs at close to $190 billion a year in the United States, with increased expenditures for items ranging from health care to worker absenteeism and even to the increased costs for jet fuel and gasoline, since more energy is required to carry heavier passengers.[7] The annual medical costs for patients who are obese are estimated to be close to $2,000 higher than for patients of normal weight.

THE FACTS ABOUT OBESITY

We are dealing with a critical issue that needs our attention and action. Obesity is not simply a condition that makes it hard to shop for clothes. Nor is obesity merely a condition associated with social anxiety because you may feel uncomfortable with your physical appearance.

Obesity is a disease. That's right. If you know someone who is obese, they have a disease. When I (Rick) was younger and heard someone use the word "obese," I immediately thought of a man or woman who was *huge*. Someone who had difficulty moving. Someone who had difficulty sitting in a standard chair. Someone who couldn't be weighed on a household scale. While this may be the case for individuals who are morbidly obese, it is clearly not the case for most who are obese. In fact, many people are clinically obese and don't even know it.

Obesity is not simply the feeling of disappointment you experience when you see your reflection in a full-length mirror and look heavier than you thought. It's not just the frustration you sense when you say to yourself, "Yikes, I can't fit into these jeans anymore!" Obesity, regardless of the degree, is a disease that over time can cause other debilitating diseases. Most people who are obese don't even realize the damage that's happening in their own bodies.

Obesity is a lifestyle disease. Obesity is linked to an individual's daily living patterns. The skyrocketing rise in obesity is directly linked to physical inactivity and poor eating habits.

Obesity is strongly linked to other lifestyle diseases. Obesity is a contributing factor for development of type 2 diabetes and cardiovascular disease. This includes high blood pressure, heart disease, and stroke. Obesity is also associated with certain types of cancer, with chronic joint pain, and with poor sleep quality.

Obesity impacts all populations, regardless of race, gender, age, or socioeconomic status. Recent CDC (Centers for Disease Control and Prevention) reports show that obesity rates are high in all states, ranging from a low of 20.7 percent of the population in Colorado who are diagnosed as obese to a high of 34.9 percent of the population in Mississippi diagnosed as obese. Table 5.1 presents recent figures for the five states with the highest incidence of obesity.

Obesity is also high for all ethnic groups, with non-Hispanic blacks topping the list (table 5.2).[8]

Obesity starts at a young age. Obesity among children and adolescents has almost tripled since 1980, with approximately 17 percent of boys and girls between the ages of two

TABLE 5.1
Highest Incidence of Obesity in the US

State	Percentage Obese
Mississippi	34.9
Louisiana	33.4
West Virginia	32.4
Alabama	32.0
Michigan	31.3

TABLE 5.2
Obesity by Ethnic Group

Ethnic Group	Percentage Obese
Non-Hispanic Blacks	49.5
Mexican Americans	40.4
Hispanics	39.1
Non-Hispanic Whites	34.3

to nineteen now diagnosed as obese. That's about 12.5 million individuals. Hispanic boys are more likely to be obese than non-Hispanic white boys, and non-Hispanic black girls are more likely to be obese than non-Hispanic white girls. Perhaps even more alarming is research from the Pediatric Nutrition Surveillance System indicating that one in seven preschool-aged children from low-income families are obese and at risk for chronic diseases.[9] Imagine walking into a nursery school classroom. You look around at the precious lives ... and one of every seven of the children is obese. Consider the pain and dangers they will face later in life.

Here is the dark picture painted by these facts:

- Obesity is a lifestyle disease with the potential to lead to other chronic diseases and death.
- Obesity rates are increasing at a rapid pace.
- Obesity impacts adults, adolescents, and children from all walks of life.
- 35.7 percent of adults are obese, up from about 13 percent just fifty years ago.
- By 2030, an estimated 42 percent of adults in the US will be obese.[10]
- 17 percent, or 12.5 million, of children and adolescents are obese.

These facts should spark great alarm in all of us. Former Surgeon General of the United States Richard Carmona warned, "Obesity is the terror within. Unless we do something about it, the magnitude of the dilemma will dwarf 9-11 or any other terrorist attempt."[11]

The problem of obesity needs to be dealt with now, but not by the government or by other organizations. By *us*. Yes, we need to do something about obesity. Like so many other issues in life, addressing the problem of obesity begins at home. Each one of us has everything inside of us to stop obesity. We need to take full responsibility for our own health. And we need to take responsibility for the health of our children. This is the only way the problem will ever be corrected. (See "The Hidden Culprit behind the Increase in Obesity Rates" on page 49.)

"AM I OBESE?"

How do you know if you're obese? You may say, "I don't want to know!" But remember, we're here to help you. So let's take a closer look.

The main tool used to classify someone as obese is the Body Mass Index (BMI). This tool is simple to use and you can easily identify your BMI using table 5.3.

Simply find your height in inches in the far left column and your body

Table 5.3: Body Mass Index

Body Weight (pounds)

Height (inches)	BMI 17	18	19	20	21	22	23	24	25	26	27	28	29	30	31	32	33	34
58	82	86	91	96	100	105	110	115	119	124	129	134	138	143	148	153	158	162
59	84	89	94	99	104	109	114	119	124	128	133	138	143	148	153	158	163	168
60 (5ft)	87	93	97	102	107	112	117	123	128	133	138	143	148	153	158	163	168	174
61	90	96	100	106	111	116	122	127	132	137	143	148	153	158	164	169	174	180
62	93	99	104	109	115	120	127	131	136	142	147	153	158	163	169	175	186	191
63	96	102	107	113	118	124	130	135	141	146	152	157	163	169	175	180	191	197
64	99	105	111	116	122	128	134	140	145	151	157	163	169	174	180	186	197	204
65	102	108	114	120	127	132	138	144	150	156	162	168	174	180	186	192	204	210
66	106	113	118	124	130	136	146	148	155	161	167	173	179	186	192	198	210	216
67	109	115	121	125	134	140	151	153	159	166	172	178	185	191	198	205	218	223
68	112	119	125	131	138	144	156	158	164	171	177	184	190	197	203	210	223	230
69	115	121	128	135	142	149	160	162	169	176	182	188	196	203	209	216	230	236
70	119	126	132	139	146	153	165	167	174	181	188	195	202	209	216	222	236	243
71	122	129	136	143	150	157	169	172	179	186	193	200	208	215	222	229	243	250
72 (6ft)	125	133	140	147	154	162	174	177	184	191	199	206	213	221	228	235	250	258
73	129	137	144	151	159	166	179	182	189	197	205	212	219	227	235	243	257	265
74	133	141	148	155	164	171	184	186	194	202	210	218	225	233	241	249	264	272
75	136	144	153	160	168	176	189	192	200	208	216	224	232	240	248	256	272	279
76	139	148	155	164	172	182	194	197	205	214	222	230	238	247	255	262	276	285
77	143	151	159	168	177	186	199	202	211	219	228	236	244	254	262	269	284	291
78	147	155	163	172	182	191	204	207	217	224	233	242	250	260	269	278	291	294

BMI categories: **Underweight** (17–18) · **Normal Weight** (19–24) · **Overweight** (25–29) · **Grade I Obese** (30–34)

This table was adapted from the following source: NHLBI Obesity Education Initiative Expert Panel on the Identification, Evaluation, and Treatment of Obesity in Adults (US), *Clinical Guidelines on the Identification, Evaluation, and Treatment of Overweight and Obesity in Adults: The Evidence Report* (Bethesda, MD: National Heart, Lung, and Blood Institute, 1998), appendix V, http://www.ncbi.nlm.nih.gov/books/NBK2003/.

weight in pounds in the table body. Then find the corresponding BMI in the bottom row of the table. This table includes a BMI from 17 to 34 (underweight to grade I obese), the range that fits the majority of individuals. However, if you find that your BMI is not identified in this table or if you want to compute a more precise value for your BMI, see "How to Compute Your Body Mass Index" on page 47 for the simple calculation steps.

Table 5.4 gives precise BMI figures for classifying individuals as normal weight, overweight, or obese.

Table 5.4: BMI Classifications

Category	BMI	Comments
Underweight	<18.5	Having too low a bodyweight may indicate malnutrition or an eating disorder.
Normal/Healthy Weight	18.5 – 24.9	This is the ideal range for most individuals; individuals with excess muscle mass may fall into the overweight category (but seldom in an obese category).
Overweight	25.0 – 29.9	Not technically obese but possibly moving in that direction; health problems may be associated with overweight status.
Grade I Obese	30.0 – 34.9	The initial stage of obesity; the likelihood of health problems may increase with this stage of disease.
Grade II Obese	35.0 – 39.9	The mid-stage of obesity; associated with approximately a 30 percent greater risk of death compared to normal weight.
Grade III Obese	≥40.0	The morbid stage of obesity; multiple health problems are associated with this stage of the disease; as with grade II obesity, this stage is associated with approximately a 30 percent greater risk of death compared to normal weight.

One flaw of the BMI tool is that it does not take into account the amount of muscle mass and fat mass of the individual. It simply measures body mass (weight) without any distinction for what the body weight is made of. My (Rick) BMI of around 25 places me toward the borderline of normal/healthy weight and overweight, even though for years my percentage of body fat has stayed in the single digits. Because of this BMI flaw, heavily muscled individuals can get bumped into the overweight or obese categories despite being in very good physical condition. This is particularly apparent in strength athletes who carry a large amount of muscle mass, such as football players, power lifters, and bodybuilders. For example, it would not be unusual for a regional-level bodybuilder who stands 5'10" and weighs 220 pounds to have just 5 percent body fat, yet the BMI would be close to 32, or grade I obese. With 5 percent body fat, this individual is not obese. However, for most people, the BMI does exactly what it is designed to do. Excess body weight means excess body fat.

The bottom line is this: If your BMI is 30 or more, you are obese. This may not sit well with some people. They associate the word *obese* with those who are morbidly obese. And they don't see themselves as *that* person. But don't be discouraged if your BMI is too high. Rather, focus on the fact that you can take control of the situation now and easily address it before it leads to other health-related problems.

WHY YOU SHOULD BE CONCERNED ABOUT OBESITY

The main reason why you or anyone else who is overweight should be concerned is that you are a precious and priceless creation of God. And like any loving father, God wants his children to be at their best—spiritually, emotionally, and physically.

Another reason is to avoid the hazards of being obese. "What hazards?" you ask. Well, for starters, if you are obese or heading in that direction, you are likely to develop certain associated lifestyle diseases, such as type 2 diabetes, high blood pressure, heart disease, and stroke. What does this mean? For many people, these conditions result in frequent trips to the doctor, routine use of medications, amputations and blindness (with diabetes), heart attack

HOW TO COMPUTE YOUR BODY MASS INDEX

The BMI (Body Mass Index) is a simple calculation that uses height and weight to determine whether a person is of normal weight or not. To compute your BMI, you need only two variables:

1. Your body weight (in pounds)
2. Your height (in inches)

The formula looks like this:

$$BMI = 703 \times Weight\ [pounds] \div (Height\ [inches] \times Height\ [inches])$$

Here is an example.

1. Weight is 182 pounds
2. Height is 72 inches (6 feet)

The BMI equation looks like this:

$$BMI = 703 \times 182 \div (72 \times 72)$$
$$BMI = 127{,}946 \div 5{,}184 = 24.7\ (Normal\ Weight\ Category)$$

Input *your* values in the following equation:

$$BMI = 703 \times Your\ Weight\ _____ \div (Your\ Height\ _____ \times Your\ Height\ _____)$$

$$BMI = _____ \div _____ = _____$$

LIFESTYLE VERSUS GENETICS

Obesity is a lifestyle disease largely determined by an individual's daily choices regarding physical activity and dietary intake. But there is a genetic component to obesity. Genes appear to regulate how our bodies accumulate, store, use, and release energy from the food we eat. Genes may also regulate how full we feel after eating, our tendency to be active or inactive, our degree of motivation and discipline to adhere to a healthy lifestyle. However, most scientists would agree that while genes may play a role in obesity, their overall impact on obesity is relatively small compared to the huge impact of lifestyle factors. Most people are obese because of their choices, not because of "bad genetics" or a "slow metabolism."

and death from heart disease, and significant impairments in quality of life with a stroke. Susan's father was only fifty-four years old when he died of a heart attack. It was the first sign that he had any heart issues. For about 30 percent of men and women with heart disease, the first symptom results in death. Just think about that. That's a big deal!

If you are obese, you are also at increased risk for developing several types of cancer, such as esophageal, breast (postmenopausal), endometrial (the lining of the uterus), colon and rectal, kidney, pancreatic, thyroid, and gallbladder.[12]

Obesity is also strongly associated with chronic joint pain, in particular in the lower extremities and the back, and poor sleep quality. This typically results in a lack of physical activity, contributing to a reduced quality of life and a progression of the obesity problem. These conditions are referred to as co-morbidities — medical conditions that may be associated with or complicated by obesity.

Consider the debilitating effect that obesity and the related health problems can have on both the quality and the length of your life, and then plan to correct the obesity problem now. Will it be easy? Probably not. But we've all known people or have read stories about men and women who finally tackled their weight issues, pressed on and did the hard work to overcome the obstacles, and gained their life back. Developing a healthy lifestyle and losing weight doesn't happen by accident. You need a plan — and the Daniel Cure can help you take the first steps.

THE DANIEL FAST AND OBESITY

Many individuals using the Daniel Fast lose weight. In our studies, we have noted weight loss of up to thirty-six pounds in just twenty-one days. This was an unusual case, and not every person who starts a Daniel Fast should expect to lose weight this rapidly. The average weight loss in our twenty-one-day studies has been about six pounds — with greater weight loss in those who have more weight to lose. (See "Lifestyle versus Genetics" above.)

Here is one story of life change from a woman named Cincy: "I started a Daniel Fast with my church four years ago. During the fast, I focused my prayer on healing for obesity. I was so tired of fighting this battle all my life. Through the fast, the Lord enabled me to continue eating healthy the rest of my life. Now, four years later, I have lost 147 pounds and feel wonderful. I praise the Lord for my breakthrough. I have been healed!"

For Cincy, the Daniel Fast was a launch pad. She used the principles of the fast to get started. Then she persisted and adopted much of what she learned to develop a long-term program of healthy eating. Most importantly, she prayed to the Lord and asked for his guidance and healing power. This is indeed a great lesson for all of us, regardless of what we might be struggling with.

THE HIDDEN CULPRIT BEHIND THE INCREASE IN OBESITY RATES

Why has the obesity rate increased so dramatically? Depending on whose information you read, you will find a variety of answers to this question, ranging from lack of physical activity to poor dietary choices. But we need to go deeper than that. And there is a significant case to be made that the main culprit is a breakdown of the traditional family unit.

Consider the fact that there are more single-parent households now than at any other time in our history. Even more disturbing is the fact that most of these cases arise from divorce and pregnancy outside of marriage. Most single-parent homes are led by women, often with little to no fatherly presence. In many cases, single parents work to provide for the family and are not available to cook regular meals for their children, to play outdoors with their children, or to ensure optimal health practices for their children or for themselves. Given the overwhelming demands they face, single parents are often weighed down and focus on basic needs — earning a living to maintain a roof over their heads, clothes to wear, and food (albeit not the best food) on the table. Exercising regularly and making certain that meals and snacks are healthy are not priorities.

In many two-parent homes, both the husband and wife now work full time outside the home. While their economic situation may be somewhat improved when compared to a single-parent home, the fact remains that neither parents nor children often have the time needed to follow a healthy lifestyle. Parents do not regularly prepare healthy meals and snacks for themselves or for their children. They rely instead on highly processed and packaged foods, fast foods, and restaurant meals. Most families lack adequate time to play together in physically active ways. Few take the time to learn about healthy lifestyle options. And many are too tired to do what is absolutely necessary to lead a healthy lifestyle. We have a mass of families with no time for and no knowledge about how to live a healthy lifestyle. They are overworked, overtired, overstressed, and overweight — even obese. A perfect recipe for a progressive disease.

We need to get back to our traditional family structure. That is, a mom and a dad, both of whom manage their lives in such a way to have time to care for themselves — to lead by example — and to care for the well-being of their children. This includes raising children in a godly home, with family-centered physical activity and regular family meals of healthy foods.

You might be wondering why the Daniel Fast is so effective for weight loss. As Cincy's words affirm, you have the power of the Lord working for you. When you embark on this plan, you ask for his guidance. You surrender yourself to his will for your life. You ask for his strength to overcome the obstacles and challenges you face. As always, he will provide for your every need. You just need to ask according to his will.

Then you do your part by focusing on the change in lifestyle. While on the Daniel Fast, you are likely to eat fewer calories. How do I know this? Because that is the evidence from the nearly 200 people who completed the Daniel Fast as part of our research studies. (See "Daniel Fast Benefits: How Does It Happen and Why Is It Important?" on page 277.) Plus, the natural food choices on the Daniel Fast — vegetables, fruits, whole grains, beans, and nuts — are very satisfying. These foods generally provide more bulk and volume than their calorie-dense counterparts and allow you to feel fuller for longer periods of time. So you eat fewer calories. The Daniel Fast foods also tend to better maintain stability in your blood sugar levels throughout the day, leading to lower and more stable blood insulin levels — which can also be beneficial when attempting to lose weight. (See "Why Am I Eating This?" above.)

> **WHY AM I EATING THIS?**
>
> When putting any food or drink into your mouth, think about what good the nutrients will do for you. Do you expect to feel better, look better, perform better? If not, then ask yourself why you are eating them. It should not simply be to fill you up. The reasons for eating should be more specific than that. In fact, to develop and maintain a healthy and aesthetically pleasing body, your reasons for eating absolutely must be clear.

DANIEL FAST WEIGHT LOSS RESULTS

As a scientist dedicated to the study of human health through nutrition, dietary supplements, and exercise, I am always pleased to see the positive results participants experience when completing the Daniel Fast. Both men and women of varying ages, with a wide range of starting body weights and BMIs, have experienced remarkable success. Tables 5.5 and 5.6 present just a few of these cases. If you decide to begin a Daniel Fast, I have no doubt that your improvement can be similar to what is presented here. Why not commit yourself today to a lifestyle of healthy eating (and living) and change your life for the better from this day forward?

Table 5.5: Daniel Fast Results: Women

Female Participant, Age, Beginning Classification	Beginning Weight	Ending Weight	Weight Loss	Beginning and Ending BMI	
Sherri, 20, grade III obese	257 lbs	221 lbs	36 lbs	40.6	34.7
MaryAnn, 23, normal weight	120 lbs	110 lbs	10 lbs	20.6	18.6
Jennifer, 27, grade I obese	189 lbs	180 lbs	9 lbs	31.7	30.3
Olivia, 29, grade I obese	229 lbs	214 lbs	15 lbs	32.3	30.2
Celia, 35, grade II obese	218 lbs	208 lbs	10 lbs	37.3	35.6
May, 36, grade II obese	203 lbs	193 lbs	10 lbs	37.5	35.3
Lucia, 45, grade II obese	245 lbs	231 lbs	14 lbs	39.9	37.6

Table 5.6: Daniel Fast Results: Men

Male Participant, Age, Beginning Classification	Beginning Weight	Ending Weight	Weight Loss	Beginning and Ending BMI	
James, 23, normal weight	172 lbs	162 lbs	10 lbs	24.0	22.7
Mark, 39, overweight	186 lbs	178 lbs	8 lbs	29.2	27.9
Jeff, 39, grade I obese	212 lbs	200 lbs	12 lbs	30.1	28.4
Phillip, 40, grade I obese	218 lbs	203 lbs	15 lbs	30.9	28.8
Charles, 42, grade I obese	226 lbs	213 lbs	13 lbs	30.0	28.3
Stephan, 52, grade III obese	288 lbs	274 lbs	14 lbs	40.0	38.1
Cameron, 58, grade I obese	256 lbs	238 lbs	18 lbs	33.6	31.3

Some people enter the fast already in excellent physical condition and lose very little body weight but improve other aspects of their health (for example, their blood cholesterol profile). Others start the fast grossly overweight, with very poor dietary habits, and lose the greatest amount of weight as they begin to eat foods conducive to optimal health.

So what type of weight loss might be possible for you? Let's assume you buy into the idea of adopting a clean-eating approach and you decide to adopt the Daniel Cure plan. You first do the twenty-one-day Daniel Fast and then begin to make certain modifications to your overall diet to meet your unique needs as part of the Daniel Cure. For example, you might decide to add one serving per day of lean meat or fish, to drink skim milk and consume low-fat yogurt, and to drink no more than one or two cups of green tea or coffee most days of the week. You also decide that you'll enjoy one cheat meal per week and one homemade dessert. A very balanced plan. So what might you expect with such a program?

Assuming your diet was in rough shape to begin with (which is the unfortunate reality for most people), you will likely experience approximately a six- to ten-pound weight loss during your initial twenty-one-day Daniel Fast. You might experience a greater loss, but don't get discouraged if you do not. You're just getting started. (See "I'm Only Successful If I Lose Weight, Right?" below.) As you continue on a modified Daniel Fast plan—possibly with the inclusion of some animal products and occasional cheat meals and desserts—you should experience continued weight loss. This might come as one to two pounds per week until you reach your optimal body weight—the weight you personally feel most comfortable at. As you get closer to your desired weight, the shedding of pounds may slow down and become more difficult. This is normal and you are not an exception. You're not in trouble. To overcome this, you might consider short periods (3–4 weeks) when you become very disciplined in your eating and do away with your cheat meals and desserts and possibly reduce your calorie intake slightly. This calorie reduction should only be temporary, as we typically do not promote a long-term reduction in calories. Following a Daniel Cure eating plan does not require you to count calories. The mere fact that you will be eating healthy foods should result in a reduction in calorie intake by default—the foods on the Daniel Cure provide greater satisfaction and "fullness" compared with unhealthy food options.

Over the initial one-year period, you might expect to reduce your body weight by as much as 50 to 75 pounds, assuming you have this amount of weight to lose and you

I'M ONLY SUCCESSFUL IF I LOSE WEIGHT, RIGHT?

Wrong! So often people become discouraged with their diet or exercise program because they haven't lost a significant amount of weight (or any weight). But keep in mind that you may have achieved many other health-related benefits that you can't observe. Healthier eating will lead to favorable changes in cardiovascular and metabolic health. In addition to these positive changes, you might find that you are more energetic, sleep better at night, and are more motivated to get up and do things. You may also find that your clothes fit better and you actually look better despite not losing any weight.

Lack of weight loss is not all that uncommon. There are many reasons for this. In fact I (Rick) have seen some people actually gain weight when starting a new dietary program and intensive exercise training program.* This can be discouraging, but know that real benefits are occurring—you just can't see them. Unfortunately, we are too often fixated on the one factor we can see (weight loss) and forget about the different internal benefits going on as a result of our lifestyle efforts. Don't get discouraged. Press on. Stick with it. You are absolutely making a difference in your health even when the scale doesn't show it.

* Intensive exercise can induce an increase in blood volume, which may equate to about a two-pound weight gain during the first week. If you have experienced such a weight gain, this might be the explanation.

diligently adhere to your plan. Not bad for a simple change in dietary intake that includes a well-balanced meal plan and an occasional cheat meal and dessert. Once you achieve your desired body weight goal, simply maintain this by adhering to your diet plan. No tricks. No special programs. No short-term diets. No packaged foods to buy. No exotic supplements. Just a simple plan that *you* develop and *you* follow. A lifestyle approach aimed at optimal health.

WHERE TO GO FROM HERE

The burden of obesity is extreme. It includes financial costs, quality-of-life costs, and, potentially ... death. The good news is that, using the tools in this book, you can control this disease. If you are obese, you have the power to overcome this condition. As a child of the living God, believe that.

Overcoming obesity requires a systematic plan, including consistent and wise changes in your everyday life. Regular physical activity and appropriate dietary intake are necessary. A social support system is also essential for success—so that others in your family and your circle of influence understand what you are attempting to do and why. Most importantly, as you tackle this challenge, you need to come to the Lord in prayer and ask for his grace and empowerment. Don't make the mistake of attempting to do this in your own power. Overcoming a lifetime of poor eating habits, possibly involving addictive behavior, is a daunting task. But remember, you have the Creator of the universe on your side, walking with you every step of the way. You truly can start today and make the *rest* of your life the *best* of your life.

■■■■■ TURN YOUR THOUGHTS INTO ACTIONS ■■■■■

1 Envision yourself with significantly less body weight holding you down —you're light, strong, fast, and full of energy. Nothing can hold you back. What would you look forward to doing that you aren't able to do now?

2 Take the first step to become more physically active. Begin with a commitment to move for fifteen minutes a day—take a walk, use the stairs instead of the elevator, park at the far corner of the parking lot. Just get up and move. Start small and then progress to twenty minutes, thirty minutes, and up to sixty minutes of activity per day. You're on your way!

3 Make your last meal of the day your dinner meal. Eat after dinner only on a rare occasion. And when you do, eat only a low-calorie snack. Going to bed *slightly* hungry can be a real advantage when attempting to lose weight.

preventing and overcoming type 2 diabetes

CARL, A SIXTY-SIX-YEAR-OLD OBESE MAN WITH TYPE 2 DIABETES, BEGAN OUR six-month clinical Daniel Fast study with a fasting* blood glucose (sugar) value of 229 mg/dL. To better understand what Carl's glucose level means, consider the reference ranges in table 6.1.

Table 6.1: Fasting Blood Sugar Ranges

Category/Classification	Value	Comments
Normal/Healthy	<100 mg/dL	Normal values typically fall between 70 mg/dL and 99 mg/dL.
Pre-Diabetes	100–125 mg/dL	This does not mean that you will develop diabetes, but your risk of doing so is higher than if your blood sugar was less than 100 mg/dL.
Diabetes	≥126 mg/dL	If your fasting blood sugar is ≥126 mg/dL, you technically have diabetes; this may be confirmed more than once and/or by using more than one type of diagnostic test.

Based on these measurement standards, it's obvious that Carl's value of 229 mg/dL was exceedingly high. But after just three weeks on a traditional Daniel Fast diet, his fasting blood glucose dropped by 21 percent to 180 mg/dL. Still high, but a significant improvement from where he started. After three months, his blood sugar dropped to 145 mg/dL, and by the end of six months,

*A fasting blood glucose sample is collected first thing in the morning, with no food or calorie-containing beverages consumed in the preceding ten to twelve hours.

it was down to 107 mg/dL. That's a 53 percent reduction in just six months based solely on a change in diet. We also measured an important variable that indicates how well the hormone insulin was functioning in Carl's system. His value improved by 66 percent—absolutely remarkable! And Carl's results are not unique. Others with type 2 diabetes who have participated in our studies have experienced similar results, providing compelling evidence about the healing power of food.

WHAT EXACTLY IS DIABETES?

Diabetes is a metabolic disease in which the body does not properly process the food you eat (particularly carbohydrates) for use as energy. The result is an elevation in blood sugar, which may be due to a variety of causes. Diabetes is typically diagnosed with three routine lab tests:

1. *Fasting blood glucose:* This test indicates what your blood sugar is at the time the blood is drawn. A value exceeding 125 mg/dL confirms a diagnosis of diabetes.
2. *Hemoglobin A1c:* This test indicates how well your blood sugar has been controlled during the several-week period prior to the measurement. A value exceeding 6.4 percent confirms a diagnosis of diabetes.
3. *Oral glucose tolerance test:* You consume a 300-calorie syrupy drink designed for the test, and your blood glucose (and possibly insulin) is measured at intervals for two hours afterward. If your body is unable to appropriately lower the sugar in your blood by the end of two hours, you may be classified as having pre-diabetes or diabetes. A value exceeding 199 mg/dL confirms a diagnosis of diabetes.

Tests for diabetes focus on sugar in the blood because blood sugar is regulated by the hormone insulin. Individuals with diabetes have one of two insulin problems (or perhaps both):

1. The inability to *produce* insulin due to cell damage. There is an autoimmune destruction of the pancreatic beta cells (the cells responsible for producing insulin). This is the problem for those with type 1 diabetes.
2. The inability to appropriately utilize insulin. This is typically the problem for those with type 2 diabetes.

Insulin is a hormone with multiple functions, but, specific to our discussion here, it regulates blood sugar levels within a fairly narrow range (70–99 mg/dL when fasting). It does this by transporting blood sugar into tissue cells (such as muscles), where the sugar is either used as an energy source or stored for later use. When insulin production or utilization is impaired, sugar in the blood can't be properly removed or utilized by tissue cells. As a result, sugar accumulates in the bloodstream and fails to reach body cells that are starved for energy. The result is twofold: First, the excess blood sugar can become chemically modified and cause severe damage to blood vessels. Second, the lack of sugar reaching the target tissues leads to decreased energy production and the feeling of fatigue.

Individuals with diabetes are treated with insulin injections and/or take medications that mimic insulin or make tissues more sensitive and responsive to insulin. Certain nutritional supplements may also prove helpful in controlling blood sugar. (See "Are Dietary Supplements Beneficial for Type 2 Diabetes?" on page 62.)

While there are other forms of diabetes besides type 1 and type 2 (for example, gestational diabetes, which is related to pregnancy), type 2 diabetes represents 90 to 95 percent of all cases and is considered a lifestyle disease. That is, the onset and progression of this disease are largely dependent on lifestyle choices—dietary patterns and activity levels.

WHY IS DIABETES SUCH A PROBLEM?

Type 2 diabetes is a significant and growing problem worldwide. The World Health Organization estimates close to 346 million cases,[13] with roughly 80 percent of people with diabetes living in low- to middle-income countries. The facts about diabetes in the United States are just as disturbing:[14]

- Approximately 18.8 million people have been diagnosed with type 2 diabetes.
- Seven million people are believed to have undiagnosed diabetes.
- Seventy-nine million people are estimated to have pre-diabetes.
- Close to two million new cases of diabetes are diagnosed each year.

While the problem of diabetes plagues all states, as with obesity, the highest incidence rates are in the southeastern part of the Unites States. And in most of these states, it afflicts more than 10 percent of the population (compared to the national average of about 8.3 percent). In those twenty years or older, the impact of diabetes is about the same in men and women. The prevalence of diabetes in different ethnic groups in the US is shown in table 6.2 (p. 58).[15]

The incidence of diabetes also increases significantly as people get older. Close to 15 percent of those over age forty-five and 27 percent of those over sixty-five have diabetes.[16] And consider these alarming projections from the CDC:[17] "As many as one in three U.S. adults could have type 2 diabetes by 2050 if current trends continue. Approximately one in ten U.S. adults has type 2 diabetes now."

Many of the problems of diabetes are linked to obesity—in particular what is known as "central obesity," or carrying excess fat in the abdomen. As discussed in chapter 5, obesity is strongly associated with the development of

WHAT CAUSES BLOOD SUGAR TO BECOME ELEVATED?

When you eat carbohydrate-rich foods, especially processed foods, high amounts of sugar enter the bloodstream. The body senses the rise in blood sugar and initiates a complex sequence of events to get it back under control (see figure). The process goes something like this:

1. The pancreas secretes insulin into the bloodstream in an attempt to remove the sugar—the greater the blood sugar, the more insulin secreted.
2. Insulin binds to insulin receptors on the surface of cells (cell membrane).
3. A complex series of signals occur inside the cell that activates a family of proteins called "glucose 4 transporters," or GLUT4.
4. GLUT4 proteins move from inside the cell (intracellular space) to the cell membrane and allow for sugar (glucose) to enter the cell from the bloodstream.
5. The GLUT4 proteins move back into the intracellular space and glucose is now available within the cell to be metabolized for energy.

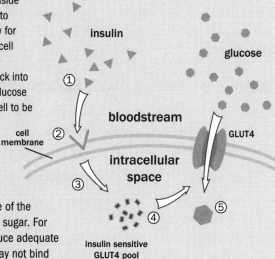

This whole process is extremely complex and highlights the human body masterpiece that God created.

Any problems with one or more of the steps can lead to a spike in blood sugar. For example, your body may not produce adequate insulin. Or the insulin produced may not bind correctly to the insulin receptors. The post-receptor signaling may be faulty. There may not be adequate GLUT4 available. Or GLUT4 is available but does not move from inside the cell to the surface of the cell. These are some of the reasons why someone with diabetes can have a high blood sugar level.

type 2 diabetes. Make no mistake—if you routinely eat a high-calorie diet comprised of processed foods, white-flour products, simple sugars, and saturated fat, there is a very good chance that one day your doctor will tell you that you have type 2 diabetes. Your likelihood of developing type 2 diabetes also increases if your lifestyle is largely sedentary and you carry a significant amount of body fat around your midsection. This applies to children as well as adults. If we fail to help our children develop healthy eating habits and stay physically active, their risk of suffering lifelong health issues increases significantly.

TABLE 6.2
Diabetes Incidence by Ethnic Group

Ethnic Group	Percent Diabetic
Non-Hispanic Blacks	12.6
Hispanics	11.8
Asians	8.4
Non-Hispanic Whites	7.1

Despite these facts about diabetes, many people continue to disregard or downplay their risk of developing the disease. They reason, "If I get diabetes, I'll just have to take pills or, in the worst case scenario, insulin injections. That's not so bad."

But here's the truth. Taking medications doesn't prevent the disease from causing debilitating health consequences, including toe, foot, or leg amputation; impaired eyesight or blindness; complications with pregnancy; kidney disease; and heart disease. Type 2 diabetes is also associated with multiple forms of cancer because cancer and diabetes share some of the same risk factors, including obesity and inflammation. The health consequences of diabetes are alarming.

CONTROLLING TYPE 2 DIABETES RISK AND PROGRESSION

If you aren't yet 100 percent convinced that taking action to reduce your risk of developing type 2 diabetes is important for your health, consider what it could cost you. For starters:

- Routine visits and co-pays/coinsurance to your primary-care doctor.
- Routine visits and co-pays/coinsurance to an endocrinologist (a specialist who treats diabetes).
- Routine visits to a variety of other specialists you will likely need to see to care for diabetes-induced conditions such as cardiovascular disease, eye disease, and kidney disease.
- Medication costs (oral hypoglycemic agents and insulin) and supplies (blood glucose test strips, lancets, needles). The average monthly costs range from $20 up to a few hundred dollars depending on medication and supplies and insurance.

- Sick leave and personal days away from work can result in lost productivity and thousands of dollars in lost wages.
- Diminished earning capacity due to time away from work for medical treatment, long-term disability, or forced early retirement due to health problems.

The collective economic burden of diabetes borne by the United States health-care system is significant, accounting for $245 billion in total costs in one year recently.[18] This includes $176 billion for direct medical costs and $69 billion for indirect costs such as disability, work loss (lost productivity), and premature mortality. The average annual medical expenses for those with diabetes is estimated to be 2.3 times higher than what health costs would be without diabetes. These statistics include only diagnosed cases. When factoring in the additional costs of undiagnosed diabetes, pre-diabetes, and gestational diabetes, the cost in the United States approaches $300 billion a year. This is a 37 percent increase in just five years, from $218 billion.[19]

Not only are the economic consequences distressing but the picture is even darker when we consider the damage to the body caused by diabetes:

- Diabetes is the seventh leading cause of death in the United States,[20] contributing to close to 230,000 deaths annually.[21] With the number of diagnosed cases increasing, this number will continue to grow.
- Diabetes is associated with a variety of macro-vascular diseases such as coronary artery disease, high blood pressure, stroke, and intermittent claudication (a condition that causes pain in the legs when walking or even standing). About 75 percent of those with diabetes die of some form of heart or blood vessel disease.[22]
- Diabetes is strongly associated with micro-vascular diseases that affect the eyes and lead to blindness, advanced kidney disease, nerve damage, and infection that can result in amputation. Diabetes is also associated with erectile dysfunction—a significant concern for many men.

These are more than statistics for me because I (Rick) know people who have suffered these terrible consequences. Several years ago, a man named Ed, who had poorly controlled diabetes, participated in a clinical study I was involved in. During the four-month study, Ed underwent two toe amputations. In another study, a forty-two-year-old man named David was unable to walk for more than a hundred yards without suffering severe leg pain due to complications of diabetic neuropathy. In early 2002, when Chrissy and I were preparing for our wedding ceremony, our pastor asked if he could use a very large type font on his version of the wedding program. He explained that he had diabetes and was going blind because of his failure to take care of himself over the years. Our wedding was just two months away, and he wasn't sure he would still be able to see by then. These are real problems suffered by real people.

Although diabetes is a costly and often debilitating disease, type 2 diabetes and the complications are largely avoidable if we simply adopt a lifestyle of regular physical activity and healthy eating. For most of us, it is just that simple.

THE DANIEL FAST AND DIABETES

We strongly believe the Daniel Fast eating plan offers significant benefits to those with type 2 diabetes as well as those who are at risk for developing the disease.* In fact, the preliminary results of our studies have been so striking, we are now interested in conducting studies focused exclusively on the Daniel Fast and diabetes.

Why does the Daniel Fast work well for those with type 2 diabetes? In short, because it stabilizes blood sugar levels by providing the body with healthy, fiber-rich, nutrient-dense food. For most of us, an ideal diet maintains stable blood sugar — avoiding highs and lows — which leads to positive effects for almost everyone. Benefits are body weight reduction, more efficient insulin action, and improvement in energy levels and mood. We can maintain stable blood sugar levels by:

- Consuming small but frequent meals. This means avoiding long gaps between meals by eating a small meal every two to three hours.
- Consuming macronutrient-balanced meals, which include small amounts of protein, carbohydrate, and fat. We'll talk more about macronutrients in chapter 11.
- Consuming nutrient-dense meals. No empty calories! Nutrient-dense foods have a high ratio of nutrients to calories. They contain the highest possible levels of quality protein, carbohydrate, fat, vitamins, and minerals for the least amount of calories.
- Consuming an abundance of fiber. Fiber is found in a variety of foods, including whole grains, fruits, vegetables, and beans.

*While those with type 1 diabetes may also benefit, we have not yet included individuals with type 1 diabetes in our research studies. Because type 1 and type 2 diabetes have different causes, we cannot state with confidence that similar benefits would be obtained.

HOW DOES EXERCISE IMPACT TYPE 2 DIABETES?

Beyond a proper diet, regular exercise is the single best thing you can do to prevent the onset or control the progression of type 2 diabetes.[†] Exercise has many health benefits. Studies indicate that those who are more physically active are far less likely to develop diabetes. Exercise may act as a preventive strategy:

1. Exercise involves energy expenditure that may lead to weight loss — and body mass is linked to the risk of developing type 2 diabetes.
2. Exercise can increase muscle mass, making more muscle available as a storage depot for blood sugar (carbohydrate).
3. Exercise improves insulin sensitivity, so less insulin is needed to perform the job.
4. Exercise improves multiple aspects of the post-receptor signaling cascade, allowing GLUT4 to move to the cell surface to take blood sugar into the cell.
5. Exercise increases the number of GLUT4 protein. More GLUT4 helps to bring more glucose into the cell.

Because exercise may have a profound effect on blood sugar, type 2 diabetics should always consult their physician before starting an exercise program. There are certain precautions to consider, such as monitoring blood sugar before, during, and after exercise by using a blood glucose meter, and having carbohydrates available if needed during or following exercise. Discuss these issues and others with your physician before beginning an exercise program.

[†] While those with type 1 diabetes will benefit from regular exercise (for reasons aside from blood sugar control), it should be understood that exercise will not prevent the disease, as the cause of type 1 diabetes is autoimmune related.

- Eliminating trans fats and limiting saturated fats, including animal fats, butter, margarine, and shortenings.
- Consuming little or no processed foods or refined carbohydrates.[*]

The Daniel Fast plan benefits people with diabetes because it does not restrict calories and calls for regular intake of food — nutrient-dense foods — throughout the day. More frequent meals stabilize blood sugar by minimizing spikes and troughs. This is important because frequent and significant spikes in blood sugar — often due to the ingestion of high-calorie, highly processed foods — likely contribute to impaired insulin action over time, which can lead

[*] Processed foods have been altered in some way, either for safety or convenience. While some processed foods (for example, pasteurized milk and flash-frozen fruits and vegetables) can be very healthy, most processed foods are not. This is because they contain many unhealthy ingredients — such as sodium, trans fats, corn syrup, sugar, additives, and preservatives. Boxed meal mixes, frozen dinners, and snack foods are typical examples of processed foods. Refined foods have been processed or altered to some degree and no longer are in their natural state. Very often, beneficial nutrients such as fiber, vitamins, and minerals are removed in the processing. White rice and white flour are examples of refined foods.

ARE DIETARY SUPPLEMENTS BENEFICIAL FOR TYPE 2 DIABETES?

Dietary supplements in general can be of benefit for those with diabetes. Beyond the commonly used supplements such as multi-vitamins and minerals and fish oil, other supplements can be useful for those with type 2 diabetes. For example, acetic acid, which is found in vinegar, has been reported to be beneficial in controlling blood sugar when 1–2 tablespoons of vinegar are taken before high-carbohydrate meals. But keep in mind, when considering supplements, that overall dietary intake and exercise will account for at least 90 percent of your success in maintaining optimal blood sugar control. Supplements can't make up for a failure to eat right and exercise.

The following supplemental nutrients have been reported to have some merit:

> blueberry bioactives
> grape anthocyanins
> cinnamon extract
> phellodendron
> crape myrtle (banaba leaf)
> chromium (polynicotinate or picolinate)
> Russian tarragon
> green tea polyphenols (EGCG)
> alpha lipoic acid
> selected fiber supplements and other agents that slow carbohydrate digestion

As with most dietary supplements, some individuals may be helped more than others. That said, if you decide to experiment with dietary supplements believed to control blood sugar, it is important to discuss your plans with your physician. You should understand that the dosage of certain diabetic medications may need to be adjusted to account for the blood-sugar-lowering effect of some supplements. This adjustment should only be done under the direction of your physician.

to both the onset and progression of type 2 diabetes.

While the Daniel Fast involves more frequent food consumption, the total calories typically are reduced because the foods are more nutrient dense but lower in calories. For example, a breakfast of oatmeal, fruit, and a soy protein powder drink not only contains fewer calories than a large bagel with cream cheese but is also more filling and much better nutritionally. Because the number of calories is generally lower when following the Daniel Fast plan, a person is likely to lose weight—and reduce the risk of diabetes.

Dietary fiber — especially in the form of legumes (beans, peas, lentils) — is also helpful for those with type 2 diabetes. In addition to providing a feeling of fullness, fiber acts to slow down the rate of absorption of foods — carbohydrates in particular — which assists in maintaining relatively stable blood sugar levels throughout the day. Dietary fat can do the same thing by essentially slowing the entry rate of glucose into the bloodstream. But it's important to note that not all fats are equal. While essential fatty acids (omega-3 and omega-6 fatty acids found in certain fish, oils, nuts, and nut butters) can improve insulin sensitivity, saturated fats (mainly animal fats) can actually damage insulin sensitivity. The important thing to note about fiber and fats is that your blood sugar is controlled by more than just the sugar (the carbohydrates) you eat. The type of fat you eat matters.

The Daniel Fast eliminates all processed foods and simple carbohydrates, such as sugar, with the exception of the fructose, a simple sugar, contained in fruit.* Eating simple carbohydrates and processed foods can lead to rapid and massive spikes in blood sugar and insulin. Remember, insulin acts to reduce blood sugar when it rises after eating a meal. A large spike in blood sugar may lead to a large counterspike in insulin—which in turn may cause a massive fall in blood sugar and a feeling of fatigue an hour or two later.

For many young and healthy individuals, occasional blood sugar spikes do not appear to present an imminent problem—yet. However, for middle-aged and older individuals—especially those with problems processing blood sugar—blood sugar spikes can pose both short-term and long-term health concerns. In the short term, people may simply not feel very good. They feel tired, irritable, and moody. In the long term, regular and significant spikes in insulin can impair the sensitivity of insulin. It is no longer as effective.

What is insulin insensitivity? In simple terms, it means that insulin does not work as well as it used to. The glucose, or sugar, cannot be adequately removed from the blood. And with the blood sugar level still high, the body senses the need to secrete even more insulin in order to get the job done. But because the sensitivity between the insulin and specific receptors that interact with insulin in an attempt to ultimately lower blood sugar is impaired, the job still doesn't get done. The result is elevated blood sugar (hyperglycemia) and elevated blood insulin (hyperinsulinemia) and body tissue cells that are not receiving glucose, a prime energy source. This is the reason diabetics often feel tired. Their muscles are not receiving the fuel they need to function properly. (See "What Causes Blood Sugar to Become Elevated?" on page 57.)

The Daniel Fast approach to eating is a powerful tool that not only limits the risk of developing type 2 diabetes but also helps in treatment by improving overall metabolic health and controlling blood sugar. A proper food plan is your first line of defense. Add to that the multiple benefits of increased physical activity and structured exercise. (See "How Does Exercise Impact Type 2 Diabetes?" on page 61.)

---

*Fruit contains fiber as well as a full complement of vitamins and minerals that may help in blood sugar control. This is why the Daniel Cure plan recommends several servings of fruit per day.

SO WHAT DOES THIS MEAN FOR YOU?

I started this chapter by describing the success of Carl, one of our past Daniel Fast study participants. You might be wondering if you could experience success with the Daniel Fast plan. Our answer is yes. Consider the results of Martha, another study participant who took control of her blood glucose in just three weeks while following the Daniel Fast. Martha was forty-one years old and not obese by BMI standards (her BMI was less than 30), but her body fat was about 30 percent. After her twenty-one-day Daniel Fast, her fasting blood sugar improved by 40 percent from a very high starting value of 330 mg/dL to an ending value of 198 mg/dL. Her insulin was functioning 23 percent more efficiently. Truly remarkable results in just three weeks — when the only change was to a diet of healthy, natural, nutrient-dense food.

Now back to you. If you have already been diagnosed with type 2 diabetes and are being treated, chances are you are familiar with some or most of what you read in this chapter. Our question is, "Are you adequately caring for yourself by putting into action the things you know are important?"

If you don't have diabetes, or if much of the information was new to you, it's likely stirred up concerns or questions about your health or your lifestyle choices. Perhaps you are now wondering if you have diabetes but haven't been diagnosed. Or maybe you recognized yourself when you read about the risk factors for diabetes, such as being overweight or obese, carrying a significant amount of abdominal fat, living a sedentary lifestyle, or eating high calorie and sugary and fatty meals. Now you are wondering if you might be heading directly toward a diagnosis of type 2 diabetes.

If anything you read prompted concerns, this may be God's invitation calling you to pay attention to the very real health risks knocking at your door. It could also be your invitation to begin a time of prayer and fasting, using the Daniel Fast as your method. By prayerfully submitting yourself to God and adopting a healthy way of eating, you will not only honor God but you'll also honor your body — the temple of the Holy Spirit that God has entrusted to your care.

■ TURN YOUR THOUGHTS INTO ACTIONS ■

1 Imagine yourself with a constant supply of energy throughout the day, with no highs and lows. Your blood glucose and insulin levels are stable. You are eating frequent meals and you feel better than you've felt in years. How different would this be from how you feel now?

2 Eat five to six small meals every day. Never go more than three hours without eating.

3 Consume small amounts of protein, carbohydrate, and fat at each meal. Split your plate into thirds—one part low-fat protein (plant- or animal-based), one part vegetable and/or fruit, one part whole grain (brown rice, barley, oats). Balanced meals are a necessity.

preventing and treating cardiovascular disease

CARDIOVASCULAR DISEASE, WITH SPECIFIC REFERENCE TO HEART DISEASE, IS the leading cause of death for both men and women in the United States. In fact, every year about 600,000 people die from heart disease. That equates to one in every four deaths, with one in every three deaths attributed to combined heart disease and stroke. Each year about 935,000 Americans have a heart attack,[23] with a large number of those occurring without any prior warning of heart disease.

"Cardiovascular disease" is an all-encompassing term that includes heart disease and blood vessel disease (including high blood pressure and stroke). The term "heart disease" covers a number of conditions, such as valve disease, congestive heart failure, and coronary artery disease. What first comes to mind for most people when they hear the term "heart disease" is heart attack — sometimes referred to as "myocardial infarction," or heart muscle death. Heart attacks are often linked to a narrowing of the arteries that supply the heart with blood and oxygen. This narrowing is typically caused by fatty plaques inside the arteries that cause the artery opening to become narrower and eventually blocked. Blood cannot flow freely to the working heart muscle, and the heart muscle becomes deprived of oxygen. The part of the heart muscle that does not receive adequate blood flow can die. The most common type of heart disease in the US, coronary artery disease, kills more than 385,000 people each year.[24]

RISK FACTORS FOR CARDIOVASCULAR DISEASE

Cardiovascular disease is a problem of lifestyle. It is well known that the following medical conditions and activities increase the risk of cardiovascular disease. (See "Assessing Your Risk for Cardiovascular Disease" on page 78.)

- overweight or obese classification
- diabetes
- smoking
- excessive alcohol use
- physical inactivity
- poor dietary intake (foods high in cholesterol, saturated fat, simple sugars)
- high blood LDL-cholesterol
- high blood pressure (hypertension)

If your goal is to live a lifestyle of health, then eat a nutritious diet, stop cigarette smoking and excessive alcohol use, and increase your physical activity. (See "What about Exercise?" on page 111.) Two other risk factors are high blood LDL-cholesterol and high blood pressure. Due to their prevalence and importance, we'll discuss these in much greater detail.

ELEVATED BLOOD CHOLESTEROL

In the opening section of this chapter, we discussed the usual cause of a heart attack — blockage in the coronary arteries. This process of blockage is traditionally thought to be linked to elevated blood cholesterol — which may lead to a condition called "atherosclerosis," a specific type of arteriosclerosis, or hardening of the arteries. In Greek, *athere* means "gruel," and *skleros* means "hard." (See "Is There a Genetic Contribution to Cardiovascular Disease?" on page 75.) Through a series of complex events, elevated blood cholesterol can ultimately lead to a buildup of dead cellular debris, called plaque, in artery walls —

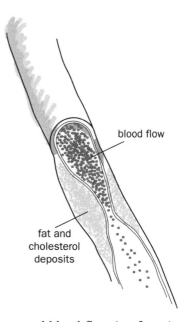

blood flow

fat and cholesterol deposits

narrowing the artery opening and preventing normal blood flow (see figure). This is why many doctors are concerned about reducing high blood cholesterol levels in their patients. They are trying to control the development of atherosclerosis, which may help reduce the likelihood of heart attack.*

---

*Atherosclerosis does not impact only the coronary arteries. It affects all arteries. In the brain, the narrowing of the arteries increases the risk of stroke. Blood vessels in the legs can be affected, leading to a condition known as peripheral arterial disease, or PAD.

For many with elevated blood cholesterol, the treatment of choice is medication with a class of drugs known as statins. These are among the most widely prescribed drugs in the world. According to documentation presented in "Understanding Statin Use in America and Gaps in Education,"[25] more than 200 million prescriptions for statins are written annually by physicians worldwide. Sales of statin drugs each year are in the multi-billion-dollar range. Clearly, high cholesterol is big business—and a big problem for many.

Cholesterol is a waxy, fat-like substance that is measured in three ways:*

- *total cholesterol:* the sum of all cholesterol particles in the blood
- *HDL-cholesterol:* the so-called good cholesterol
- *LDL-cholesterol:* the so-called bad cholesterol

An easy way to remember which cholesterol is good and which is bad is to know that you want to have a **H**igh good HDL-cholesterol count and a **L**ow bad LDL-cholesterol count. HDL-cholesterol is viewed as a healthy form of cholesterol because it acts to remove harmful LDL-cholesterol from where it doesn't belong. High levels of HDL-cholesterol reduce the risk for coronary artery disease, whereas low levels increase the risk. Elevated LDL-cholesterol is thought to contribute to blood vessel disease, which can lead to heart attack and stroke. For these reasons, your physician pays close attention to your blood cholesterol profile. The current recommended values for fasting blood cholesterol are shown in table 7.1.[26]

TABLE 7.1: Blood Cholesterol Profile

Cholesterol Type	Desirable Value	Comments
Total cholesterol	<200 mg/dL	At one time, the upper limit for total cholesterol was 240 mg/dL. However, in recent years, the suggested value for total cholesterol of less than 200 mg/dL is desirable.
LDL-cholesterol	<100 mg/dL	For anyone with no history of heart disease, 130 mg/dL is sometimes used as an upper limit.
HDL-cholesterol	>40 mg/dL (men) >50 mg/dL (women)	HDL-cholesterol helps to clear cholesterol from the body. A high HDL-cholesterol, preferably over 60 mg/dL, is better. Women tend to have much higher HDL-cholesterol than men.

*These forms of cholesterol are measured as part of a blood lipid panel, a routine blood test conducted as part of a physical examination. One other important variable measured is blood triglycerides. For more information, see the appendix "The Science behind the Daniel Fast" on page 281.

A low HDL-cholesterol and a high LDL-cholesterol may promote a buildup of fatty plaque on the walls of your arteries, possibly resulting in a heart attack or stroke. If your cholesterol levels are outside the recommended ranges, your doctor may prescribe a statin drug as a first step in protecting your health. As with all drugs, there exists the minor chance for adverse side effects. Potential side effects with statins include muscle pain and weakness, liver damage, neurological effects, and increased blood sugar. The increase in blood sugar could lead to the development or progression of type 2 diabetes.[27] Many people accept the risk of statin use, but some prefer alternatives to reduce their blood cholesterol. Enter the Daniel Fast.

Over the last few years, we have witnessed both men and women of varying ages significantly improve their overall cholesterol profile, with dramatic decreases in both total and LDL-cholesterol. Table 7.2 presents just a few of these cases and should provide encouragement to you concerning your own ability to simply change to a healthy eating plan and lower cholesterol without the use of medication.*

TABLE 7.2: Impact of the Daniel Fast on Total Cholesterol over 21 Days

Participant, Age, and BMI Classification	Starting Total Cholesterol	Ending Total Cholesterol	Percentage Reduction
Nicole, 24, normal weight	182 mg/dL	129 mg/dL	29%
Liz, 28, normal weight	219 mg/dL	134 mg/dL	39%
Mark, 33, normal weight	152 mg/dL	106 mg/dL	30%
Martin, 39, obese	211 mg/dL	155 mg/dL	26%
Julio, 39, overweight	174 mg/dL	123 mg/dL	29%
Levi, 42, obese	177 mg/dL	135 mg/dL	23%
Harriette, 43, normal weight	194 mg/dL	134 mg/dL	31%
Kathy, 49, normal weight	201 mg/dL	130 mg/dL	35%
Robin, 52, normal weight	192 mg/dL	145 mg/dL	24%
Debbie, 55, overweight	216 mg/dL	174 mg/dL	19%

Note three things about the information in the table. First, regardless of age or sex, we see a significant decrease in total cholesterol. Second, the changes occur despite the fact that the participants' starting cholesterol values are not very high — six of the ten participants started the fast within the "normal"

---

*While many people may be able to control blood cholesterol by adopting a lifestyle of increased physical activity and optimal dietary intake, others may still require the assistance of medication. You should always consult your physician for guidance on this important issue.

range. It is possible that those with higher starting cholesterol values may experience an even more pronounced decrease. Third, most of the participants are of normal weight, highlighting the fact that body weight alone does not provide a complete indication of overall health.

In many cases, these impressive reductions in cholesterol are similar to reductions achieved with the use of prescription statins. The results listed in the table are not unusual for those using the Daniel Fast. Many on the Daniel Fast, regardless of age, experience a 25 percent or greater reduction in total cholesterol. This includes those who have low levels to begin with, like Mark in table 7.2.

These results are achieved simply by following the Daniel Fast plan for twenty-one days. No doctor visits. No drugs. No adverse side effects. No out-of-pocket expenses. Just a lifestyle change. And the benefits aren't limited to lowering total cholesterol. In our studies, we have observed corresponding decreases in LDL-cholesterol as well as a 10 percent reduction in triglycerides —another important component of the overall lipid panel.*

ELEVATED BLOOD PRESSURE

Blood pressure is defined as the pressure exerted by blood against the walls of blood vessels, in particular the arteries. Hypertension, or high blood pressure, is a problem for two reasons:

1. It can lead to blood vessel damage. This damage can then complicate the problem of elevated blood cholesterol—leading to both heart disease and stroke.
2. It can lead to heart failure, as high pressure forces the heart to work harder and harder to pump blood. Over time, the heart muscle becomes weaker and cannot pump as much blood out of the heart as it should. This is called congestive heart failure.

Although there is some debate about the role cholesterol plays in the development of cardiovascular disease (see "Does Cholesterol Really Contribute to Cardiovascular Disease?" on page 72), there is general agreement that elevated blood pressure plays a significant role.

Blood pressure is measured in millimeters of mercury (mmHg) with two numbers—a systolic pressure and a diastolic pressure, shown as 120/80 mmHg, for example. The top number, or systolic reading, is the pressure in

---

*To learn more about cholesterol and triglycerides, see "The Science behind the Daniel Fast" on page 281.

your arteries when the heart contracts. The bottom number, or diastolic number, is the pressure in your arteries when the heart is relaxed. Table 7.3 provides the reference ranges for blood pressure values in assessing health and hypertension. Note that for diagnostic purposes, blood pressure should be measured at rest (at least five minutes of quiet, seated rest before reading is obtained).

TABLE 7.3: Reference Ranges for Blood Pressure

Category/ Classification	Systolic Value	Diastolic Value	Comments
Normal/ Normotensive	<120 mmHg	<80 mmHg	Ideal blood pressure
Pre-Hypertension	120–139 mmHg	80–89 mmHg	Carefully monitor values; lifestyle intervention warranted
Stage 1 Hypertension	140–159 mmHg	90–99 mmHg	Initial stage of hypertension; lifestyle intervention warranted; discuss with personal physician
Stage 2 Hypertension	160–179 mmHg	100–109 mmHg	Highly problematic; work with your physician to lower blood pressure
Stage 3 Hypertension	≥180 mmHg	≥110 mmHg	May indicate a hypertensive crisis and may require emergency care; significant intervention warranted; will likely require use of medication (at least in the short term)

When blood pressure is elevated for an extended period of time, it can lead to various long-term problems, especially blood vessel damage, which can develop into coronary artery disease and/or stroke. When blood surges through the vessels under high pressure, the vessels are more prone to damage. Think of a standard garden hose subjected to excessively high water pressure. Since the hose isn't designed to handle such high pressure, over time it will likely become weaker or brittle and develop bulges, cracks, or tears. With hypertension, blood vessels experience the same kind of damage.

When damaged, blood vessels are more susceptible to the small and dense LDL-cholesterol particles getting deep inside the wall of the blood vessel, where they are eventually "modified" by molecules called free radicals. This is discussed in the next section. (See also "The Science behind the Daniel Fast" on page 281.) This modification leads to formation of fatty plaques that can eventually block blood flow and lead to heart attack and stroke. Smoking can worsen this problem, as the chemicals in cigarette smoke can damage blood vessels and modify LDL-cholesterol in negative ways. This is one reason why smoking is a risk factor for cardiovascular disease. If you smoke, do whatever you have to do to quit. It's vitally important to your health.

Heart failure is another potential consequence of chronic high blood pressure. Each time the heart beats, it must overcome the blood pressure in the aorta in order to push its oxygen-rich blood out into circulation. The aorta is the large main artery connected to the heart. A valve, called the aortic valve, regulates the blood flow between the heart and the aorta. Blood is ejected from the heart through the valve into the aorta and then makes its way throughout the body.

The issue with heart failure lies in the effort required by the heart to open the valve so blood can get through. The higher the blood pressure, the harder

DOES CHOLESTEROL REALLY CONTRIBUTE TO CARDIOVASCULAR DISEASE?

The answer for most physicians and scientists ten to twenty years ago would have been a clear "yes." However, more recent evidence calls that assumption into question. Much of the controversy stems from the aggressive and widespread treatment of elevated blood cholesterol with statin drugs—in particular with patients who do not yet have a history of cardiovascular disease or many risk factors for cardiovascular disease. In addition, it has been suggested that national guidelines for cholesterol levels have been inappropriately influenced by individuals with a financial interest in drug companies that sell medications used to treat elevated cholesterol. And, perhaps of greatest importance, recent evidence indicates no clear association between total cholesterol levels and cardiovascular disease. All of this has prompted many scientists to question the importance of total cholesterol levels with regard to cardiovascular disease.

What most scientists do seem to agree on is that the entire lipid panel—not merely *total* cholesterol—needs to be taken into consideration in assessing a patient's risk for cardiovascular disease. The entire lipid panel includes values for:

  total cholesterol
  triglycerides
  LDL-cholesterol (called "bad" cholesterol)
  HDL-cholesterol (called "good" cholesterol)
  sub-fractions of both LDL-cholesterol and
    HDL-cholesterol

It's also important to know the potential for LDL-cholesterol modification (oxidation) by free radicals—as the modification of LDL-cholesterol appears more important than the actual amount of LDL-cholesterol circulating in the blood.

Bottom line: A complete picture is needed to fully understand the role of cholesterol in cardiovascular disease. In general, the most desirable profile has low triglycerides, low total cholesterol, and low LDL-cholesterol, and high HDL-cholesterol and high blood antioxidant capacity.

the heart must work—every beat, every minute, every hour—to open the valve. Like other muscles in the body, if the heart works harder against a higher resistance (in this case, the pressure in your aorta), it gets bigger. Up to a point, this is not necessarily a problem. But there is a threshold at which an increase in heart size leads to a "stretched out" and much weaker heart muscle—one that can no longer effectively pump blood to body tissues.

When this happens, the heart is like an overstretched rubber band. When a rubber band is new and tight, you can stretch it out and it recoils with great force. However, if you continue to stretch it out over and over again, it eventually loses its elasticity and its ability to recoil is reduced. When chronically overworked, the heart does the same thing—it becomes larger in a non-functional way. It no longer is capable of generating sufficient force to move blood through the body. Over time, the reduced blood flow leads to severe fatigue, heart failure, and possibly death.

This is why it is critical to have annual physical exams in which your doctor checks your blood pressure and other items, such as your blood cholesterol and blood sugar. At some point, your doctor may also check your heart function with a more sophisticated test such as an echocardiogram. You may never feel a heart problem brewing. And if you routinely avoid an annual exam—which men are prone to do—you may discover a problem when it is too advanced, making it more difficult to treat. The CDC estimates that of the 68 million adults in the US who have elevated blood pressure, only half have been diagnosed and have the condition under control.*

FREE RADICALS, INFLAMMATION, AND CARDIOVASCULAR DISEASE

While high blood cholesterol and high blood pressure have been considered risk factors for cardiovascular disease for many years, two new risk factors have been identified. These are elevated oxidative stress and inflammation. We'll take a closer look at inflammation in chapter 8, and you can read more about oxidative stress in "The Science behind the Daniel Fast" on page 281. But here's a brief introduction to both topics.

Oxidative stress occurs when your body's capacity to detoxify certain substances (specifically, free radicals) is inadequate. Free radicals are molecules that can have both beneficial and hazardous roles in the body. At relatively low concentrations, free radicals are helpful and act to send signals to other

---

* http://www.cdc.gov/chronicdisease/resources/publications/AAG/dhdsp.htm.

molecules, telling them what to do to aid normal biological functioning. How-ever, too many free radicals can overwhelm the body's antioxidant defense system. When this happens, free radicals can lead to disease-promoting mod-ifications of proteins, lipids, and DNA. This process is what we call oxidative stress.*

When you are under a lot of stress, the formation of free radicals increases. A lot. While psychological stress may lead to an increase, one of the primary triggers of free radical formation is the ingestion of high-calorie, high-saturat-ed-fat, sugar-rich meals. In fact, aside from cigarette smoking, in our research we have noted no other stressor that compares to high-fat meal ingestion. This is one reason why attempts should be made to reduce the intake of saturated fat.

Free radicals are a big problem in association with LDL-cholesterol mole-cules, since free radicals modify LDL-cholesterol to become more harmful. In fact, it's the modification of LDL-cholesterol (as opposed to simply the amount of LDL-cholesterol) that appears most problematic with regard to the devel-opment of atherosclerosis. In our work, we have noted a decrease in oxidative stress when participants follow the Daniel Fast plan.

Inflammation is the immune system's defense against injury or disease. But chronic inflammation, or systemic inflammation, is linked with various dis-eases. In fact, it might be an initiating factor in certain cardiovascular diseases such as atherosclerosis. In our clinical studies, we have documented significant decreases in systemic inflammation when participants follow a Daniel Fast for as little as twenty-one days.

The fact that the Daniel Fast plan can significantly improve the cardio-vascular disease risk profile in a wide variety of individuals should be strongly considered as we explore this next section pertaining to the cost of cardiovas-cular disease. All of these factors are largely, if not totally, influenced by the lifestyle choices you make. That's what's so amazing. You can control your risk of developing cardiovascular disease ... if you choose to do so.

THE COST OF CARDIOVASCULAR DISEASE

Each year in the United States, the cost of treating coronary heart disease alone well exceeds $100 billion—this includes the cost of health-care services, med-ications, and lost productivity. Treating other forms of cardiovascular disease increases this total to an estimated $444 billion—a sum that continues to

---

*In an attempt to combat oxidative stress, many people take antioxidant dietary supplements. For more information about antioxidant supplements, visit *www.DanielCure.com/supplements*.

rise each year.[28] According to the American Heart Association, the projected cost of treating coronary heart disease, stroke, heart failure, and high blood pressure in the US in 2030 will be $818 billion — nearly triple the $272 billion spent in 2010. An estimated 40 percent of the US population (116 million people) are projected to have some form of cardiovascular disease by 2030. The economic projections alone are staggering, but the implications of 40 percent of the population suffering from cardiovascular disease have catastrophic meaning.

Despite all the money spent to treat heart disease, interventions performed to correct blocked heart vessels, particularly bypass surgery and angioplasty, produce poor results overall. For example, each year Americans spend more than $100 billion in surgical interventions to treat heart disease. Yet, the success of these interventions in terms of prolonging life and preventing future heart attacks is only about 5 percent. Because this cost is borne primarily by Medicare and other insurers, the overall cost is passed on to taxpayers and

IS THERE A GENETIC CONTRIBUTION TO CARDIOVASCULAR DISEASE?

Yes, there is. In fact, some individuals do everything right — follow a healthy diet, exercise regularly, maintain an ideal body mass, don't smoke, don't drink, and because of family history, still die at a very early age from cardiovascular disease. But this is uncommon, and it does not give you an excuse for failing to do everything possible to help control this genetic influence.

I (Rick) have had people say to me, "Why should I bother following a healthy diet and exercise regularly when both my parents died prematurely from heart disease?" My response is something like this: "Well, you can adopt that defeated mentality, do absolutely nothing to improve your health, and possibly die prematurely. That's one option. Or you can do everything possible to take control of your health, including adopting a program of structured exercise and optimal dietary intake, and possibly extend your life to sixty, seventy, or even more than eighty years." Of course, there

is still the possibility that a person who opts for a healthy lifestyle might die at the "early" age of sixty-five. Was the choice to live healthy worth it? Absolutely. The fact remains that the quantity of this person's life was likely much longer than it otherwise would have been, and the quality of life was also likely much better. It's tough to argue with that.

The idea that genetics predetermines every aspect of your existence, including disease onset and life expectancy, assumes that your actions have no impact on how your genes respond to what you do — which is not accurate. While all of us may have a certain genetic makeup, our actions can regulate the genetic response (a scientific field known as epigenetics or epigenomics). Your actions may have such a profound impact on your genetics that you never develop the condition you were concerned about in the first place. The bottom line is this: You should do everything in your God-given power to improve and maintain your health.

those who purchase insurance policies. That means we are paying billions of dollars annually for largely ineffective surgical procedures.

In contrast, the United States spends next to nothing on lifestyle approaches used to prevent cardiovascular disease despite strong evidence supporting the great success of preventive strategies. For example, the INTERHEART study followed 30,000 men and women on six different continents and determined that changing the lifestyle could prevent at least 90 percent of all heart disease (with specific reference to heart attacks).[29] Clearly, our health-care decisions and priorities need to be reevaluated.

THE DANIEL FAST AND CARDIOVASCULAR DISEASE

If you agree that preventing potential disease is preferable to treating existing disease, we strongly encourage you to consider launching your approach to healthy eating by using the Daniel Fast. This plant-based dietary strategy promotes lifestyle changes that can significantly reduce the risk factors for developing cardiovascular disease.

- The Daniel Fast typically results in weight loss, which often leads to corresponding reductions in cholesterol, blood glucose, blood pressure, oxidative stress, and systemic inflammation.
- Eliminating or reducing animal products reduces intake of dietary cholesterol and saturated fat—both of which are found almost exclusively in animal foods. This in turn reduces blood cholesterol.
- Increased consumption of dietary fiber leads to a reduction in blood cholesterol, as fiber helps to carry cholesterol from the circulation to the liver for removal from the body.
- Daniel Fast plan foods include a rich source of dietary antioxidants in the form of fruits and vegetables, in addition to whole grains. These antioxidants combat the potential damage of free radicals and lessen or prevent oxidative stress.
- The Daniel Fast involves "clean" eating without additives, preservatives, saturated fat, and processed foods. This may be one explanation for the significant reduction in inflammation.
- The high volume of vegetables consumed on the Daniel Fast offers a high nitrate content, which is associated with increased nitric oxide levels in the blood. This enables blood vessels to relax and open more fully, which may in turn reduce blood pressure—the tube is bigger, therefore the pressure in the tube is reduced. (For more information on nitric oxide, see "The Science behind the Daniel Fast" on page 281.)

Table 7.4 demonstrates the dramatic changes in blood pressure experienced by participants in our Daniel Fast studies.

TABLE 7.4: Impact of the Daniel Fast on Blood Pressure over 21 Days

Participant, Age, BMI Classification	Starting Blood Pressure	Ending Blood Pressure
Jerome, 28, obese	141/98 mmHg	113/68 mmHg
Louise, 41, normal weight	147/85 mmHg	115/73 mmHg
Johnny, 58, obese	134/98 mmHg	121/78 mmHg
Vivian, 58, obese	147/87 mmHg	130/71 mmHg
Seth, 60, obese	162/80 mmHg	128/66 mmHg

The blood pressure values presented yield a decrease in both systolic and diastolic pressure of close to 20 percent. All participants were classified as hypertensive at the start of the fast. At the conclusion of just twenty-one days, all participants' values were below the cutoff for hypertension. This *is* a big deal.

One potential reason for the significant reductions in blood pressure with the Daniel Fast is the noted increase in nitric oxide associated with increased vegetable intake. In our Daniel Fast studies, we have documented increases in nitric oxide levels of 64 percent, 116 percent, and 238 percent in men, as well as increases of 160 percent, 188 percent, and 319 percent in women.* These are remarkable findings and support the results of other studies using specific dietary approaches to increase nitric oxide, which relaxes blood vessels, to reduce blood pressure.

IT'S YOUR TURN NOW

Every day in the United States, close to 1,650 people die of cardiovascular disease — that's more than one person every minute. Perhaps the saddest thing is that most of us know what to do to reduce our risk of this disease, but we simply choose not to do it.

So, what about you? Are you ready to do something about your risk?

The Daniel Cure involves a lifestyle approach to healthy eating that can dramatically reduce certain cardiovascular disease risk factors. These include obesity, type 2 diabetes, blood cholesterol, and blood pressure. It also results in a significant reduction in systemic inflammation — an emerging risk factor

---

* Nitric oxide is a short-lived molecule with multiple functions within the body. With regard to blood pressure, it helps blood vessels to relax, allowing blood to flow more freely.

for most human diseases and discussed in detail in the following chapter. We presented the evidence. Now it's up to you to take action.

Perhaps you are overweight. Maybe your doctor recently informed you that your cholesterol is too high. You might have a demanding job, get little sleep, and are concerned that your blood pressure is elevated. A twenty-one-day Daniel Fast followed by the Daniel Cure approach can help you. It's a realistic plan and can have a measurable and lasting impact on your overall health. Believe it.

ASSESSING YOUR RISK FOR CARDIOVASCULAR DISEASE

Some physicians like to use a risk assessment when determining an individual's long-term (ten-year) risk of having a cardiovascular event (usually a heart attack). While a risk assessment is not 100 percent accurate, it does provide information to help you gauge where you are and what you might need to focus on in terms of lowering your risk.* Although other factors such as obesity, diabetes, dietary intake, and physical activity are now considered by many physicians when calculating risk, the variables in the table have been used historically and are well-known risk factors for cardiovascular disease.

Cardiovascular Risk Factors

Variable	Description / How to Lower Risk
Age	The higher the age, the higher the risk; cardiovascular disease is age related.
Sex	Earlier in life, men are more prone to cardiovascular disease than women.
Total Cholesterol	Should be less than 200 mg/dL.
HDL-Cholesterol	Should be greater than 40 mg/dL.
Smoker	Quite simply, you should not smoke cigarettes.
Systolic Blood Pressure	Should be less than 120 mmHg.

If you have certain risk factors for cardiovascular disease, seriously consider doing something to get these under control now, before it is too late. Embarking on the Daniel Cure is a great start.

---

*A frequently used risk calculator is that of the National Cholesterol Education Program, available at *http://hp2010.nhlbihin.net/atpiii/calculator.asp.*

▰▰▰▰ TURN YOUR THOUGHTS INTO ACTIONS ▰▰▰▰

1 Think of your body as a well-tuned machine. You provide it what it needs to function at peak performance.

2 Eat *at least* 20 grams of fiber every day if you're a woman and 30 grams if you're a man (more fiber if you are under the age of fifty). For example: one cup of raspberries has about 8 grams; one-half cup cooked beans (any variety) about 5 grams; one cup cooked broccoli about 5 grams; one-half cup uncooked oats about 4 grams; one large banana about 3 grams; one-half cup cooked brown rice about 2 grams.

3 Consume at least five servings of vegetables every day. A typical vegetable serving is equal to one-half cup; a serving of green leafy vegetables is equal to one cup. These are rather small amounts and are easily obtainable on a daily basis.

CHAPTER 8

fighting inflammation
and associated diseases

As I (Rick) sat down to write this chapter, I stretched my arms back above my head and immediately felt a dull pain in my biceps and shoulders—a "good" pain—called delayed onset muscle soreness (DOMS). You may know the feeling. You complete a really tough workout, and during the following days your muscles feel sore or stiff. Sometimes it's even a source of pride: "I really must have worked those muscles hard to feel *this* sore!"

When you exercise vigorously, you induce microscopic tears in your muscle fibers. Your body experiences this as an injury and responds by increasing blood flow to that area, sending white blood cells and other immune cells to promote healing. This inflammatory response helps promote recovery of your damaged muscle tissue—in fact, the tissue regenerates and is actually stronger than it was before the injury. This is why the first time you do certain exercises, you may feel excruciating soreness afterward. But the second time you do the exact same exercises, you are not nearly as sore. Your muscles have adapted and can now better handle the workout. This is known as the "repeated bout effect."

Traumatic injuries—such as burns, frostbite, and infection—also prompt an inflammatory response. This short-term inflammation is part of the highly complex biological response God created in order for our bodies to heal. However, inflammation is problematic when it becomes a long-term, or chronic, condition. In fact, chronic low-grade systemic inflammation is associated with a variety of diseases and has received a great deal of attention in recent years.

INFLAMMATION AND DISEASE

Scientists have discovered links between chronic inflammation and a variety of diseases. In fact, some researchers suggest that inflammation could be the single most significant factor regulating disease.[30] However, while few doubt that inflammation is associated with disease, it's not yet clear if inflammation plays a role in causing the disease or if it is a consequence of having the disease. In either case, inflammation is a complicating factor linked to diseases such as asthma and allergies (inflammation impacts the airway), osteoarthritis (inflammation impacts the joints), diabetes (inflammation impairs insulin sensitivity), and atherosclerosis (scientific focus so far has been on inflammation as a major contributing factor).

As discussed in chapter 7, atherosclerosis involves a progressive narrowing of the arteries that supply blood to our body tissues. When narrowed or blocked, blood flow to the heart or the brain or other tissues is reduced or stops, leading to tissue death. This happens with a heart attack or a stroke. Atherosclerosis is a highly complex, age-related disease. As you get older, the degree of artery narrowing increases. Inflammation is thought to be involved in all stages of the disease, from initiation to progression and finally to the formation of a potentially fatal clot.

The inflammatory cells and free radicals interact with LDL-cholesterol and promote the formation of fatty plaques in blood vessels. Over time, these plaques reduce the opening in blood vessels and ultimately reduce blood flow. Because of this link between LDL-cholesterol and inflammatory

EATING AND INFLAMMATION

High-calorie, high-fat, high-sugar meals can induce a state of systemic inflammation, which may persist for several hours following a meal. If you eat such meals regularly, you may find yourself in a state of chronic inflammation. This is why a healthy eating plan should include small and frequent meals of lean protein, fiber-rich carbohydrates, limited saturated fat, and a wealth of vitamins and minerals.

A main focus of research in my (Rick's) lab over the past several years has been the study of metabolism after eating. We focus on the biochemical changes that occur in the body following meals with high fat and high sugar. (See "The Science behind the Daniel Fast" on page 281.) We focus both on how free radicals modify important molecules, such as protein and lipids, as well as the interplay between free radicals and inflammation.

The take-home message from our work and the work of other scientists is that when you consume high-calorie, high-saturated-fat, sugar-rich meals, you (1) produce a significant amount of free radicals that can damage important molecules such as proteins, lipids, and DNA; and (2) induce a significant increase in inflammation (possibly related to the increase in free radicals).

The combination of excess free radical production and increased inflammation may lead to the development of disease or accelerate aging. Adopting a clean-eating approach, coupled with regular exercise, can lessen both free radical production and inflammation — leading to improved quality and quantity of life.

cells, many physicians, when evaluating heart disease risk, are interested not only in measuring cholesterol levels of their patients but also in measuring their degree of inflammation.

HOW IS INFLAMMATION MEASURED?

With acute conditions like infection or muscle injury, you can actually feel or see the inflammation. When I was in graduate school, I worked on a study that used a high-tech computerized exercise device to induce muscle trauma in our subjects and we then assessed the degree of injury over a period of days. We measured muscle girth with a tape measure to determine the degree of swelling. Where there is pronounced swelling, there is inflammation, which involves increased blood flow to promote healing. Many of us exercise enthusiasts experience this regularly, and it has no effect on our overall health. Remember, the body generally repairs itself to a stronger state than it was in before the injury. So don't use this as an excuse not to exercise.

Beyond feeling and seeing inflammation, we can also measure it with blood tests that analyze inflammatory biomarkers. These biomarkers provide a quantitative assessment of the degree of systemic inflammation. The most commonly used inflammation biomarker in clinical practice is something called C-reactive protein (CRP). CRP is an acute-phase protein, meaning that the level of CRP rises or falls in response to a short-term change in inflammation in the body. For example, the CRP level in your blood may rise in the days before, during, or after you have an acute illness or infection. Your CRP also may increase following strenuous exercise or even after ingesting a high-fat meal. When you have your CRP level measured, it is important to do so when you are in a healthy, rested, and fasting state. Table 8.1 shows typical values for CRP in relation to disease risk.

TABLE 8.1
C-Reactive Protein Levels

< 1.0 mg/L	Lowest Risk
1.0 – 3.0 mg/L	Average Risk
> 3.0 mg/L	Highest Risk

Doctors use CRP to assess chronic systemic inflammation, a condition in which the inflammation persists over time and is not tied to one specific event (such as an illness or strenuous exercise). If you are obese or have diabetes or cardiovascular disease, chances are good your CRP is elevated. But it's not something you can feel. There are no symptoms associated with elevated CRP. If your CRP is elevated, it may indicate an underlying problem that needs to be addressed. The good news is that CRP levels are very responsive to healthy eating and regular exercise, especially when these changes result in weight loss. These lifestyle changes may significantly reduce your CRP levels—and that's a good thing.

THE DANIEL FAST AND INFLAMMATION

If you want to increase systemic inflammation, routinely consume meals that are high in calories, saturated fat, sugar, and processed foods. If you want to decrease systemic inflammation, consume meals—similar to those of the Daniel Fast—that are low in or devoid of these things. (See "Eating and Inflammation" on page 81.)

The men and women who participated in our research on the Daniel Fast have experienced remarkable effects on their CRP levels, reducing their CRP levels by an average of 40 to 50 percent in just three weeks. And many who were obese and started the study with very high CRP levels experienced an even greater reduction. One participant, Antonio, reduced his CRP from 2.6 mg/L to 0.3 mg/L—an 88 percent reduction. Of great interest to us was the simultaneous reduction in CRP and body weight experienced by many who followed a traditional or slightly modified Daniel Fast for six months—highlighting the interplay between excess body weight and increased inflammation.

Table 8.2 demonstrates the dramatic changes experienced by four of our participants.

TABLE 8.2: **Impact of a Traditional or Modified Daniel Fast on CRP and BMI over Six Months**

Participant	Diet	Starting CRP/ Ending CRP		Starting BMI/ Ending BMI	
Janie, 22	**Modified Daniel Fast:** adding 3 ounces of lean meat and 8 ounces of skim milk per day	2.8 mg/L	0.8 mg/L	33.1	30.7
			71% reduction	Grade I obese to approaching overweight category	
BethAnn, 35	**Modified Daniel Fast:** adding 3 ounces of lean meat and 8 ounces of skim milk per day	2.6 mg/L	0.8 mg/L	37.3	32.9
			69% reduction	Grade II to Grade I obese	
Charlotte, 46	**Traditional Daniel Fast:** no animal products	3.9 mg/L	0.6 mg/L	29.1	24.5
			85% reduction	Overweight to normal weight	
Elijah, 52	**Modified Daniel Fast:** adding 3 ounces of lean meat and 8 ounces of skim milk per day	6.6 mg/L	3.6 mg/L	39.9	34.4
			45% reduction	Grade II to Grade I obese	

These people made dramatic improvements in their health by eating a traditional or modified Daniel Fast diet. They learned to eat "clean" by reducing their intake of saturated fat and eliminating processed foods, simple sugars, additives, and preservatives. And while we cannot state with certainty that their dietary changes guarantee a prolonged lifespan, the scientific evidence is clear that a lifestyle of clean eating and regular exercise will absolutely reduce the risk factors for a variety of diseases and improve the overall quality of life. The men and women in our clinical studies were amazed at how quickly their bodies responded to their changes in diet. Many were on a sure road to serious health risks but now have experienced the powerful results of eating a healthy diet.

INFLAMMATION AND YOU

So what does inflammation and CRP mean for you? It means that being healthy is about more than simply losing a few pounds and looking better. Reducing systemic inflammation—indicated by your CRP level—has significant implications for improving your overall health. The potential benefits include avoiding certain diseases, reducing joint pain, becoming more physically active, and leading a more fulfilling and enjoyable life. Just because you cannot *see* the improvement in systemic inflammation by looking in the mirror does not mean that improvement in your overall health is not present. In fact, when you adopt the Daniel Fast eating plan, the improvements you cannot see are often more important than those you can see.

This opportunity to dramatically change your health is open to you. *You can do this.* You can literally choose life when you step out in faith and begin to make the necessary step-by-step changes for health.

■ TURN YOUR THOUGHTS INTO ACTIONS ■

1 Think of yourself as having lower systemic inflammation within your body—allowing for healthy blood vessels, reduced joint discomfort, and lowered risk for chronic disease.

2 Choose to eliminate one or all of the following from your diet: fried foods, processed lunch meat, and calorie-containing soft drinks and other calorie-containing beverages (aside from milk and natural fruit and vegetable juice).

3 Consider taking a daily fish oil supplement. Read the nutritional label and choose a supplement that includes 1,000–2,000 mg (combined) Eicosapentaenoic acid (EPA) and Docosahexaenoic acid (DHA). Studies on the omega-3 fatty acids in fish oil have repeatedly demonstrated a reduction in systemic inflammation. See *www.DanielCure.com/supplements*.

PART 3

getting started

preparing for the daniel cure

The Camino de Santiago is a beautiful 500-mile trek across northern Spain. Thousands of people complete this pilgrimage every year, and most begin preparing for it months in advance. In addition to physical conditioning, it's essential for walkers to have the appropriate gear for a thirty- to forty-day walk—sturdy boots, a few pairs of thick socks, a good backpack, and comfortable hiking clothes.

I (Susan) had long dreamed of making this trek and finally got my chance a couple years ago. The first day was grueling as I slowly made my way up the steep trail through the Pyrenees Mountains that divide France from Spain. In the space of thirteen miles, the elevation of the trail rises from 600 feet to more than 4,700 feet. I had trained for the long-distance trek and had good boots and equipment, but I hadn't anticipated how challenging that first day would be. I was fatigued, but I also had confidence that the time I'd invested in preparation and training had given me the stamina I needed to keep moving forward, step by step.

Along the way, I met a thirty-something woman from Canada who was also struggling—and it wasn't hard to see why. Instead of good walking boots with a sturdy tread, she wore white Keds—a lightweight canvas sneaker with thin rubber soles. Instead of a backpack, she was pulling a rolling suitcase—yes, the kind designed as carry-on luggage for air travel. Clearly, she was not prepared for a 500-mile, month-long trek through the mountains and across the plains.

I stopped where she was resting and we chatted for a few minutes. Her decision to embark on the 500-mile walk had been motivated by a recent breakup with a long-time boyfriend. She thought the experience would take her mind off her troubles. We talked a little about her equipment, but she didn't seem too concerned and was sure her determination was enough to keep her going. As we parted, I told her I looked forward to seeing her at the little hostel along the trail where we had both planned to stop for the night.

Several hours after I reached the hostel, my Canadian friend finally hobbled in. Her feet were covered with blisters, and she was so exhausted she could barely hold up her head. The owner of the hostel checked her in and then advised her to discontinue the walk. He offered to make arrangements to have a car come the next morning and return her to the little village at the base of the mountains where she could rest and decide what to do next. I'm glad she heard the wisdom in the hostel owner's words and accepted his offer.

Perhaps you already understand why I tell this story. The invitation of the Daniel Cure is to embark on a beautiful journey — one that may include spiritual, emotional, and physical challenges. The experience people have on the journey is determined in large part by how well they prepare for it. Like my Canadian friend on the Camino de Santiago, those who fail to adequately prepare mentally, spiritually, and physically — whether for a twenty-one-day Daniel Fast or for the Daniel Cure lifestyle plan — may begin with high hopes and great determination, but there is a reasonably good chance they'll make it only a couple of days before they call it quits.

Lack of preparation is the biggest reason people quit. I often receive emails from people who confess to feeling defeated, weak, and ashamed when they fail to complete the twenty-one-day Daniel Fast. When they ask for counsel, my response is always the same: "Try again." But before they do, I encourage them to learn from their mistakes. Before trying again, they must prepare and equip themselves with the necessary tools to ensure success. As Maya Angelou teaches, "When you know better, you do better."

As you anticipate your initial fast and the lifestyle approach that follows, try thinking of it as you might think about planning for an extended vacation or an overseas journey. These aren't typically the kinds of trips we decide to take at the last minute. Invest in yourself and in your journey by taking time to prepare for the amazing faith adventure the Lord has in store for you. Preparing for the Daniel Fast includes identifying your purpose and spiritual practices, preparing yourself logistically and physically, planning meals, and consecrating yourself and your fast to God.

IDENTIFY YOUR PURPOSE AND SPIRITUAL PRACTICES

The Daniel Cure involves a lifelong approach to healthy living—including both spiritual and physical components—and we would like for you to begin this lifelong approach with a twenty-one-day Daniel Fast. The same general guidelines and suggestions can be followed as you transition from a twenty-one-day Daniel Fast into the Daniel Cure lifestyle.

Because your fast is a journey, it's essential before you begin to be very clear about where you want to go and how you will get there. You do that by identifying the central purpose of your fast and making decisions about how you will act and what tools you will use.

Identify the Purpose of Your Fast

One way to think about the purpose of your fast is to consider your challenges, needs, and desires. For example, are there obstacles—physical, emotional, and spiritual—that keep you from growing or moving forward in some area of your life? Have you come to that place where you know it's time to honor your physical body and get healthy? Do you have a loved one with a specific need? Are you facing a major decision and desire to seek the Lord's guidance? Do you want to experience greater intimacy with God or develop a more consistent practice of daily prayer and study? Is there a self-defeating behavior you're struggling to overcome? What is it you hope God might change—in you, your relationships, your circumstances—as a result of your fast?

I hear from many people who feel drawn to use their fast to intercede for a friend or family member, as Rick's wife Chrissy did when she prayed for their daughter's health during her initial fast. Others pray that a husband or wife will find a job. Parents pray for rebellious children. Couples pray for their marriage or other family relationships—perhaps a major decision that needs to be made. Still others focus on someone they care about who needs healing, guidance, or salvation. In addition, you might use your fast strictly as a form of praise, giving thanks to the Father for all the good he has done, is doing, and will do in your life.

Rick and I both routinely fast at the beginning of each year. I focused my most recent fast on health for my spirit, soul, and body. Specifically, I asked the Lord to show me anything that might be keeping me from living the kingdom-of-God life Jesus died to give me. During my twenty-one days, I deepened my commitment to physical health and well-being by identifying areas in my eating and exercising habits that needed attention. I also targeted work and home projects I wanted to complete so I could decrease distractions, increase simplicity, and focus more of my time and energy on fulfilling the call Jesus has for me. This commitment included reading through the *One Year Chronological Bible*, attending a Christian conference, joining an association of Christian authors, business owners, and pastors, and continuing my morning time of prayer, mediation, and study. My commitments to health were to drop those stubborn unwanted pounds ... walk ten miles each week ... and to not purchase potato chips (my greatest weakness) for at least a year.

As you consider the purpose of your fast, resist the temptation to take on too many goals. Focus on just one or two — three at the most. If you have trouble narrowing your focus, make a list of everything that comes to mind and then pray through your list. Which ones stand out most to you? If you don't have a strong sense about what to focus on during your fast, continue to seek the Lord's guidance and open your heart to him. Every time I've done this, the Holy Spirit has revealed the answer to me within a matter of days. He is faithful to lead us as we put our trust in him.

DANIEL CURE STEPS TO SUCCESS

1. Start with a twenty-one-day traditional Daniel Fast. This will allow you to dedicate yourself to the Lord and to ask for his strength and guidance as you begin your new healthy eating plan. The twenty-one-day fast will also teach you about the new foods that you will be eating (and those you will not be eating), which makes it easier to comply with the Daniel Cure way of eating.

2. Start each day with prayer, asking for God's strength as you encounter potential difficulties and temptations. We all need help, and God is the greatest of all Helpers. Why would you ever attempt to do this in your own strength alone?

3. Make exercise a regular part of your week — ideally set aside a specific time for a specific activity three to five days per week. Aside from such formal exercise, remain as physically active as you can every day.

4. Once your twenty-one-day Daniel Fast is complete, you can begin to include additional healthy foods in your overall dietary plan, such as lean meats and low-fat dairy products. You may also want to schedule regular "cheat" meals/snacks into your overall dietary plan. This means one or two such meals or snacks per week, including an occasional dessert. Remember, the goal is long-term progress, not perfection. Eating clean is important, but you should enjoy your life too — and food (including dessert) is part of that enjoyment. Do not overlook this important aspect of long-term dietary success.

5. Consider informing the people who make up your social support system about your newly adopted dietary plans. Doing so may help to keep you accountable. Some may even choose to adopt the same dietary approach. Set short-term and long-term goals, reassess and make changes as needed, and stay focused. You really can do this!

Write down your purpose in a journal or on a piece of paper you can place in your Bible. Then listen with your spiritual ears as the Holy Spirit confirms your commitment and continues to guide and support you in this desire.

Choose Your Spiritual Practices

Once you've identified the purpose of your fast, consider the spiritual practices you'll use throughout the experience. Daily fellowship with God and prayer along with study are the foundational disciplines of every fast, but there are nearly limitless ways to practice both. For example, do you want to practice a specific kind of prayer, such as silent prayer, praying through Scripture, or using your body in prayer (raising hands, kneeling, lying down)? Do you want to focus your Bible study on the Beatitudes, reading through one of the Gospels, or on passages about a specific issue or theme?

In addition to prayer and Bible study, are there other spiritual disciplines that would support the purpose of your fast? For example, keeping a journal, taking a one-day silent retreat, or donating time or resources to a nonprofit or ministry organization. Keep in mind that additional spiritual disciplines may not be necessary or even advisable. The goal is not to pile up spiritual activity, but to choose the spiritual practices that best support the purpose of your fast.

It's wise to also make a specific commitment about the time and duration of the spiritual practices you choose. For example, you could choose to pray and study for thirty minutes every morning before breakfast, to read Scripture for ten minutes on your lunch hour each day, or to devote fifteen minutes every morning and evening to silent prayer. Depending on your situation, you might establish one pattern for weekdays and another for weekends. Whatever you choose, keep your commitment simple, specific, and doable.

Consider Keeping a Journal

I first started journaling decades ago when I gave my life to Christ. I use my journal primarily for prayer, and so all my entries start with "Dear Father." Then I write about whatever is on my mind. I'm frequently stunned by the wisdom that comes as I journal—and I know it's not from me, but from the Spirit of God working in me. I open my heart to God and write until I sense it's time to sign off. Although many people later go back and reread their journals, I rarely do. Instead, I use my journal primarily as a tool that helps me to communicate with my heavenly Father in the moment.

In addition to using a journal as a tool for prayer, you might also use it to reflect on your physical, emotional, and spiritual experiences during the fast.

For example, during the first week of the fast, you might make observations like these: "I really miss my coffee—and so does my body. I was so tired this afternoon!" "My body is craving sugar. I never realized I was so addicted to the sweet stuff." "I was feeling discouraged this morning, but the praise music I listened to at lunch helped to redirect my focus to God."

Gather Resources

Now it's time to gather the soul-nourishing resources you'll need to sustain yourself during the fast. I sometimes think about my fast as a college-level course in the powerful truths of the gospel. During my time in "higher learning," I choose a study tool that helps me to feast on God's Word. My "professors" might be authors of Christian books or Bible teachers who share their knowledge on DVDs, CDs, podcasts, or online videos.

In addition to your Bible, what other resources would best support the purpose and spiritual practices of your fast? Do some research by asking trusted friends for recommendations or by investigating appropriate resources online. We've included a twenty-one-day devotional in part 5 of this book to support you during your fast. Perhaps there is a Bible study course you want to use each morning in your quiet time. Or a book that will teach you practical how-to steps for prayer, studying the Bible, or learning more about patience or self-control.

As you consider what you might need, don't limit yourself to just one kind of worship or study resource or even a once-a-day study. For example, I sometimes listen to recorded Bible teaching while I'm creating meals. Several years ago, I prepared for an upcoming fast by installing a small CD player on a shelf in my kitchen. Now all I need for my "higher learning" class is to pop in a CD while I'm cooking. Rick listens to sermons in his car while driving to and from work, and he occasionally uses his audio player to listen to Bible teaching while working out at the gym.

And don't forget music! Tap into the abundance of great worship and praise music for your fast. I have a playlist of favorite inspirational music loaded into my iPhone and often listen to it on my morning walks outside, on the treadmill, or sometimes through the car stereo when I'm driving. Praise music is a great encouragement throughout the fast and can usher us into a place of sweet worship as we focus our minds on God and his glory.

Create a Space

Consider establishing a specific place in your home where you'll meet with the Lord each day. I call this my "secret place," after the psalmist's words, "He who dwells in the secret place of the Most High shall abide under the shadow of the Almighty" (Psalm 91:1 NKJV). My secret place is a loveseat in my bedroom with a nearby end table and lamp. Next to the loveseat is a basket that holds my Bible, journal, study books, notepaper, pens, and colored markers. When I'm fasting, I nestle into my secret place with a cup of hot water with lemon slices (no coffee or tea on the Daniel Fast) and begin each day with prayer.

PREPARE LOGISTICALLY

One problem I often hear about is people trying to fit the fast into their already too busy lifestyles. As much as possible, you need to plan logistically for your fast so it can be the center of your daily life.

Determine the Length of Your Fast

Most people use the Daniel Fast for twenty-one days, based on the prophet Daniel's fasting experience recorded in Daniel 10:2–3. I have used the fast for as few as seven days and for as many as fifty days. In the midst of a fast, don't be surprised if you sense the Lord prompting you to fast longer. Not long ago, I had committed to fasting for twenty-one days but sensed the Holy Spirit leading me to fast an additional three days. On another occasion, I felt the Lord prompting me to add an additional ten days to my fast.

Since your health is one of the priorities for using the Daniel Cure, we encourage you to fast for at least twenty-one days. This will give your body enough time to experience the amazing physical benefits of the Daniel Fast. You can then make the transition into the Daniel Cure lifestyle plan, as discussed in the next chapter.

Put It on Your Calendar

Review your calendar and choose an optimal time for your fast. The best time to schedule your fast is when you can limit your daily commitments and, ideally, avoid traveling away from home. After choosing the best time for your fast—including sufficient time to prepare—mark the days on your calendar and make plans for that start date.

Limit Your Commitments and Activities

While you can easily engage in activities and keep appointments during your fast, we encourage you to limit your commitments and activities. This will not only enable you to devote more time to prayer and study but also free up time for preparing meals and getting sufficient rest.

Limiting activities is one of my biggest challenges. For example, my love of learning is a strength, but it can also be a weakness when I am trying to simplify my days and create more space for quiet time, rest, and prayer. I can't count the times when I've gone web surfing for something specific, only to look up and realize two hours have vaporized into the abyss of lost time. I can also lose myself in "quality" television—especially British dramas. The story lines are rich, the sets enchanting, the costuming stunning, and the performances excellent. What's not to like?

I know these things about myself, and so I have to be intentional about countering these distractions with simple routines and habits. I have my quiet time with the Lord first thing in the morning, before I can be sidelined by distractions. I limit the time I watch television, record favorite shows to watch later, and have a set time in the evening for prayer and study. Rick prefers to eliminate nighttime television when he fasts, with the goal of using his evenings to study and spend quiet time with the Lord.

Take a few days to observe yourself and how you spend your time. Identify any routine obligations you can cancel or reschedule until after the fast. Note the distractions that tend to eat up time on your schedule and limit or eliminate the distractions you can control. Set up some boundaries or routines that will protect the time you need for quiet time, prayer, and digging into God's Word.

Include Family and Friends

Your fast is between you and God, but it also impacts your relationships. You honor your friends and family members when you include them in your fast. Including them could be as simple as letting them know in advance about your decision to fast so they understand why you might be bowing out of things like the weekly pizza lunch or late-night movie marathon.

If you're the only person fasting in your family or circle of friends, be gracious in responding to social invitations and accommodating the needs of others where you can. When I am invited out for meals or parties, I sometimes eat at home and then have just a salad or a side of vegetables at the restaurant. When I am invited to someone's home for a meal, I explain that I'm fasting and ask if we can either get together after the fast or if they don't mind preparing vegan foods for me. My experience is that friends and family members are not only respectful of my requests but also very interested to learn more about the fast.

If possible, we encourage you to go beyond just telling others about your decision to fast by actively enlisting their support.* Ask a close friend or your small group to pray for you. Consider gathering with others for dedicated times of worship, prayer, and study. If your church is fasting, take advantage of any additional resources or worship experiences that might be offered to support those who are fasting.

Note that your fast could also impact those who don't know Christ. I've heard from many people who said their fast was a powerful witness to their "pre-Christian" family members. One woman wrote to me about the impact the fast had on her husband. "He noticed that I was much more peaceful during my fast and more loving toward him," she wrote. "This was an unexpected blessing for me and taught me a lot about the ministry I have within my own marriage and family."

PREPARE PHYSICALLY

A common reason people compromise or quit the Daniel Fast is because they fail to adequately prepare their bodies. Two key factors in preparing yourself physically are anticipating withdrawals and getting sufficient rest.

Anticipate Withdrawals

The biggest culprit in the withdrawal category is caffeine, found primarily in the coffee so many of us drink every day, and to a lesser extent in tea and soft drinks. Caffeine withdrawals are well-documented and the pain can range from mild to excruciating, with headaches being the most common symptom. Some people also feel pain in their lower back or leg cramps. There have been times when I've had no withdrawal symptoms and other times when the discomfort and fatigue have been severe. The lesson I've learned? Always prepare for withdrawals by tapering off of caffeine ahead of time.

To minimize caffeine withdrawal, begin decreasing your caffeine intake at least one week before your fast. Start by mixing in some decaf with your regular coffee, and cut back on sodas and tea. Begin the habit of making water your beverage of choice. Continue to taper off until you're totally free of all caffeine the day you begin your fast. Not only will you minimize the harsher symptoms of cold-turkey caffeine withdrawal, you'll also feel less fatigued

---

*We understand Jesus' words in Matthew 6:16 when he teaches about fasting as a private discipline. We are in no way suggesting that you attempt to seek glory for yourself by informing others of your fasting practice. We simply believe that a support system may help you — and informing others may provide an opportunity to teach them about fasting. That said, if you feel more comfortable doing your fast in private, this is your choice.

during the first few days of your fast, which is a common complaint of many caffeine users.

Sugary and highly processed foods are also withdrawal culprits. If you regularly consume sugar-rich or highly processed convenience foods,* you'll want to begin tapering off these as well. For example, exchange a sugary breakfast cereal or pastry for soy yogurt and fresh berries. Instead of chips or candy, try snacking on a handful of almonds or a piece of fruit. Avoid foods typically considered "fast food" and opt for a salad or other whole foods for lunch. Drink more water. If you follow these simple guidelines, you'll be less likely to experience withdrawal and fatigue and will enter into your fast well prepared.

Even if you do experience withdrawals, they will likely pass in a few days. You'll soon begin to feel more alert and stronger, and your sense of well-being will increase. It's at this point in the Daniel Fast that people write me emails like this: "I have not felt this good in more than fifteen years. I can't believe the food I was eating had such an impact on me! I want to feel this good all the time." The same will likely be true for you. Within a short amount of time, your body will respond positively to healthy foods and adequate water, and withdrawals will be behind you.

Get Sufficient Rest

When you enter your fast, do so well rested. Again, think of this in terms of starting a journey. Just as you wouldn't embark on a 500-mile walk in a stressed, fatigued, and harried state, don't start your fast that way.

Life is challenging and often unpredictable, so you may not always be able to get the ideal amount of rest you need during the fast. But starting the fast in a sleep-deprived state is a setup for failure. For at least a week prior to starting your fast, plan to be in bed early enough to get seven to eight hours of sleep. No late-night cramming for work or school, no midnight movie marathons, no web surfing into the wee hours. Clear your calendar of evening commitments. Rearrange your schedule if necessary. Adequate rest is essential — both in preparing for the fast and in maintaining it.

PLAN YOUR DANIEL FAST MEALS

Keep one word at the forefront of your mind as you plan what you'll eat during your Daniel Fast: balance. Over and over, I've seen people who get so caught

---

* So-called convenience foods are commercially prepared foods designed to be ready to eat right out of the package or with minimal preparation. They can be room temperature, refrigerated, or frozen. They are typically low in nutrients and high in fat, sugar, sodium, and chemical additives.

up in the foods they can and can't have and in the details of meal planning that they miss the life-changing power of fasting.

Yes, this is a partial fast that allows us to eat food, and enjoying meals is a good thing. But if we devote most of our time, energy, and thought to worrying about food, preparing complicated recipes, or using the fast primarily to experiment with new foods, we can soon find ourselves on a diet rather than a fast. Experimenting with new ways of preparing and enjoying food is definitely part of the Daniel Fast, but we lose balance when food itself becomes the primary focus of the fast.

I find that people who flourish on the Daniel Fast are those who choose about three breakfast meals, three lunch meals, six to eight dinner meals, and a few snack recipes. (See chapter 11 about eating five or six small meals throughout the day.) Studies show that this is how people eat most of the time anyway. We have our favorites and those foods make up most of our meals. We might try a new recipe from time to time and may even find we like it so much that we add it to our regular rotation. But for the most part, we need only a few recipes to satisfy our desire for an enjoyable variety of meals.

Part 4 of this book includes plenty of recipes to get you started on your Daniel Fast. And you'll find even more on our website (*www.DanielCure.com*) and in my previous book, *The Daniel Fast: Feed Your Soul, Strengthen Your Spirit, and Renew Your Body*. Both sources provide a variety of recipes you can consider for your personal collection. We'll also go into greater detail about meal planning and preparation in chapter 12.

CONSECRATE YOURSELF AND YOUR FAST TO GOD

Fasting is a time of consecration. To consecrate something is to set it apart for a holy purpose.* That's what we do when we fast—we consecrate the time and ourselves to God, asking him to use our fast for a holy purpose. In committing to the Daniel Fast, we submit all of who we are to the Lord. We use the fast as a means of surrender, to "offer [our] bodies as a living sacrifice, holy and pleasing to God" (Romans 12:1).

---

*The Old Testament writers described how God's people consecrated such things as altars, priests, firstborn sons, animal sacrifices, fasts, monetary gains, and themselves. In the New Testament, we read that it is Jesus who consecrates us: "Therefore, brothers and sisters, since we have confidence to enter the Most Holy Place by the blood of Jesus, by a new and living way opened for us through the curtain, that is, his body, and since we have a great priest over the house of God, let us draw near to God with a sincere heart and with the full assurance that faith brings, having our hearts sprinkled to cleanse us from a guilty conscience and having our bodies washed with pure water" (Hebrews 10:19–22). Jesus consecrated a new way of living by shedding his blood, making it possible for us to come to God as clean, pure, and righteous.

The psalmist describes the kind of "living sacrifice" that pleases God: "The sacrifices of God are a broken spirit, a broken and a contrite heart—these, O God, You will not despise" (Psalm 51:17 NKJV). God wants us to be wholly his so we can be united with him, set apart for his purposes, and a living demonstration of the love of Christ.

Your Daniel Fast is intended to be a powerful time of growth and renewal —for your spirit, soul, and body. The Daniel Cure extends this short-term fast into a lifestyle of health and continued growth. (See "Daniel Cure Steps to Success" on page 92.) Prepare yourself to commune with the Lord and thank God in advance for all he will show you as you put your trust in him and begin your journey.

■■■■■■■■ TURN YOUR THOUGHTS INTO ACTIONS ■■■■■■■■

1 Get out your calendar and identify a specific block of time this week to think and pray about the purpose of your upcoming Daniel Fast.

2 Choose a start date for your twenty-one-day Daniel Fast. Select a three-week period when you foresee no major distractions and will have sufficient time to study, meditate, and prepare your meals.

3 Select and gather the tools you want to use to support you during your fast. Purchase a journal if you plan to journal during your fast. Find books or other study materials that you will use over the twenty-one days.

CHAPTER 10

making the daniel cure
a way of life

I (SUSAN) RECEIVE COUNTLESS EMAILS FROM MEN AND WOMEN WHO ARE amazed at the health results they experience while on the twenty-one-day Daniel Fast. They write to me almost as though they are asking permission to continue on the fast and eat this way for the rest of their lives. My response is typically some version of both "No" and "Yes." No, because being on a continual spiritual fast is an oxymoron—fasting is intended to be a temporary experience. But I also say a resounding "Yes" because changing eating habits to a natural, whole-food plan can provide remarkable and rapid health benefits —as described in detail in chapters 5 to 8.

We hope you are truly interested in moving away from the disease-promoting eating habits that are so prevalent today and in adopting the principles of the Daniel Cure, a healthy eating plan that can last a lifetime. Choosing this way of eating as a lifestyle begins with the twenty-one-day Daniel Fast. During the fast, you'll cleanse your system from sugar, fat-laden foods, and chemical additives. Plus your body will be more adequately hydrated.

As you reset your body for optimal health, you'll find that your cravings for unhealthy foods will diminish, your taste buds will be recalibrated, and you will feel better because your body is operating more efficiently. After completing the fast, you can use the knowledge and experience gained, coupled with the Daniel Cure lifestyle principles, to develop a sustainable, healthy eating plan.

DANIEL CURE LIFESTYLE PRINCIPLES

The guidelines for a twenty-one-day Daniel Fast are based on the fasting experience of the prophet Daniel (Daniel 1 and 10) and are clear about the foods that can and cannot be eaten. However, choosing a lifestyle of healthy eating based on the Daniel Fast requires adapting the fast and personalizing it into a plan you can follow long term. For example, you may choose to maintain a strictly plant-based eating plan, or you might decide to follow a plant-focused plan but add a small amount of low-fat meat, skim milk, and yogurt to your weekly menu, recognizing the health benefits of these foods. (See "Do I Really Need to Eat Animal Products for Adequate Protein and Calcium?" on page 108.) But how will you make these decisions, and how will you know that your choices are aligned with the Daniel Cure? The answer? You build on the foundation of the Daniel Fast and make choices using five foundational Daniel Cure principles.

1. *Make a firm commitment to be healthy.* This is most important and is your first step to success. If you recognize that your current lifestyle plan is not conducive to optimal health, acknowledge this and seek an alternative. Once you commit yourself to becoming healthy, you can then determine your specific course of action. This should include physical action, such as adopting an appropriate dietary and physical activity plan, and spiritual action, such as engaging in daily prayer and Bible study. As you get started, consider completing the Daniel Cure Pledge (see page 276).

2. *Eat natural, clean, nutritious foods regularly throughout the day.* The right foods (including both plant and animal products) will provide your body with the nutrients it needs for optimum health. Frequent meals will allow you to maintain stable energy levels throughout the day, without crashes. You will function at your best when you regularly eat natural, clean, nutritious food throughout the day.

3. *Drink adequate water to keep your body well-hydrated.* As with food intake, consuming water regularly throughout the day is of vital importance. (See "The Health Benefits of Water" on page 29.)

4. *Get adequate exercise and sleep to maintain your health.* While nutritional intake is the focus of this book, regular exercise should be a part of every healthy lifestyle. (See "What about Exercise?" on page 111.) Getting enough quality sleep each night will help greatly in your quest for improved health. Proper sleep allows for greater productivity in all aspects of your life.

5. *Seek the Lord in all you do and accept his gift of grace as he empowers you to adopt a lifestyle of health.* If you attempt to make this lifestyle change on your own, the chance for long-term success is not good. This is the unfortunate reality. Our advice: Start your journey with the God of the universe as your guide. He will take you exactly where you need to go.

Each of these principles has been independently touched on in this book. However, when pulling the nutrition-specific principles together, we generate a plan very similar to the "modified" Daniel Fast that Rick's research team studied and noted similar benefits compared with the traditional plant-based Daniel Fast in which no animal products are consumed. (See Study 5 on page 281 in the appendix "The Science behind the Daniel Fast.")

Remember, although a traditional Daniel Fast includes only plant-based foods, the Daniel Cure allows for additional freedom of food choices. Specifically, the Daniel Cure plan proposes that all clean, natural, and non-processed plant- and animal-based foods are acceptable — recognizing the fact that much nutritional value comes from both plant and animal foods. For example, lean meats and low-fat dairy products are excellent sources of protein and micronutrients — with research supporting the opinion that restricting all animal products from your diet is not necessarily the best idea. In fact, Rick's studies found that even for vegetarians, including small amounts of meat and dairy was a better option for overall health than restricting all animal foods.

The diagrams on page 104 provide a representation of what your nutritional intake might look like when following either a traditional plant-based Daniel Fast or the Daniel Cure approach. In both plans you'll eat small and frequent meals throughout the day, with an abundance of dietary fiber, fruits, and vegetables, while minimizing processed foods and saturated fat. You'll also drink plenty of water.

You'll notice that for each plan (and ideally, for each of your meals) your plate should be split into three even sections — one part low-fat protein (plant- or animal-based), one part vegetable/fruit, one part whole grain. If you are using meal-replacement shakes as discussed in chapter 13, simply follow the recipes provided and you will be adhering closely to the three-section split — albeit in a blender.

On each plate you will notice that for both the Daniel Fast and the Daniel Cure plans, two of the three sections are essentially the same. The only difference is that you have a bit more freedom in the Daniel Cure plan to consume bread as a whole grain. Other than that, the plans are technically identical, with your goal to consume natural fiber-rich fruits, vegetables, and whole grains throughout the day. The main difference between the two plans lies in the protein sources. Specifically, the Daniel Fast includes only plant-based protein sources, including protein powders such as soy and pea. The Daniel Cure allows for a wealth of protein options, including poultry, beef, pork, fish, and dairy, in addition to all forms of protein indicated for the Daniel Fast. Of course, both plant- and animal-based protein powders are also options with the Daniel Cure.

As for the amount of food to consume, eat as much as you would like. But keep in mind that your goal with each meal should be to walk away feeling satisfied but never "stuffed." An example dinner meal when following the Daniel Cure approach might consist of a 4–5-ounce chicken breast, a large sweet

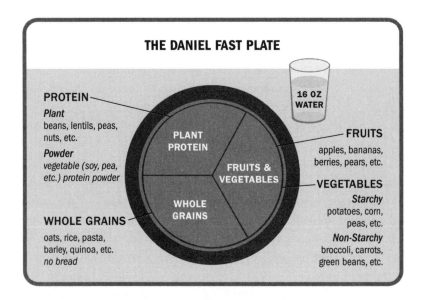

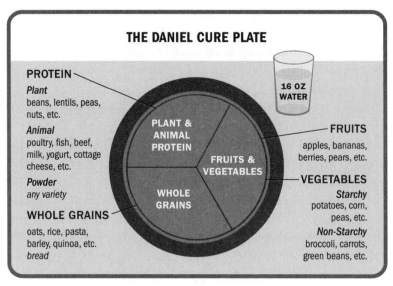

potato, one cup of steamed vegetables, and one piece of fruit. Simple, clean, balanced eating designed for health success! See chapter 22 for sample menus.

For both plans, the small amount of fat that you receive will likely be contained in the actual foods you consume (nuts, nut butter, meat, dairy, etc.). Of course, you may also receive small amounts of fat in the form of oil used to season and cook your food.

The bottom line is this: Both plans represent a very healthy way for you to take control of your life through dietary intake. If you are committed to a twenty-one-day Daniel Fast for spiritual growth, we suggest that you adhere to the traditional plant-based Daniel Fast plan. However, once you complete this and are seeking a plan that can be maintained long-term, you might feel more comfortable with the Daniel Cure approach due to its flexibility.

For example, while some men and women are perfectly fine giving up all animal products for the long-term, many are not. Some would like to enjoy a juicy burger on occasion or a perfectly seasoned and grilled medium-cooked steak. Some might enjoy a breakfast with egg whites or a snack of low-fat cottage cheese and pineapple. Others might indulge with a glass of red wine and a few small slices of cheese. All of these food choices are acceptable to consume while following the Daniel Cure approach—as long as you do so in moderation.

The key to your success is to adopt an approach that includes natural, unprocessed foods—whether plant based or not. Changing the lifelong habits of the way you eat will take time and commitment. But keep your eyes on the goal and the life-changing benefits of clean eating. Keep in mind that your new way of healthy living doesn't mean you can never have a piece of cake or a Coke. We know that you will not eat clean food for every meal from this day forward for the rest of your life. Such a goal is an invitation to failure. It's special to enjoy an occasional sweet dessert, a few slices of pizza, or a plate of homemade lasagna. Foods are pleasurable and you want to have the option to appreciate certain foods — on occasion. However, your path to success is to not consume such foods on a regular basis. Develop a "new normal" for you and your daily eating plan that has health and vitality as its guaranteed results.

With that in mind, note that the Daniel Cure plan also includes the option of consuming items such as coffee, tea, and occasional sweeteners. You should also consider including a cheat meal in your weekly menu and possibly a dessert. Doing so may help you remain on track, knowing that you do not need to be perfect in order to make progress. (See "Dietary Perfection versus Progress" on page 106.)

EATING TO LIVE

If you feel that food is controlling your life, you might ask yourself the following question: Are you eating to live or living to eat? Food is nourishment—a way to fuel our bodies with macro- and micronutrients so we can be at our best—physically, emotionally, and spiritually. World-class athletes understand this principle, but many of us tend to treat food more as a way to "fill up" or to experience pleasure. Again, it's important to enjoy food and to make meals satisfying to the taste buds. But if our food choices are part of the reason we are sick, overweight, chronically fatigued, or out of shape, then we need to shift our perception of food and why we eat. That means resetting our minds and our actions toward eating to live. Eating to live means eating for nourishment and to care for the body—the temple of the Holy Spirit—with which each of us has been entrusted.

DIETARY PERFECTION VERSUS PROGRESS

Most people start a dietary plan believing that they need to adhere to it perfectly. Not so. In fact, the perfectionist mentality is likely responsible for the massive failure rate among so many who set out to change their diets. I (Rick) have talked with many people who believe if they are not perfect, they may as well just give up. As you embark on a new way of eating aimed at optimizing your lifelong health, I encourage you to include "cheat" meals in the plan. One or two such meals per week will work well for most people. Now, I know the diehard dieters may not agree with this, as they maintain the all-or-nothing mentality. I was once one of those people and can appreciate the discipline displayed by those who can eat perfectly every day, day in and day out. But few such people exist, and it's clearly better to have 90 percent dietary success all the time (for the remainder of your life) than it is to have 100 percent success for only a short time. That's what happens for most people—they start out strong, their enthusiasm wanes after the first two to three weeks, and they quit.

This is not the way to adopt a healthy way of eating for life.

Your cheat meals might include dinner at your favorite restaurant or a great meal at home with the family, followed by an ice-cream sundae. Whatever you crave, treat yourself to something special—but don't go overboard. The next day, get right back to the dietary plan you set for yourself. Remember, the goal is not perfection, but progress. If you have been struggling with your dietary plan (30 percent of your meals are of good quality; they're relatively low in calories and high in nutrients), great progress would be moving up to 75 to 80 percent of all meals being of good quality. For example, you eat four meals per day, or twenty-eight meals per week. If you decide to have one cheat meal on Wednesday and another on Saturday (along with a dessert), we'd call that three "cheat meals." Now your success rate has moved up to 89 percent (twenty-five of the twenty-eight meals are good meals). It may not be perfection, but it's great progress!

MAKE A QUALITY DECISION

Changing deeply entrenched eating habits is hard, but it's far from impossible. It all starts with a decision, or what we call a "quality decision." A quality decision requires thorough consideration and prayer. It requires thinking about the kind of person you want to become as well as the decisions you need to make. It means you've weighed the benefits and the consequences of the decision. You've presented the matter to God and asked the Holy Spirit for direction. You've studied what the Word teaches and applied its truths to the matter you're considering.

Once made, your quality decision then fuels your thoughts and your actions. It informs what you do and how you go about doing it. For example, when you make a decision to pursue healthy eating as a lifestyle, you no longer need to go on a series of temporary diets that lead you to say, "I can't have that candy bar." Instead, you operate from a different mind-set: "I don't want that candy bar because it interferes with obtaining my goals and becoming the healthy and fit person I want to be."

To pursue your goal of developing a healthy lifestyle, you'll experience the temporary hardship of forgoing foods you may have really liked but now realize are incompatible with your goal. You may need to consistently get up earlier and go for that daily walk, even if that self-defeating voice in your head puts up a fight and says, *Oh, you can always go tomorrow.* Or *You're okay. You walked a few days last week. You deserve a day off.* I know from experience that sitting on a couch or munching on a bag of potato chips doesn't move me closer to who I want to be. So I leave the potato chips on the grocery store shelves, get myself up off the couch, and go for a walk. That's the kind of shifting that's not only possible but becomes routine when we can make a quality decision that enables us to become who we want to be.

GETTING STARTED

Making significant changes in daily habits is difficult. That's why so many people start off with great enthusiasm and determination but ultimately fall back into their comfortable routines. But you can be successful if you set yourself up for success. Studies indicate that there are four essential components for reversing bad habits and developing new habits for lasting change in one's life.

1. Increase Your Awareness

Increasing awareness means learning more about the subject you are pursuing. When it comes to health, we hope you now are more aware of the opportunity you have to adopt a healthy lifestyle. We also hope that you have a better understanding of the very real threats you face if you don't take good care of your body. But it's important to keep pouring information into your mind. Start reading health magazines or watching educational television programs related to health and fitness. Be more aware of television commercials for certain foods and recognize that what "they are selling" isn't really what you want to buy.

2. Develop New Habits

The key to eliminating old habits is to replace them with new habits. When it comes to taking better care of your health, this includes habits related to what you eat, how you exercise, and how you rest. If you've had unhealthy eating habits, you can replace them by planning a new healthy dietary plan and incorporating it in your daily life. This will involve experimentation with a variety of foods as well as collecting and experimenting with recipes that you find satisfying and enjoyable. Although not a focus of this book, developing the habit of simple exercise that you can do consistently is crucial to your overall health success. (See "What about Exercise?" on page 111.)

DO I REALLY NEED TO EAT ANIMAL PRODUCTS FOR ADEQUATE PROTEIN AND CALCIUM?

No, you don't need animal products to obtain protein and calcium in adequate amounts. With proper planning, you can get all of the protein, carbohydrate, fat, and micronutrients you need from a 100 percent plant-based diet. This includes all nine of the essential amino acids and all of the essential fatty acids (for more information on amino acids, see "What Are Amino Acids?" on page 120). However, most vegetable proteins are incomplete—they do not contain all nine essential amino acids you need in order to manufacture new proteins in your body. If you plan to avoid eating animal protein, you need to educate yourself on "complementary" protein sources.

Certain food protein sources are incomplete in their amino acid profile (for example, brown rice). However, when eaten along with other food protein sources that contain "complementary" amino acids, such as corn, beans, nuts, and seeds, you can generate a meal that contains a complete protein. Various examples of these complementary proteins are rice and tofu, whole-wheat pita bread and hummus, rice and lentils. Soy is a complete source of plant protein. You might consider using a soy protein powder as discussed in chapters 11 and 13. (See www.DanielCure.com/supplements.) By following the simple guidelines of mixing incomplete protein sources to ensure complete protein nutrition and/or using a soy protein powder, you should be able to obtain adequate protein of sufficient quality.

It's important to note that the overall quality of animal protein is generally superior to

Find creative ways to make exercise enjoyable—prayer walking, playing basketball, joining a cycling class, or dancing to an exercise DVD. Add some weight training a few days a week and you'll be surprised how quickly your health will improve and your self-image will mend. Finally, make health a significant part of your prayer life. Allow the Lord to change you from the inside out. Open your heart to his loving encouragement and direction. Know for sure that his will for you is to be healthy, strong, able, and full of joy.

3. Change the Way You Think

Growth and change require changing the way you think, or what the apostle Paul described as "the renewing of your mind" (Romans 12:2). Embrace what the Bible says about your health, your body, and your life. How do these truths impact your daily life? For example, one way to renew your mind is to develop a better understanding of nutrition and how it can change the way you think about the foods you'll eat. We've heard this countless times from those following the Daniel Fast as they began for the first time to read food labels.

Become a lifetime student of health, well-being, and nutrition. Be aware of the words used in our culture to describe food and make sure you understand

plant-based protein. This is why I (Rick) do not believe a strict vegetarian/vegan diet—no animal products—is ideal for extended periods. Rather, a slight modification of the Daniel Fast (which is essentially an extremely purified vegan diet) that includes small quantities of animal protein (lean meat and dairy) is ideal for most people. Now, I understand that many people who follow a vegan plan believe their eating plan has changed their life. Certainly, a vegan plan can have many advantages if adhered to in a purified form. And a vegan plan is a good alternative to the high-calorie, high-fat, high-sugar diets many people consume daily. However, my view is that it may be a good approach, but it is not the best approach.

Getting enough calcium is another concern with a vegan plan. The recommended daily allowance for calcium for men is 1,000 mg/day and for women is 1,200 mg/day. This can easily be obtained by taking a dietary calcium supplement, which is likely a good plan for anyone who decides to forego animal products, especially dairy. Calcium supplements should generally be taken with food twice a day to enhance absorption (for example, 500 mg in the morning with breakfast and 500 mg in the evening with dinner). In addition to a calcium supplement, you might choose to routinely eat a variety of the following foods: broccoli, cabbage, kale, and certain calcium-fortified food items such as tofu, cereals, and fruit drinks.

Bottom line: You can obtain the nutrients you need to survive, and in some cases thrive, by adhering to a plant-based diet. But the addition of small amounts of animal products (lean meats and dairy) might make your diet even better.

the true meaning. For example, I took a lunch break while writing this chapter and decided to watch a show on the Food Network. The chef was demonstrating how to prepare a dinner menu that included beef with root vegetables, a cheesy potato dish casserole, and a sugary chocolate dessert. In her excitement about the meal, she kept saying things like, "This is so good. The flavor is amazing! Oh, and it's so easy to make, even if you're not a trained chef."

I could tell the meal was full of sugar and fat, but I was curious about the nutritional specifics, so I downloaded the recipes and entered the ingredients into a recipe analyzer. I was astounded at the results. An individual serving of the complete meal totaled 2,320 calories. That's more calories than most adults need for a full day! Yet this chef described the meal as "good." I knew my definition of a good meal was completely different — and this meal was definitely not good. In fact, it's this kind of "good eating" that leads to obesity and life-threatening health conditions.

As we renew our minds, we need to clearly define what is truly good for us. We need to stand firm and decide upfront what is acceptable. Then, when faced with a challenge, we want to maintain our position.

4. Surround Yourself with Support

Developing new habits requires support. I tell my blog readers, "Health is the latest fashion statement and it will always be in style." Seek out and surround yourself with people who want to live and eat healthy. Start a support or study group at your workplace or your church. Maybe you belong to a social group or have a couple of neighbors you can recruit to join you in your quest to develop and maintain a healthy lifestyle. Change is typically much easier and longer lasting with support.

Understanding the need for support, we have created the Daniel Cure Pledge. This pledge can be reviewed on page 276 and is also available at *www.DanielCure.com*, where an opportunity to sign the pledge is available. We encourage you to read it, commit to it, sign it, print it, frame it, and then live it. Your best days are ahead of you!

CHOOSING A LIFESTYLE OF HEALTH

For nearly twenty-five years, I've joined a growing group of friends and family for an annual reunion in Puerto Vallarta, Mexico. I usually stay for about fifteen days, and the time is restful, enjoyable, and gives me precious time for contemplation and planning. It was during one of these times about ten years ago when I made a quality decision to pursue the kingdom-of-God lifestyle

Jesus came to give all those who follow him—a decision to live every day in the joy, peace, rest, power, and security of the gospel. Part of that decision included presenting my body to the Lord as a living sacrifice (see Romans 12:1). I wanted to joyfully submit myself to God by caring for the body he created and entrusted to me. I wanted to choose life—to be healthy—and I knew my choice required actions consistent with my goal. "For the kingdom of God is not a matter of talk but of power" (1 Corinthians 4:20).

The choice is ours. We each must take responsibility for where we are today concerning our own health. The great news is that taking responsibility means that we have a wonderful opportunity to choose life. Just like God says in his Word, "I have set before you life and death, blessings and curses. Now choose life, so that both you and your children may live" (Deuteronomy 30:19). We hope that as you read these words, you accept the invitation and make a firm resolve within yourself to choose life ... so you may live.

As followers of Christ, we have the most powerful change agent living inside of us. God's Holy Spirit is in you and he's your teacher, comforter, companion, and encourager. Engage the Holy Spirit in your decision to live a lifestyle of health. Ask for his guidance at the start of each day. Let him become your personal trainer. He never fails.

WHAT ABOUT EXERCISE?

As an exercise enthusiast with formal training in exercise physiology, I (Rick) would be remiss if I failed to at least comment briefly on exercise. Of course, to do things correctly, we would need an entire book dedicated to the how and why of exercise that included both cardiovascular (aerobic) and resistance/weight (anaerobic) training. Exercise has been demonstrated not only to help people look and feel better but also to function as "medicine" to our ailing health. In fact, a recent joint initiative of the American College of Sports Medicine and the American Medical Association titled "Exercise Is Medicine" (*http://exerciseismedicine.org*) aims to increase awareness of the medicinal qualities of exercise. It's that powerful.

In brief, make regular physical activity (for example, light walking, housework, yard work) and structured exercise (brisk walking, jogging, resistance training) a priority in your life. It is a great privilege and blessing to be able to exercise regularly. There are many people who would give anything to be able to exert themselves physically. Don't take your own opportunity for granted. It may not last forever.

What follows are general guidelines for both cardiovascular exercise and resistance exercise. You should be doing both. Some health experts claim you can get by with a few brisk walks per week, as such activity does favorably impact the cardiovascular and metabolic systems. However, brisk walking or jogging does little for the skeletal and muscular systems, in particular the upper body. Weakness in both increases the risk of falling and of fractures. Every year, thousands of older adults suffer fractures of the hip, spine, leg, ankle, and wrist due to falls. These fractures typically are linked to low bone mineral density. Correctly prescribed resistance exercise (not walking) may help to improve bone strength. Bottom line: Make both cardiovascular and resistance exercise a priority in your life. They are both important for different reasons.

Guidelines for Cardiovascular Exercise

Frequency	3 to 5 days per week
Intensity	65 to 90 percent of max predicted heart rate (220 – age = max predicted heart rate; multiply this number by 0.65 to 0.90; use a higher percentage if you are in good physical condition and a lower percentage if you are in poor physical condition); exertion rating of "somewhat hard" to "hard"
Duration	20 to 60 minutes of continuous activity
Mode	walking, jogging, cycling, stepping, elliptical machine, aerobic class, swimming, hiking, jumping rope, inline skating, boxing, etc.

Guidelines for Resistance/Weight Training Exercise

Frequency	2 to 4 days per week (with each muscle group trained once every 3 to 6 days, depending on personal recovery)
Intensity	5 to 15 repetitions per set performed at a slow speed of movement such as 2 seconds to lower the weight and 2 seconds to lift the weight); exertion rating of "somewhat hard" to "hard"
Duration	30 to 60 minutes of intermittent activity (1 to 2 minutes of rest between each set)
Mode	All major muscle groups including chest, shoulders, upper and lower back, biceps (anterior upper arm), triceps (posterior upper arm), quadriceps (anterior thigh), hamstrings (posterior thigh), glutes (butt), calves, and abdominals.* A combination of free weights and machines may be used.

*These muscle groups may be split into two or more groupings, depending on how often you plan to exercise, or may be performed on the same day (during times when you will not have an opportunity to exercise more than one to two days in a week).

Follow these guidelines, work hard, and be consistent. The results will follow!

Oh ... and when is the best time of day to exercise? When you can do it and feel your best. For me, it's first thing in the morning (4:30 a.m.) before I'm presented with the demands of the day. For you, it might be on your lunch break or right after work. It really doesn't matter. Just get it done. There is absolutely no evidence that exercising at a certain time of day is best for everyone.

▰▰▰▰▰▰ TURN YOUR THOUGHTS INTO ACTIONS ▰▰▰▰▰▰

1 Think of three things you can do to increase your awareness about food, exercise, and healthy eating. Maybe this involves reading a book on the subject. Maybe it includes a subscription to a health-specific magazine. Think of what will work for you and write it down.

2 Choose two new habits you want to develop that will contribute to your goal for a healthy lifestyle. This may be going to bed one hour earlier each night, going for an evening walk four days a week immediately after dinner, or limiting television watching to five hours each week so that you can devote additional time to prayer.

3 Design a specific plan to act on your hopes. When will you create an outline of your meals? Set a time. How will you exercise? Create a program. What will you do to make sure you have the support for your success? Develop a plan and reach out to others for support if you believe this will help.

nutrition
for life

DIET PLANS CAN BE COMPLICATED. I (RICK) KNOW THIS FIRSTHAND BECAUSE I have personally experimented with a multitude of plans over the years, and I have worked with several hundred clients in designing their own dietary plans. In most situations, I can design a dietary plan on paper that will guarantee success. However, the problem is, most people can't follow a stringent and detailed plan. There is a big gap between what may be optimal and what is realistic. This is why I am so excited about the Daniel Cure plan. It is realistic, economical, doable, and yields excellent results that will make a real difference in improving your overall health.

We've already presented the scientific evidence to support a nutritional program of clean eating in accordance with the Daniel Fast. Our objective in this chapter is to provide information that will help you to more fully understand basic nutrition — in the context of incorporating foods into your lifestyle that meet the guidelines of the Daniel Cure. With a more complete understanding of how and why certain nutritional principles should be followed for optimal results, you will be empowered to do exactly what you need to do to take control of your health through dietary change.

Once your twenty-one-day Daniel Fast is complete and you construct your own specific dietary program in line with the Daniel Cure, sit back, take a good look at it, and ask yourself, "Is this something that I can implement as part of a lifestyle change?"

If the answer is no, and you feel uncertain about your ability to follow such a plan, press pause and reevaluate. Address any potential weakness now, before you begin, and design a plan that is workable. Don't start by setting yourself up for failure.

Remember, our objective with this book is to motivate, challenge, and encourage you to try the Daniel Fast way of eating as a lifestyle—a realistic and effective way for you to get into and maintain the best physical condition that your genetics will allow. Commit to it. Pray about it. Ask the Holy Spirit to guide you and give you the strength and discipline you'll need to follow through—for life.

There are five essential components you need to be aware of in planning your Daniel Cure lifestyle eating plan: meal frequency, meal size, meal timing, meal composition, and water and other fluid intake.

1. MEAL FREQUENCY

While most diet plans involve reducing meal frequency and cutting calories, the Daniel Cure approach actually calls for an increase in the number of meals consumed each day—specifically, five to six meals as the ideal. This may be welcome news for you if you've spent years starving yourself in an attempt to lose weight. But the Daniel Cure is so much more than losing weight. It's about gaining life and doing so through healthy eating.

Much health literature is available discussing the benefits of eating five to six small meals* throughout the day in an attempt to improve overall health and physical conditioning. Here is the science behind eating more frequently:

As discussed in chapter 6, the hormone insulin is released every time you eat, and the amount released corresponds to the size and the nutrient content of the meal. One of insulin's main roles in the body is to lower blood glucose (sugar) when it increases after you eat. Insulin also acts to increase fat storage and to decrease the breakdown of stored fat to be used as a fuel source. And fluctuating (low and high) blood sugar due to infrequent eating and/or consumption of large meals followed by excess insulin secretion can lead to headaches, feelings of fatigue or irritation, and intense cravings. The scenario you want to avoid looks like this:

| infrequent eating | ⟹ | unstable blood glucose | ⟹ | increased cravings for carbohydrates | ⟹ | tendency to consume large high-carbohydrate meals | ⟹ | excess insulin secreted |

---

*While we refer to each "feeding" as a meal, you might think of a smaller portion (such as a bowl of cottage cheese and fruit) as a snack rather than a meal. That's your choice and the terminology really doesn't matter. The important thing is that you are eating a balance of protein, carbohydrate, and fat in healthy food form several times each day.

The objective in consuming smaller but more frequent meals—those rich in dietary fiber and balanced in protein, carbohydrate, and fat—is to minimize insulin secretion and maintain insulin at relatively low and stable levels throughout the day. Your goal should be to never get to the point of "feeling" very hungry. When you get to this point, it's too late—most people lose the mentality of "I will choose the best food option" and instead go for instant gratification. This usually means eating more food of poor quality. In the same way that people take their daily medicine before they begin experiencing a problem, you should be using the medicinal properties of quality food to prevent the potential problem of intense hunger and the chaos that often follows by consuming high-calorie, high-fat, high-sugar meals.

As you begin to develop a new way of eating, plan for five to six smaller meals a day, rather than two or three large meals. This should allow for much more stable blood glucose and insulin levels throughout the day, which will likely allow you to immediately feel a whole lot better. Over time, this way of eating should result in weight loss and an overall improvement in your health. (For examples of what a typical daily meal pattern looks like, see chapter 22.)

Here are just a few of the benefits of eating more frequently:

- You'll avoid "crashes" and feel more consistently energetic throughout the day.
- You'll have more control over feelings of hunger, which minimizes the urge to consume high-calorie meals. For example, when you allow yourself to get too hungry, your ability to choose appropriate foods may be compromised—you choose the whole pizza over the grilled chicken breast sandwich.
- You'll maintain stable blood glucose and insulin levels, potentially enabling your body to more readily access stored body fat for energy.
- You may increase your metabolism, as energy is required to digest and absorb the foods you eat.

I have witnessed these results with hundreds of individuals and have personally followed this approach for over twenty years. Of course, meal frequency is only one component in our overall plan. We also need to focus on meal size.

2. MEAL SIZE

When you think about meal size, think about how many calories are in the meal—not necessarily how much food is on your plate. I say this because some foods are very "calorie dense." They contain a high number of calories despite a relatively small size. This is true for many high-fat foods and desserts. For example, 3 ounces of cheddar cheese contains about 340 calories and 27 grams of fat! For most people, this calorie allotment is appropriate for a complete lunch or dinner meal. For the same number of calories, you might opt for a 6-ounce marinated and grilled chicken breast, one cup of steamed broccoli, and a large orange, a very balanced meal. To improve your overall dietary plan, it's essential to focus on selecting the right foods—and know the calorie and macronutrient content of the food you eat. (See "Read Labels and Understand Calories" on page 138.)

Meal size can vary from person to person based on body weight, amount of muscle mass, and activity levels. Table 11.1 provides a general guideline for both women and men.

You might initially view these numbers and consider them to be low. But when you eat healthy, low-fat foods, you will be surprised at how much food you can actually eat for these calorie levels. In fact, when the people I counsel first see these calorie recommendations, they often say something like, "There is no way that I can eat only that amount of calories and be satisfied." Then, after a few days of following the plan, they com-

TABLE 11.1

General Guidelines for Meal Size (Calorie Amount) for Daily Meals

Time	Meal	Women / Men
6:30 a.m.	Breakfast	400 calories / 500 calories
9:30 a.m.	Mid-Morning Shake	250 calories / 350 calories
12:00 p.m.	Lunch	450 calories / 600 calories
3:00 p.m.	Mid-Afternoon Shake	250 calories / 350 calories
6:00 p.m.	Dinner	350 calories / 450 calories
Total		**1,700 calories / 2,250 calories***

* See "How Many Calories Do I Need?" on page 118.

plain that they're having trouble eating all the food. This is the beauty of the Daniel Cure plan. You choose the right foods and you can have as much as you would like. You will not run into the problem of overeating in calories because the foods you will be eating are not calorie dense. And you will be reading food labels and developing knowledge of what is contained in the foods you eat. So you'll have the ability to check up on yourself. (See "Making Sense of Ingredients on Food Labels" on page 138.)

I don't want you to be obsessed by how many calories you take in each day. I simply want you to be aware of what you are eating. Keep in mind that calorie intake that is more than you actually need is usually stored as body fat. Don't make the mistake of thinking that low-fat or fat-free foods can be eaten in large quantities without consequences. They cannot. Be sure to review food labels and become familiar with the nutritional value of ingredients contained in the foods you regularly consume. Some things might really surprise you. (See "Zero Grams of Fat? Let's Take a Closer Look" on page 129.) After reviewing

HOW MANY CALORIES DO I NEED?

People often ask, "How many calories should I be eating?" Although our objective is not to focus on calorie counting, understanding what is in most commonly consumed foods will help you to design a dietary plan that is both satisfying and effective. Once you learn this basic information, you can — and should — simply eat as much good-quality natural food as you feel comfortable eating. For most people, this means the precise amount that their body needs to maintain ideal health.

For those who still want information regarding calorie needs, consider the following. The total amount of calories needed per day in order to maintain body mass and optimal physical functioning can vary greatly from one person to the next, depending on genetically regulated metabolic rate, degree of physical activity, amount of muscle mass, and the amount and type of foods eaten. Here is a general suggestion for overall weight maintenance:*

0.5 to 0.7 calories per pound of body mass per hour (1 kg = 2.2 lbs)

Example:	187 lbs:	$0.5 \times 187 \times 24 = 2,244$ calories/day
Example:		$0.7 \times 187 \times 24 = 3,142$ calories/day
Example:	132 lbs:	$0.5 \times 132 \times 24 = 1,584$ calories/day
Example:		$0.7 \times 132 \times 24 = 2,218$ calories/day

Your weight: _____ lbs: $0.5 \times ($ _____ $) \times 24 =$ _____ calories/day

_____ lbs: $0.7 \times ($ _____ $) \times 24 =$ _____ calories/day

The daily calorie range for most of us will fall somewhere around that calculation. Of course, exceptions exist, with some needing fewer calories and others, perhaps due to increased physical activity, needing more. You will need to figure out for yourself, through experimentation, what range is most appropriate for you.

One advantage of the Daniel Cure plan is that you eat as much food as you want, and you find that you just don't eat as many calories as you might think. Because you are now eating clean, wholesome, and natural foods that are nutrient dense but not calorie dense, you are much more satisfied with what you eat, you tend to feel fuller for a longer period of time, and you don't ingest as many calories as you once did — a real blessing for those who have long struggled with diets and calorie restrictions. The Daniel Cure plan is not about counting calories and starving yourself. The Daniel Cure plan is all about learning what is in the foods you eat, consuming natural foods exclusively, eating until you are satisfied, and doing so from this day forward — a lifestyle approach to optimal health.

---

*To calculate calories for losing weight rather than maintaining weight, reduce calories per day by 10 to 20 percent. Note that several reputable medical sources, such as the Mayo Clinic, offer calorie calculators on their websites to make it easier to calculate calories for losing weight.

food labels for a few weeks, you'll be familiar with the amount of calories, protein, carbohydrate, and fat (in addition to other nutrients such as vitamins, minerals, cholesterol, and sodium) contained in your most commonly consumed foods. This will provide you with the knowledge needed to help you make wise food choices throughout your life.

When discussing meal size, we must also mention meal frequency, as both are related. If you will be eating frequent (five to six) meals throughout the day, each of these meals should be small—smaller than the typical meal consumed in the three-meal-per-day regimen. This is illustrated in the table giving guidelines for meal size and calorie counts (table 11.1). Keep in mind that the total amount of food/calories consumed in the five or six meals per day should be similar to the amount consumed in the traditional three meals a day. In other words, I am not suggesting that you consume your typical three meals containing the same amount of food/calories as you are currently consuming, and add two to three more meals. Rather, you are restructuring your entire dietary plan to include smaller, more frequent meals.

3. MEAL TIMING

Another important component to a successful nutrition plan is meal timing—when you will consume your meals. There are three basic guidelines to follow.

1. Consume your first meal of the day within one hour after waking in the morning. An exception may apply if you are a morning exerciser, in which case you may choose to wait until after you finish exercising. When you wake up in the morning, your body has been deprived of nutrients for an extended period (typically six to eight hours). Failing to supply the body with adequate calories (energy) and nutrients by skipping breakfast is a mistake—a big mistake. Why? Because your body may feed on itself to provide the energy you need. Specifically, during acute periods of starvation, the body may rely on its own protein stores (amino acids in your muscle tissue) in order to provide energy. That is not a desirable situation when your goal is to maintain muscle tissue, reduce body fat, and feel healthy and lively. (See "What Are Amino Acids?" on page 120.) Eating stimulates your metabolism, so a morning meal should be a staple in all eating plans.

2. Never allow more than three hours to pass without consuming a small meal. If you are like many people, you might start the day at 7:00 a.m. with coffee and a bagel with cream cheese. Then you head off to work and eat lunch around noon. Because your breakfast was five hours earlier and nutritionally

WHAT ARE AMINO ACIDS?

Amino acids are the building blocks of proteins. The number and type of amino acids linked together to form proteins dictate the actual function of that protein. There are twenty-one amino acids (or twenty, depending on who you read): nine essential (the body cannot make these and they are needed in the diet) and the remainder nonessential (the body can make these and they are not absolutely required in the diet). Complete proteins (animal products and soy) contain all nine essential amino acids. Incomplete proteins (rice, beans, grains) do not contain all nine essential amino acids. Vegetarians need to consume all nine essential amino acids, which can be accomplished by combining two incomplete protein sources or by using a protein supplement, such as soy. If you are following a traditional Daniel Fast and avoiding all animal products, you too will need to consider combining incomplete protein sources to ensure that you get adequate protein to supply your body's needs. If you complete the Daniel Fast and decide to adopt the Daniel Cure lifestyle approach to healthy eating — including lean meat, fish, and dairy products — you should have no trouble getting all the essential amino acids you need for optimal physical functioning.

poor (predominantly carbohydrate and fat), you are quite hungry by lunchtime and over-consume in calories. You then head back to work feeling lethargic and you struggle to make it through the afternoon. You head home and have dinner around 7:00 p.m. and again over-consume in calories due to the large time gap since your lunch meal. This is *not* an eating plan conducive to optimal health.

3. Consume your last meal of the day based on your schedule and what is realistic for you. There is no one time that works best for everyone. If you work late, you may eat dinner at 10:00 p.m. If you follow a more typical routine, dinner could be anytime between 5:00 p.m. and 7:00 p.m. Either is fine, as long as you do not exceed your calorie total during the course of the day. There is some evidence that metabolic rates, which are higher in the morning, may slow somewhat as the day proceeds and be lower in the evening. Therefore, a moderate restriction of calories during the hours immediately before bedtime is probably a smart strategy. If your objective is weight loss, try to avoid consuming anything after your dinner meal and go to bed slightly hungry each night.

4. MEAL COMPOSITION: MACRONUTRIENTS AND MICRONUTRIENTS

The foods we eat contain both macronutrients and micronutrients. As the names depict, macronutrients are large and micronutrients are small. The three macronutrient classes are proteins, carbohydrates, and fats. The two micro-nutrient classes are vitamins and minerals. You should be able to purchase excellent quality food packed with nutrients simply by shopping at your local grocery store, with a possible need for "health food" store shopping on occasion as well as the inclusion of organic food. (See "Is Organic Necessary?" below.)

The following sections provide an overview of these nutrients and why they are important as you develop your Daniel Cure plan.

Macronutrients (Protein, Carbohydrate, and Fat)

Our bodies function optimally with an intake of macronutrients—protein, carbohydrate, and fat—specific to the level and kind of physical activity we engage in. For example, compared to most sedentary individuals, athletes who do a lot of resistance training typically consume a diet with a higher proportion of protein (40 percent) and lower amounts of carbohydrate (40 to 50 percent) and fat (10 to 20 percent). In contrast, endurance athletes generally consume much more carbohydrate relative to protein (60–70 percent carbohydrate; 10–15 percent protein) and a moderate (20 percent) proportion of dietary fat. The average American consumes 10 to 15 percent protein, 30 to 40 percent fat, and the remainder carbohydrate (often highly processed carbohydrate). Keep in mind that the precise ratios of these macronutrients will always be specific to each individual. It is a mistake to apply one set ratio to all people.

IS ORGANIC NECESSARY?

This is a topic that merits its own chapter—or perhaps its own book. However, the simple answer here is no, organic is not necessary. Although organic foods should contain limited or no pesticides or chemical fertilizers and may be better for you than their nonorganic counterparts, there are differences in the "degree" of organic. This can result in packaging and advertising that may be somewhat misleading or difficult to understand—suggesting benefits that may not be realized.

Considering this fact, coupled with the reality that many people simply cannot manage to purchase organic food exclusively, while following the Daniel Fast, the Daniel Cure, or any other health-focused nutrition plan, you can eat whatever fruits, vegetables, grains, and animal products that you would like as long as they are natural and ideally without additives and preservatives. Organic options are great if you can afford to pay the price. If there were no price difference, we would suggest you consume organic entirely. But we need to be realistic. Most of us can't afford to spend $4 on a pound of organic apples. However, certain foods (generally, those that do not have a peel that will be removed prior to eating) do make sense to purchase organic if you can afford to do so. Do some investigating and determine what will be best for you and your family.

However, you might be asking, "What is best for me?" While your plan may need to be tweaked a bit here and there, a good starting guideline that works well for most people who aspire to consume a healthy diet is the following:

Protein: 20 percent of caloric intake*
Carbohydrate: 60 percent of caloric intake
Fat: 20 percent of caloric intake

To generate a visual of this breakdown, simply think of a typical plate divided into three equal parts. One part will contain a low-fat protein source and two parts will contain a carbohydrate source. Aim for at least half of the carbohydrate portion to be vegetables or fruit, with the other half consisting of whole grains (for example, brown rice, barley, pasta, oats). If you're wondering where the 20 percent fat content is, it's in your protein and carbohydrate portions. Rarely will you need to go out of your way to add dietary fat to your meals. In some cases, you might opt to add a very small amount of healthy oil to your meal to increase the fat content. (See food "plates" for both the Daniel Fast and Daniel Cure plans as examples on page 104.)

Here is a brief overview of the three macronutrients, including examples of each.

Protein (4 calories per gram)

Proteins are large molecules that consist of "building blocks" called amino acids. Proteins are essential to human life and participate in virtually every process in cells, including metabolic reactions and muscle growth. Table 11.2 (see next page) lists good sources of protein, in no particular order of quality.

How Much Protein?

Now that you have an idea of good protein sources, it's important to understand how much protein you need to consume each day—or on average over the course of a few days. The current recommended intake for protein for sedentary adults is 0.8g/kg/day (1 kg = 2.2 pounds). For example, a man weighing 180 pounds (81.8 kg) would require only 65 grams of protein per day.† However,

---

*While a traditional Daniel Fast plan tends to follow these ratios overall, we have found that for most people the protein intake is closer to 12 to 15 percent of daily calories, while the carbohydrate and fat intake is slightly higher than the numbers indicated. See "Are Certain Ratios of Protein, Carbohydrate, and Fat Optimal?" on page 141.

† One ounce of meat or fish contains approximately 7 grams of protein. Therefore, a 5-ounce piece of beef, chicken, or fish (about the size of an average-sized fist) would supply about 35 grams of protein, or one-half of the daily protein requirement of 65 grams. Animal products such as meat and milk generally provide more protein per unit volume as compared to plant-based foods. Check labels to determine how much protein is in the foods you routinely consume.

Table 11.2: Proteins

Category	Source	Comments
Animal	Fish	Some fish is very high in fat, although it is typically the so-called "good" fat (polyunsaturated). Choose fish high in omega-3 fatty acids, such as salmon, mackerel, lake trout, sea bass, sardines, and tuna (bluefin and albacore).
Animal	Chicken/Turkey/ Pork	White meat is preferred, as this is lowest in fat content. Dark meat is acceptable but contains more dietary fat. You should minimize processed lunch meats.*
Animal	Beef	Extra-lean cuts are preferred. According to the USDA, extra-lean beef (top sirloin, top and bottom round, eye of round) contains less than 5 percent fat. Lean beef (flank, brisket, chuck shoulder roast, shoulder steak) contains less than 10 percent fat.† Trim visible fat before eating.
Animal	Eggs	Egg whites are best, but whole eggs are fine on occasion. While there are only 2 to 3 grams of saturated fat in a jumbo egg, there are also 250 mg of cholesterol in that same egg.
Dairy‡	Cottage Cheese	Choose a low-fat or fat-free variety.
Dairy	Yogurt	Plain yogurt is the best option nutritionally. However, some flavored Greek yogurts are also very good and contain little added sugar (Greek yogurts may also contain slightly less calcium; check the label). Many traditional yogurts taste great but contain a significant amount of added sugar. Read the labels.
Dairy	Milk	Choose skim or 1 percent milk, as these varieties contain a much lower amount of fat but the same amount of protein as 2 percent or whole milk (8 grams of protein per cup). In an 8-ounce cup, the fat content of milk is as follows: Skim (0 grams); 1 percent (2 grams); 2 percent (5 grams); whole (8 grams).
Plant	Beans/Lentils	These contain roughly 7 grams of protein and 5 grams of fiber per cooked ½ cup.
Plant	Whole Grains	Grains are primarily a source of carbohydrates, but for those following the traditional Daniel Fast, whole grains provide a moderate amount of protein and are an adequate vegetarian protein source. As a source of protein, whole grains should be combined with other vegetarian protein sources, such as beans.
Supplement	Protein Powder	Protein powder is manufactured from animal, dairy, and plant sources to contain essentially pure protein — with very little carbohydrate or fat. Protein powder can be an excellent adjunct to your whole-food protein sources, in particular when used in meal-replacement shakes (see chapter 13). Many excellent sources are available. For more information, see www.DanielCure.com/supplements.

* Lunch meats often contain more sodium and less protein on a gram-weight basis than meats you can cook and prepare yourself. Lunch meats often contain other ingredients, such as binders, fillers, sodium, and preservatives, and they cost two to three times more than their unprocessed counterparts.

† Keep in mind that the percentage of fat is based on product weight (for example, 10 grams of fat per 100 grams of beef), not product calories. Therefore, considering the water content in the beef, a 10 percent fat product yields a dietary fat content closer to 50 percent.

‡ Dairy products are derived from animals.

keep in mind that these guidelines are for sedentary adults. If you are involved in regular exercise, you need more than 0.8g/kg/day. Or if you are older than 65, you too need more protein. This is what the scientific research shows, despite the government recommendation for only 0.8 g/kg/day. It's that simple.

I suggest a general guideline of 20 percent of daily calories coming from protein, 60 percent from carbohydrate, and 20 percent from fat. For an example of quantities and total calories using these percentages, see table 11.3.*

Table 11.3: Gram Quantities for Macronutrients

Macronutrient	Women (1,700 calories)	Men (2,250 calories)
Protein	85 grams	112 grams
Carbohydrate	255 grams	338 grams
Fat	38 grams	50 grams

This plan works well for most people. It provides a protein amount that matches the scientific evidence (1.2 g – 1.4 g/kg/day) for active adults and allows for a realistic intake to be consumed. For example, a woman eating approximately 1,700 calories per day and 85 grams of protein might split her meal plan into breakfast, lunch, and dinner, plus two meal-replacement shakes (one mid-morning and one mid-afternoon). Protein intake for each of these five meals would be 15 – 20 grams, providing the total of 85 grams per day. Such a plan should provide all the necessary protein for optimal health and physical functioning.

Carbohydrate (4 calories per gram)

Carbohydrates are the most important source of energy for your body. The carbohydrates are broken down by the body into glucose, which first enters the bloodstream and then enters various tissues to be used as a fuel source. Although carbohydrate is not essential for life (your body can create energy from protein and fat), you would not feel very good if you decided to eliminate carbohydrates from your diet. Table 11.4 (see next page) lists good sources of carbohydrate, in no particular order of quality.

How Much Carbohydrate?

Up until about ten years ago, there existed no minimum recommended intake for carbohydrate. However, the Institute of Medicine now recommends a minimum daily intake of 130 grams of carbohydrate for children and adults.

---

* See also "How do I Compute the Calorie Contribution of Protein, Carbohydrate, and Fat in Foods?" on page 246.

Table 11.4: Carbohydrates

Category	Source	Comments
Fruit	Fruits	Any variety of fresh, frozen, or canned fruit is acceptable. However, make certain that the frozen and canned varieties do not contain added sugar. The ingredient list should simply include the fruit itself, with the possible addition of fruit juice (in canned varieties). Heavy syrup or other sweeteners are unacceptable. Aim for at least five servings of fruit each day (one serving is equal to ½ cup or one medium piece of fruit).
Vegetables	Vegetables (Non-Starchy)	All varieties of fresh, frozen, or canned vegetables are acceptable. Make certain that the frozen and canned varieties do not contain added ingredients. Many canned vegetables have added sodium — read labels carefully. Non-starchy vegetables generally contain fewer calories than starchy vegetables. Aim for at least five servings of vegetables each day (one serving is equal to ½ cup; a serving for green leafy vegetables is equal to 1 cup).
	Vegetables (Starchy)	Common starchy vegetables include any variety of potato (red, purple, white, sweet) in addition to corn and peas. Include the skin of potatoes when possible, as it contains micronutrients and fiber. Starchy vegetables typically contain more calories than non-starchy vegetables.
Grains	Rolled Oats (or Steel-Cut Oats)	Both old-fashioned (slow cooking) and "quick" oats are acceptable. However, you should note that many flavored instant oatmeal products contain more sugar and less fiber than traditional oats. Because of this, flavored instant varieties are inferior nutritionally and should not be used regularly.
	Rice	Choose brown rice over white, and regular (slow cooked) over instant. Brown rice is moderately higher in fiber than white, and regular rice has a lower glycemic index than instant rice. Perhaps most important, slow-cooked brown rice seems to provide a much greater feeling of "fullness," or satiety, after eating, as compared to white or instant.
	Barley	Pearled barley provides about 7 grams of fiber per ½ cup cooked. It is a great high-fiber substitute for rice.
	Quinoa	Quinoa provides about 4 grams of fiber per ½ cup cooked. It is also relatively high in protein, containing about 7 grams per ½ cup. It is another great substitute for rice.
	Cereal	Choose only those cereals without added sugar (read the label) and those with a high-fiber content — shredded wheat is a good option.
	Pasta	Whole-wheat is preferred over white pasta, as it contains much more fiber. Pasta is a very calorie-dense food and should not be consumed regularly. For example, ¼ lb. plain pasta contains over 400 calories. Add the sauce and some meat and you can easily be up to 800 calories. For most, this is too many calories for any one meal. Save the pasta for cheat meals.

(continued)

Category	Source	Comments
Grains *cont.*	Bread/ Bagels/Pitas	Whole-wheat/whole-grain products are preferred over white-flour products. Like pasta, calories can add up quickly with these items.
Legumes	Beans and Lentils	All varieties of beans are excellent. If choosing cooked, canned beans, make certain that sodium is not added and consider rinsing the beans in a strainer before eating. Beans and lentils are an excellent source of dietary fiber, providing about 5 grams of fiber per cooked ½ cup.

The 130-gram figure was supposedly based on the suggestion that the brain uses this amount of carbohydrate, or glucose, each day for optimal functioning. This recommendation has been scrutinized by proponents of low carbohydrate diets who claim that many people can function perfectly fine with far less carbohydrate than 130 grams per day. Regardless of your view on this, when following a Daniel Fast plan, based on the nature of the plant-based program, you will easily consume carbohydrate in an amount that exceeds the 130-gram-per-day minimum value.*

While you should attempt to consume a mix of carbohydrate sources, as provided in table 11.4, another goal should be to consume 25–40 grams of fiber per day—with specifics based on sex and age.† Adequate daily intake levels for fiber, as recommended by the Institute of Medicine, are shown in table 11.5.

Following the Daniel Fast plan should easily get you to that amount. For example, my fiber intake is close to 70 grams per day when I'm following the Daniel Fast.

Note that there are two kinds of fiber: soluble, which dissolves in water, and insoluble, which resists digestion and does not dissolve in water.

- *Soluble fiber* includes items such as oats and oat bran, legumes, beans, barley, bananas, oranges, apples, pears, and blueberries. The soluble fiber is thought to assist in transporting cholesterol from the body, stabilize blood glucose levels, delay stomach emptying and help you to feel full longer, and promote a feeling of fullness.

---

* Most people consume far more than 130 grams of carbohydrate per day. One large piece of fruit, one cup of cooked corn, one cup of cooked oats, ⅔ cup of cooked rice, and ¾ cup of cooked beans each contain about 30 grams of carbohydrate.

† The differences in fiber intake are based on the number of total calories consumed. For example, men typically require more calories than women, while younger adults—possibly due to increased physical activity—typically require more calories than older adults. Hence, fiber requirements are higher for these groups.

• *Insoluble fiber* includes items such as wheat bran, whole wheat and whole grains, dark leafy vegetables, grapes, nuts, seeds, brown rice, and fruit and vegetable skins. It may help prevent constipation, maintain regular bowel function, aid in the prevention of colon cancer, and reduce inflammation, which may slow the development and progression of various diseases.

The benefits of fiber intake are significant. For example, it has been noted that for every 10 grams of fiber eaten per day, the risk of coronary artery disease death is decreased by 27 percent.[31] In terms of longevity, it has been reported that men and women who ate the most dietary fiber every day (about 26–29 grams) were 22 percent less likely to die over the course of a nine-year study period, compared to those who consumed the least amount of fiber daily (about 10–13 grams).[32] With these facts in mind, consider increasing your dietary fiber intake to improve your overall health and increase longevity.*

TABLE 11.5:
Recommendations for Daily Fiber Intake

	Men	Women
Age 19–49 years	38 grams	25 grams
Age 50 years and above	30 grams	21 grams

When choosing carbohydrate foods, you should aim for foods in their most natural state. In chapter 3 we discussed the glycemic index (GI), a scale originally developed for diabetics that evaluates how quickly (or slowly) various nutrients are released into the bloodstream and, therefore, how these nutrients will affect blood glucose (and insulin) levels.† Your goal if you desire to reap the most benefits from your nutritional plan is to maintain relatively stable blood sugar and insulin levels throughout the day. As stated earlier in this chapter, eating small and frequent meals will assist greatly in that. Including low GI foods, such as the examples of carbohydrate provided in table 11.4, will enhance this plan.

Fat (9 calories per gram)

If you've been paying attention to the calorie quantities indicated in parentheses next to the macronutrient name, you've noticed that while protein and carbohydrate contain only 4 calories per gram, fat contains more than double that amount.‡ This should help you to understand why it can be easier to gain

---

*It is imperative that as you increase your fiber intake, you also increase your water intake. High fiber diets without adequate water can lead to constipation. Aim for one gallon of water per day.
† For additional information on the GI, see the Glycemic Research Institute at *www.glycemic.com*.
‡ These are approximate values used and widely accepted in the food and diet industry. Actual values are slightly different. Alcohol contains approximately 7 calories per gram.

weight when eating high-fat foods and why restricting high-fat foods often results in weight loss. It's a function of calorie intake.

There are four kinds of dietary fat you need to be concerned with. The so-called "bad" fats are saturated and trans fats (also referred to as hydrogenated fats). Limit consumption of saturated fats and avoid trans fats altogether. Healthier fats are monounsaturated fats and polyunsaturated fats (which include essential fatty acids). Eat these fats in moderation.

TABLE 11.6: Fats

Kinds of Fats	Sources
Bad fats*	Animal fats (saturated fat)
	Dairy fats: milk, cheese, butter, cream (saturated fat)
	Margarine (trans fat)
	Shortening (trans fat)
Healthier fats	Olive oil
	Peanut oil
	Soybean oil
	Corn oil
	Sunflower oil
	Safflower oil
	Flaxseed oil
	Borage seed oil
	Fish oil
	Olives
	Avocados
	Nuts and nut butters†
	Seeds

*Trans fats (contained in margarine and shortenings and identified on most packaged snack foods as "hydrogenated" or "partially hydrogenated") are most problematic for health. Fried foods are often very high in unhealthy saturated and trans fats and should be eliminated or significantly limited in a healthy food plan.
†While nuts and nut butters may be a healthier source of fat, they are not a good source of protein, as is commonly believed. Just because a food has protein in it does not mean that the ratio of protein to other nutrients is optimal. To consume an adequate amount of protein from nuts, you will consume a very high amount of fat and calories. Nuts and nut butters contain 75–80 percent of calories from fat.

Table 11.6 identifies some sources of bad and healthier fats.

Although saturated fat is considered a "bad" fat, a small amount of saturated fat in an otherwise healthy diet should not be a problem. You should not be afraid to consume low-fat animal products simply because they contain some saturated fat. They also contain many health-enhancing nutrients—complete protein, iron, zinc, calcium, and B vitamins—that can be beneficial to your body. Moderation is the key here.

How Much Fat?

While consuming enough fat is never a concern for most individuals, consuming the right type of fat may be, specifically essential fatty acids (EFAs). You need to obtain EFAs from your diet. Your body cannot make them. The daily amount of the healthier EFAs needed by adults, as recommended by the Linus Pauling Institute, is shown in table 11.7.

If in a typical week you are consuming a variety of the healthier fats as indicated in table 11.6, you should have no difficulty meeting the minimum requirements for EFAs. For

TABLE 11.7: Essential Fatty Acids (EFAs)

Women	Men
12 g/day omega-6 (linoleic acid)	17 g/day omega-6 (linoleic acid)
1 to 2 g/day omega-3 (alpha-linolenic acid)	1 to 2 g/day omega-3 (alpha-linolenic acid)

Note: 1 gram = 1,000 mg

example, 1 tablespoon of flaxseed oil contains roughly 14 grams of fat, of which about 10 grams are EFAs. For those who don't regularly eat fish, it will be more difficult to get enough omega-3 fatty acids as compared to the omega-6 fatty acids. The use of fish oil supplements, at a daily dosage of 1,000 – 2,000 mg in the form of Eicosapentaenoic acid (EPA) and Docosahexaenoic acid (DHA) as a combined supplement may be considered in consultation with your physician

ZERO GRAMS OF FAT? LET'S TAKE A CLOSER LOOK

Food labels often boldly claim their contents to be "fat free" or "low fat." But such statements are often misleading. For example, in order for a nutrition label to claim "fat free" status, the product needs to have less than ½ gram of fat per serving. Manufacturers are sneaky in that they make the serving size small enough to meet this criterion, leading consumers to believe that the entire contents of the product is fat free, when in fact it may actually contain a significant amount of fat when consumed in large amounts.

The most blatant abuse of this guideline is found in cans of cooking spray. The label claims that the product contains zero grams of fat and zero calories from fat, yet the product is literally a can of oil! How can a can of oil contain no fat? Well, the suggested serving size is a ¼-second spray, and, by law, if the fat content per serving is less than ½ gram, the label can claim zero grams of fat. I don't know anyone who sprays a pan for a mere fourth of a second. Now, while these cooking sprays are a better choice than pouring oil into a pan, they do contain essentially 100 percent fat. Consumers should understand this and not think they can use as much spray as desired with the impression that the spray contains no fat or calories.

Here's some science to put this into perspective. In analyzing one can of spray, I (Rick) noted a serving size to be 0.25 gram, with about 200 grams in the entire can. Since one tablespoon of oil is 14 grams, the can contains a bit more than 14 tablespoons of oil (200 / 14 = 14.3). There are about 125 calories in one tablespoon of oil, which means the can contains 1,750 calories of oil (14 tablespoons × 125 calories per tablespoon = 1,750). Therefore, in the can of oil that supposedly contains zero fat and zero calories, there are approximately 200 grams of fat and 1,750 calories. This is simply one example of how food labels can be misleading.

It's important to take a very close look at labels before you purchase and consume foods. Educate yourself concerning what exactly is in the foods you plan to eat — the content may not match the marketing claims. Your newfound knowledge might dramatically alter what you eat and what you decide to feed your family.

or other qualified health-care provider. See *www.DanielCure.com/supplements* for more information.

Micronutrients (Vitamins and Minerals)

The food compounds we've been discussing—proteins, carbohydrates, and fats—are called macronutrients. Micronutrients, which are the vitamins and minerals, are also necessary for optimal health. In some cases, adequate intake of the micronutrients can be obtained through consumption of a well-balanced, diverse, fresh, and nutrient-dense diet that includes both whole foods and meal-replacement shakes. Foods such as fruits, vegetables, grains, legumes,

DIETARY SUPPLEMENTS

While dietary supplements certainly will not make up for a poor diet, they can be of assistance if used in conjunction with a well-balanced diet. In fact, most of us would benefit from some dietary supplements.

Not all dietary supplements are created equal. Some supplements provide little benefit, in part because they contain too little of the active ingredient to be beneficial.* The question "Does that supplement work?" really needs to be followed by another question: "Does it work for what?"

My (Rick) short list of dietary supplements really do work—for aiding overall health. These supplements support consistent intake of quality whole-food macronutrients (protein, carbohydrate, fat) and micronutrients (vitamins and minerals), as well as assist in maintaining and/or improving multiple aspects of overall health.

1. Protein powder (whey isolate and casein in particular): to use as needed by men and women in meal-replacement shakes, as an adjunct to whole foods.

2. Multi-vitamin/multi-mineral supplement (typically 1 tablet/capsule per day—see manufacturer guidelines): for daily use by men and women. Although certain nutritional differences do exist between men and women, a general-purpose multi-vitamin/multi-mineral supplement will work fine for most people. Seek a product that contains 100 percent or more of the daily value for all nutrients listed.

3. Vitamin D_3 (at a dose ranging from 2,000–4,000 IU per day; this value far exceeds the current recommended daily value but is consistent with the scientific literature demonstrating a benefit with use): for daily use by men and women.

4. Fish oil supplement providing both EPA and DHA (at a combined dose of 1,000–2,000 mg of total EPA and DHA): for daily use by men and women.

These supplement staples—which should be considered by virtually everyone—are an inexpensive "health insurance policy." It's interesting that many people have no problem spending money on physician office visits, co-pays and coinsurance, and medications, yet they are concerned about spending $40 a month on dietary supplements that could likely alleviate many of the same simple problems for which they tend to seek medical care. Prevention is preferred over treatment.

In addition to these supplements, others

meats, and dairy products have an abundance of micronutrients. If a wide variety of foods from these groups is consumed on a regular basis, there is less need for supplemental micronutrients in most diets.

However, as more research continues to become available regarding selected vitamins and minerals and their role in health maintenance, enhancement, and disease prevention, it is reasonable to consider supplementing an already balanced diet with certain micronutrients, depending on the situation. This would come in the form of a dietary supplement or supplements. For example, athletes, individuals on a low-calorie intake, pregnant or nursing mothers (or simply women of child-bearing age), and individuals with diabetes,

that have an abundance of data in support of their use include creatine monohydrate and methylsulfonylmethane (MSM). Although initially marketed to athletes as a performance aid, more data now focus on the benefits of creatine monohydrate in older adults, those with neurological disorders, and those with depression. A common dose is 5 grams (5,000 mg) per day (equal to 1 teaspoon), which is typically sold as a powder that can simply be mixed into your favorite beverage.

MSM also has been demonstrated in several scientific studies to decrease inflammation — which has far-reaching implications, ranging from alleviating joint pain to improving cardiovascular health. A commonly consumed dose is 3 grams (3,000 mg) per day, which is typically sold in capsules of 500 – 1,000 mg. These two relatively inexpensive ingredients may provide significant benefit to many.

Finally, a well-balanced antioxidant blend that includes a variety of plant-based nutrients and extracts can prove very helpful to overall health. An example of such a blend is a fruit and vegetable powder concentrate, which may be encapsulated or sold as a powder that can be mixed into a beverage. I personally believe that such a product is a wise choice to add to your overall supplement regimen. Due to the complexity of antioxidant dietary supplementation, you will need to do more research. More information is available at our website, *www .DanielCure.com/supplements.*

With the advancement in nutritional science research and dietary supplement development, other ingredients may soon emerge for consideration. Some that are of interest to me and many other scientists include ubiquinol (reduced co-enzyme Q10), resveratrol, curcumin, and others in the family of phytochemicals.

If you would like to learn more about dietary supplements in general, or if you have specific questions regarding the efficacy of certain dietary supplements, visit *www.DanielCure .com/supplements.* As with any change to your nutritional regimen, it is always best to first consult with your physician or other qualified health-care provider before starting any dietary supplements.

---

* Unfortunately, many dietary supplement manufacturers choose to use less than optimal dosages of key active ingredients in their products. This decision is largely influenced by the cost of the ingredients and possibly by a lack of understanding regarding the scientifically demonstrated effective dose. For more information on the topic of inferior dosing in many dietary supplements, visit *www.DanielCure.com/ supplements.*

heart disease, or other inflammatory-related diseases may benefit from taking a micronutrient supplement. Because the topic of dietary supplementation can be quite complex, here are a few simple guidelines to get you started on the path to optimal health.

- Consume a well-balanced, diverse, fresh, and nutrient-dense diet — with both whole foods and meal-replacement shakes. Following the guidelines presented for the Daniel Cure will ensure such a diet.

- For additional assurance that you are nutritionally complete in the micronutrient category, consider using a good multi-vitamin/multi-mineral supplement. These typically contain needed micronutrients at or above the recommended daily intake level. They serve as an inexpensive health insurance policy and can be easily used by almost anyone.

- Consider using individual micronutrient supplements. These are provided at much higher dosages than what is contained in multi-vitamin/multi-mineral supplements. See "Dietary Supplements" on page 130 and visit *www.DanielCure.com/supplements* for more information.

5. WATER AND OTHER FLUIDS

An often overlooked component of many dietary plans is fluid intake — in particular, water. So let's be clear. You need to seriously consider what you will drink every day (water is ideal), how much you will drink, and how you will make this happen. Just as you will determine the answers to these questions for your food intake, you need to develop the same plan for your fluid intake. Here are some general guidelines.

What to Drink

- Pure water is the ideal fluid to consume. And you do not need to drink bottled water. Many city drinking waters are of excellent quality. You can make the choice for yourself based on taste preference and water quality in your area. (See "The Health Benefits of Water" on page 29.)

- Non-calorie beverages such as diet sodas and flavored waters are generally fine on occasion, but should not make up a significant amount of your daily fluid intake. These products typically contain artificial sweeteners, flavorings, colorings, and other chemicals — potentially unhealthy items that you do not want to consume regularly. For example, some scientific literature suggests that artificial sweeteners may increase sweet cravings and dependency and may be associated with weight gain.[33]

- Calorie-containing beverages (soft drinks, lemonade, teas, etc.) are usually loaded with sugar and provide little nutritional value. For example, one 12-ounce can of soda contains about 40 grams of sugar. This is equal to 10 teaspoons of sugar and 160 calories of sugar. You are better served by eating calories rather than drinking them. Meal-replacement shakes and milk are the exception.

- Alcohol and caffeinated beverages, such as coffee and tea, act as diuretics and may cause your body to lose fluids. While you should understand this, it's not necessary to totally eliminate these beverages from the diet. In fact, much research indicates the health benefits of coffee and tea, as well as of alcohol when consumed in moderation (for example, one 5-ounce glass of wine per day). It is of no concern if you drink one or two cups of coffee or tea each day—preferably without sweetener and in addition to your plain water intake.

How Much to Drink

- Make it a goal to consume one gallon (sixteen 8-ounce cups) of water each day.* Drink more when you're in a hot, humid environment and when exercising.

- Assess your fluid intake by the color and odor of your urine. When you are adequately hydrated, your urine should be clear or pale yellow and mostly odorless. If not, increase your fluid intake. (Note that certain medications, vitamin supplements, and foods—such as asparagus— can impact urine color and/or odor.)

How and When to Drink

- Fill a one-gallon container with water each night and place it in the refrigerator so it is cold in the morning. Keep it with you—in your office, at home, wherever. People might think you're weird for bringing a gallon of water to work. But you're in the business of getting healthy. And it's a good conversation starter.

---

*This amount exceeds what is generally recommended by many other sources. For example, the Institute of Medicine suggests total fluid intake to be about three-fourths of a gallon per day for men and a half gallon per day for women. But this is the volume deemed to be adequate for most people. We are not satisfied with adequacy. We can do better. When considering the benefits of water related to hydration status, reduction in food consumption, importance when consuming a high-fiber diet, and the impact on physical performance during exercise and physical activity, we suggest that you aim higher and set your goal on one gallon of water per day. It may take you a while to get there, but you can do it.

- Buy yourself a cup or bottle you really like and fill it frequently from your gallon container. Then keep it within reach throughout the day. The main excuse people have for not drinking fluid is a failure to have something to drink. Start planning ahead and include this on your "get healthy" list.

- Drink two 8-ounce cups of water before every meal. This may reduce your food intake and aid in weight loss.

- Drink fluids regularly throughout the day and attempt to finish the entire gallon at least one hour before bedtime. Drinking water too close to bedtime may result in awakening to use the restroom in the middle of the night.

DESIGNING A PLAN OF YOUR OWN

We have covered a good amount of information in this chapter, and now it's time to bring it all together. You need to decide how you will use this information to construct your own Daniel Cure eating plan. If you're planning to follow a traditional Daniel Fast for the initial twenty-one-day period, which is recommended, simply consume a purified plant-based diet. The information contained in chapter 3 provides the guidance you need.

However, if you are now ready to embark on the Daniel Cure plan, your options increase and you can be more creative in your dietary design. Specifically, you can consider animal products such as lean meat and dairy. You can also consider caffeinated beverages, such as coffee and tea. Finally, you can consider an occasional cheat meal or dessert each week, which may provide you peace of mind, knowing that you do not need to be perfect in order to make great progress.

Chapter 10 provides food "plates" for both the Daniel Fast and Daniel Cure plans on page 104. Chapter 22 provides some sample menus for both the traditional Daniel Fast and the Daniel Cure. Of course, the essential guidelines of consuming frequent, small, clean, and healthy meals, along with adequate water intake, are similar for both plans and should be adopted as your new lifestyle approach. Fully understand what is in the foods you are eating. (See "Making Sense of Nutrition Facts" on page 139.) Then decide to choose only the best foods—those that you know will improve your overall health and lead you to your goal.

Let's end with a recap of what we learned, focusing on seven key principles to ensure your success using the Daniel Cure plan.

Eat Frequently

- Eat five to six meals per day, every day.
- Never skip meals.
- You should never feel excessively hungry during the day. If you do, you waited too long to eat.

Manage Portion Sizes

- Eat the appropriate amount of calories/food for you, divided over five to six meals per day.
- You should never feel excessively full during the day. If you do, you ate too much.

Adjust Your Plate

- Divide your plate into three equal parts, with one part containing a low-fat protein source and two parts containing a carbohydrate source (one part vegetable or fruit, one part grain). Add small amounts of healthy dietary fats if desired.
- If you are using meal-replacement shakes, start by adding 15 to 20 grams (2 to 2½ tablespoons) of protein powder to your carbohydrate source (fruit juice, fruit, oats). Then, add a small amount of healthy fat such as flaxseed oil or natural peanut butter (½ tablespoon) if desired.

Consume Natural Foods

- Eat a wide variety of fresh foods — purchase most of your groceries from the perimeter of the supermarket and shop minimally from the aisles.
- Avoid packaged and processed foods.
- Consume a nutrient-dense diet. Attempt to get as many quality nutrients — protein, carbohydrate, fat, vitamins, minerals — in the least amount of calories. Eating the healthy foods indicated in the tables provided in this chapter will allow you to consume a nutrient-dense diet.
- Understand that it can be challenging to eat healthy foods away from home and consider bringing your own lunch to work each day.

Aim High for Fiber

- If you are a man younger than 50, aim for 38 grams of fiber daily. If you are a man 50 or older, aim for 30 grams daily. If you are a woman younger than 50, aim for 25 grams of fiber daily. If you are a woman 50 or older, aim for 21 grams daily.

Drink Water

- Drink one gallon of water every day—consistently throughout the day.
- Consider drinking plenty of water prior to each meal (16 ounces).

Enjoy Yourself

- Determine which healthy foods you enjoy eating and consume those foods regularly.
- Experiment with different recipes to add some pizzazz to your overall diet. There are so many easy-to-prepare and great-tasting recipes that involve healthy ingredients. See part 4 of this book for examples. These can be modified with the inclusion of low-fat animal products if desired.
- Splurge with one or two cheat meals, and possibly one dessert, each week. Remember, if you're eating five meals per day, that's 35 meals per week. If only 33 are healthy and in line with the Daniel Cure guidelines, you're still 94 percent compliant!

NOW LET'S GET STARTED

From a basic nutrition perspective, you now have all the information you need to get started on a healthy nutrition plan. The material presented in chapters 10 and 12 should help you incorporate this information into a workable plan. The sample menus provided in chapter 22 show you how this can be done very easily. So what now?

The first thing you need to do is abandon your current unhealthy diet (assuming this is the case) and make a commitment to the Daniel Cure lifestyle. (See "The Daniel Cure Pledge" on page 276.) This may not be easy for you, but it can be done. It's the committed step, and it will guide you on the remainder of the path. You'll then need to determine which healthy foods you will eat—simply plant-based food or a combination of plant and animal foods. This chapter provides a wealth of examples for both types. The food "plates" provided in chapter 10 on page 104 provide additional guidance. Then, it's a matter of putting together meal plans that include your favorite foods. The final task is follow-through—you actually need to do this!

And while we certainly understand that change can be difficult, we also know that it is absolutely possible if you truly desire it. As a follower of Christ, you have the power of the one true God living inside of you. If he can create the universe out of nothing, form human beings from the dust of the earth, and rise from the grave in a glorious and life-giving manner, he can most certainly help you commit to a lifestyle change. Just ask him.

■ TURN YOUR THOUGHTS INTO ACTIONS ■

1 Think of yourself as the nutrition leader in your circle of family and friends—the go-to person for information and encouragement related to optimal dietary intake. You know what to do and you actually do it!

2 Pack your lunch each day and bring it to work with you. Spend the first half of your lunch break going for a brisk walk. Spend the second half eating a nutritious meal and thanking God for granting you the power to take control of your health. You'll be a great example to others in your workplace.

3 Accept the idea that eating five to six small meals per day is best for your overall health. Then follow through on this plan. Finally, once or twice a week, treat yourself to a cheat meal or dessert and know that you can comfortably enjoy this because you are in control.

READ LABELS AND UNDERSTAND CALORIES

One comment we have heard over and over again from those participating in our Daniel Fast studies is that reading food labels has greatly increased their knowledge of what is in the foods they eat. They have been shocked at the amount of added fat, sugar, sodium, and preservatives contained in packaged foods. They are also concerned about the amount of calories in certain foods. For these reasons, we recommend that you get into the habit of reviewing food labels. This includes ingredient lists, macronutrient content, and calories. Once you do this for a while, you'll find that it takes less and less time because you will become "nutritionally informed."

While we urge you to read food labels and take the time to learn of the calorie content of various foods, regularly counting daily calorie intake is not something we endorse in this book. If following the Daniel Cure plan, you should be able to eat freely without concern over the exact amount of calories consumed. If you are eating clean, wholesome foods, you need not worry about calories. By default, your overall calorie intake will likely be at or below the level you need to maintain your current body weight—or far lower than this amount if you just recently abandoned a high-calorie diet in favor of the Daniel Cure plan. Having the knowledge of what is contained in the foods you eat—including calories—will help you in making better nutritional choices, in particular when you are away from the home. Equip yourself with knowledge by reviewing the food labels.

MAKING SENSE OF INGREDIENTS ON FOOD LABELS

When buying packaged foods, try to choose items with only a single food in the ingredient list —such as fruit, vegetables, oats, brown rice, beans, lentils, and nuts. If you must purchase other packaged food items containing more than the actual food itself, select those with the fewest ingredients. For example, peanut butter should contain simply peanuts (and perhaps a small amount of added salt). However, if you look at the different labels on peanut butter at the local supermarket, you'll find long lists of ingredients that include things like corn syrup solids, sugar, hydrogenated vegetable oils, etc.

Ingredients on food labels are listed in order of greatest to least quantity. For example, the ingredients for a barbecue sauce might list high fructose corn syrup, distilled vinegar, tomato paste, food starch, salt, smoke flavor, garlic, and sugar. This indicates that there is more high fructose corn syrup in the sauce than any other single ingredient. Sugar is present in the least amount. What we do not know is the precise contribution of any of the listed ingredients. When considering the purchase of a packaged food item, look carefully at the ingredient list as well as the nutrition facts. If you see ingredients at the top of the list that you know should be avoided when present in abundance (such as high fructose corn syrup and hydrogenated oils), recon-sider your purchase. There are healthier alternatives. Of course, if you are simply planning to use certain food items on rare occasions (such as the barbecue sauce), you do not need to be so critical. Enjoy yourself and then get back on track. One "cheat" meal is not the end of the world. But it is important to understand and recognize what you are eating and to make the healthiest choices. You're not aiming for perfection; you're aiming for progress and understanding. You can do it!

MAKING SENSE OF NUTRITION FACTS

If you've ever tried to read the nutrition facts panel on packaged food and felt confused, you're not alone. To give you a better idea of what each variable on the label means, read through this breakdown of the basic nutrition information for rolled oats.

NUTRITION FACTS: 100 Percent Whole-Grain Rolled Oats

Variable (In order of appearance on label)	Explanation
Serving Size: ½ cup uncooked (40g)	The amount of oats (in this case uncooked) that will yield the calories and nutrients indicated on the label. If you consume more or less than this serving size, adjust the nutritional values up or down.
Servings Per Container: about 30	If you use the indicated serving size of ½ cup uncooked oats, the container (in this case, 42 ounces) will yield about 30 servings.
Amount Per Serving:	All nutritional values on the label are what you get if you consume the serving size of ½ cup uncooked oats (which makes about 1 cup of cooked oats).
Calories: 150 Calories Calories from Fat 25	150 calories total, with 25 calories from fat. There are about 9 calories per gram of fat. One serving contains 2.5 grams of fat (9 × 2.5 = 22.5). The food manufacturer rounds up to 25 calories from fat. This amounts to about 17% of calories from fat (25 / 150 = 16.7) — a very healthy percentage of fat.
Total Fat: 2.5 g 4% Daily Value*	Total fat content is 2.5 grams per serving.
Saturated Fat: 0 g 0% Daily Value*	There are 0 grams of saturated fat (regardless of serving size – oats do not contain saturated fat). Saturated fat is mainly contained in animal products. Saturated fats are generally viewed as unhealthy fats and should be minimized. The term "saturated" indicates that the fatty acid chain of carbon atoms has no double bonds and is fully "saturated" with hydrogen atoms.
Trans Fat: 0 g	There are 0 grams of trans fat. Like saturated fat, trans fats (also known as hydrogenated or partially hydrogenated fats) are considered unhealthy fats and should be minimized or eliminated.
Polyunsaturated Fat: 1 g	There is 1 gram of polyunsaturated fat (generally viewed as a healthier fat). The term "polyunsaturated" indicates that the fatty acid chain of carbon atoms has more than one double bond.
Monounsaturated Fat: 1 g	There is 1 gram of monounsaturated fat (viewed as a healthier fat). The term "monounsaturated" indicates that the fatty acid chain of carbon atoms has one double bond.
Cholesterol: 0mg 0% Daily Value*	There are 0 mg of cholesterol (regardless of serving size – oats do not contain cholesterol). Cholesterol is contained in animal products, with only trace amounts in certain plants.
Sodium: 0 mg 0% Daily Value*	There are 0 mg of sodium. Note that ¼ teaspoon of table salt contains about 600 mg of sodium. The maximum recommended daily allowance for sodium is 2,400 mg.

(continued)

Variable (In order of appearance on label)	Explanation
Carbohydrate: 27 g 9% Daily Value*	There are 27 grams of total carbohydrate per serving. There are about 4 calories per gram of carbohydrate. One serving contains 27 grams of carbohydrate (4 × 27 = 108). This amounts to about 70% of calories from carbohydrate (108 / 150 = 72). Note: because oats contain 4 grams of dietary fiber and fiber is not digested like other carbohydrate sources, these 4 grams may not be "counted" in the calculation of calories. This is why the total percentage of all fat, carbohydrate, and protein does not equal exactly 100% (slightly over in this case: 17% fat + 70% carbohydrate + 16% protein = 103%).
Dietary Fiber: 4 g 17% Daily Value*	There are 4 grams of dietary fiber per serving. Fiber is considered a carbohydrate.
Soluble Fiber: 2 g	Of the 4 grams of dietary fiber, 2 grams are soluble fiber. (See chapter 11, pages 126 – 27, for more information on soluble and insoluble fiber.)
Insoluble Fiber: 2 g	Of the 4 grams of dietary fiber, 2 grams are insoluble fiber. (See chapter 11, pages 126 – 27, for more information about soluble and insoluble fiber.)
Sugars: 1 g	There is 1 gram of sugar per serving. This is excellent and rare for a carbohydrate-rich food. For example, many processed carbohydrate-rich cereals have similar total carbohydrate loads as oats (about 30 grams per serving) but contain approximately 20 grams of sugars in the 30 gram total. One teaspoon of sugar contains about 4 grams. Hence, a 20-gram sugar content is the equivalent of adding five teaspoons of sugar per serving – highly undesirable.
Protein: 6 g	There are 6 grams of protein per serving. This equates to about 16% of all calories. There are approximately 4 calories per gram of protein. One serving contains 6 grams of protein (4 × 6 = 24). This amounts to about 16% of calories from protein (24 / 150 = 16) – a very healthy percentage of protein.
Vitamin A: 0%	Each serving contains 0% vitamin A – the percentage is based on daily requirements for healthy adults. Rolled oats obviously are not a good source of vitamin A.
Vitamin C: 0%	Each serving contains 0% vitamin C – the percentage is based on daily requirements for healthy adults. Rolled oats obviously are not a good source of vitamin C.
Calcium: 2%	Each serving contains 2% calcium. Daily requirements for calcium vary depending on age and sex. Assuming a value of 1,000 mg/day, a 2% value indicates a calcium amount of 20 mg per serving.
Iron: 10%	Each serving contains 10% iron. Daily requirements for iron vary depending on age and sex. Assuming a value of 8 mg/day, a 10% value indicates an iron amount of 0.8 mg per serving.

* Percent Daily Values are based on a 2,000 calorie diet. Your daily values may be higher or lower depending on your calorie needs.

ARE CERTAIN RATIOS OF PROTEIN, CARBOHYDRATE, AND FAT OPTIMAL?

Healthy percentages of protein, carbohydrate, and fat are approximately 20 percent, 60 percent, and 20 percent, respectively. When putting together a meal, try to stay close to this overall recommendation. You do not need to adhere to this for each food item, understanding that you will mix and match different foods to comprise your overall meal — and the overall meal is what you should be focusing on. You don't want meals to regularly contain 5 percent protein, 70 percent carbohydrate, and 25 percent fat. This ratio is unfortunately commonplace for many and is very unlikely to yield optimal results in terms of physical health and performance. Most people do not process this much carbohydrate well — especially if much of the carbohydrate is processed. Packaged foods usually are lacking in protein, not carbohydrate or fat. This is why I (Rick) suggest the use of protein powder (see *www.DanielCure.com/supplements* for more information). You can easily turn an unbalanced meal into a balanced meal with the addition of 10 to 20 grams of protein powder. Just stir it into water and drink. Easy and healthy — every time.

It's worth noting that nutrition panels (and governmental nutrition guidelines) often suggest a higher percentage of fat (30 percent) and a lower percentage of protein (10 percent). From a health standpoint, there is little rationale for the higher fat percentage, as many studies using a very low fat percentage have yielded outstanding results. The recommendation has more to do with the fact that most people eat a lot of fat (more than 30 percent) and agencies are attempting to provide a guideline that might serve as a realistic target. Since most people consume fat percentages that greatly exceed 30 percent, reducing that to 30 percent would be viewed as progress. The recommendation has little to do with what is optimal. It's important that you consider what is best for you, and not what might be just okay.

I disagree with this higher fat percentage and especially the lower protein percentage. In working with many clients over the years, I have observed too many individuals who simply cannot get into their best state of physical health with such a low protein intake.

Consider the typical 2,000-calorie diet. Government agencies suggest a ratio of 10 percent protein, 60 percent carbohydrate, and 30 percent fat. This amounts to only 50 grams of protein per day (2,000 calories × 0.10 = 200 calories from protein / 4 [calories per gram of protein] = 50 grams). For a person weighing 165 pounds (75 kg), this protein intake is only 0.66 grams/kg (50 grams / 75 kg) — which is far less than the already low RDA (Recommended Daily Allowance) of 0.8 grams/kg.

I recommend almost twice as much protein — close to 20 percent of total calories. This is particularly important if you are active and/or an older adult (65 or older), as protein requirements increase with strenuous physical exercise and advancing age.

meal planning
and recipes

meal planning
and preparation

MEAL PLANNING AND PREPARATION ARE ESSENTIAL FOR STAYING ON TRACK with the Daniel Fast and Daniel Cure plans, especially when facing temptations or cravings. Developing this habit of planning will serve you well after the fast, as you move into the next phase of your long-term healthy lifestyle.

FIVE STEPS FOR YOUR SUCCESS

Throughout our years of guiding men and women through their Daniel Fast experiences, we've identified five key steps that consistently help people to successfully keep their commitment—to the fast and to a long-term healthy lifestyle.

1. Make a Weekly Menu Plan

Planning a week's worth of breakfasts, lunches, dinners, and snacks will not only help you comply with a fast or your long-term eating plan, it will also organize your shopping list and save you time at the supermarket. For additional help with weekly meal planning, use "The Daniel Cure Meal-Planning Worksheet" (on page 273 or available for download at *www.DanielCure.com*).

Follow these guidelines as you plan your weekly meals:

- Set aside two to three hours each week for meal planning and shopping. Write it on your calendar.
- Review your calendar for the week ahead to determine how many meals you'll need to prepare.
- Select the recipes you'll prepare, keeping in mind that you might want to use dinner leftovers for lunch the next day or double a recipe and freeze a portion for later.

- Create a shopping list from the recipes, checking first for what you may already have on hand.

- Shop for your groceries on one day. Most large supermarkets will carry everything you need, though you may occasionally need to visit more than one store for a specialty item. You do not need to shop at a health-food store in order to consume healthy foods.

- Wash produce as soon as you return from the grocery store, and cut up vegetables and fruit so they're ready to eat or use in recipes.

- Cook one or two large recipes that can be stored in containers and placed in the refrigerator or freezer for easy access during the week.

These steps of planning, shopping, and up-front food prep are invaluable time savers, especially for busy families and for those who work outside the home — particularly when children are involved who may not be eating the same foods you are.

2. Plan for the Unexpected

No matter how carefully you plan, something unexpected is sure to pose a challenge to your fast or your usual clean-eating plan. You might be following a Daniel Fast and need to attend a lunch or dinner meeting at a local restaurant. If you have time, check the restaurant's website and review their menu to identify potential Daniel Fast–compliant foods. At the restaurant, talk with the server about your special dietary requirements. Most establishments are willing to prepare something on request if it is not on the menu.

There may also be times when an unplanned event disrupts your meal preparation. Or you might have an especially tiring day and don't feel up for spending time in the kitchen. For times like these, I (Susan) keep cans of beans, vegetables, and tomato sauce in my pantry. I mix and heat everything in a large pot, toss in some dried herbs, and in minutes I have a nutritious and hearty soup. If I have greens in the fridge, I can easily add a salad. Preparing some meals in bulk is another great idea — and you can start this process during the weeks leading up to your fast. Simply choose a few meals that can be prepared in advance and then frozen. When needed, defrost and enjoy. Items that work well for advance preparation include soups, bean recipes, and vegetable stews.

It's also good to plan for smaller meals or "snacks." We recommend eating one or two healthy snacks or small meals as part of your daily meal plan. You may find yourself craving a "little something" between your main meals of the day or a couple hours after dinner. Plan for these times by keeping healthy snacks available—or consider the use of meal-replacement shakes, which can be made very simply and with few calories (see chapter 13).

Rick prefers shakes and I typically prefer whole foods. A favorite snack of mine is plain rice cakes with peanut butter. Add a few slices of banana on top for an even more tasty and nutritious snack. I also like carrot sticks with hummus. And I keep almonds and walnuts around as they are easily transportable and great for satisfying hunger. These and other nuts can be added to raisins and other dried fruit for a healthy snack. Consider keeping a few small snack-sized bags of almonds or walnuts in your car or in your office, as well as a few bottles of water. With a little advance planning, you will always be prepared when your body clock tells you it's time for a small amount of nourishment.

3. Invest in Planning and Preparation

Decide now to invest time in meal planning and food preparation each week. Although food manufacturers are getting better about producing convenience foods that are healthy and may comply with the Daniel Fast, you'll still find that preparing meals from scratch is necessary for most of your meals during the fast. (See "Are There Kitchen Gadgets That Will Aid with Fast Compliance?" below.)

Some people enjoy cooking and others dread the thought of preparing meals. Either way, you can maximize your meal prep and cooking time by using it for more than just cooking. For example, listen to biblical teaching or an audio book on CD or podcast while you chop vegetables. Play praise and worship music while cleaning up the kitchen. Invite children or your spouse to help in preparing meals and enjoy spending time together in a new way.

ARE THERE KITCHEN GADGETS THAT WILL AID WITH FAST COMPLIANCE?

When you have the right tools for a job, everything is a lot easier. This is certainly true when it comes to the Daniel Fast—especially when considering the abundance of vegetables and fruits you'll prepare and eat while fasting. The following list has items you will be using regularly if you adopt the Daniel Cure plan as your new dietary lifestyle.

Cutting board
Knife set
Blender (one with a large-capacity jar
    of approximately 60 ounces)
Immersion blender
Multi-level food steamer

Rice cooker (if you do not have the food
    steamer)
Food processor
Food dicer
Crockpot
Hot air (or microwave) popcorn popper
Airtight food storage containers

If you're pressed for time, meal-replacement shakes—which will be covered in the next chapter—are a great option for mid-meal "snacks." Meal-replacement shakes are especially helpful for nurses and other health-care professionals, teachers, real estate agents, college students, or others who are constantly on the go and who don't have a lot of time to eat nutritious whole food meals during the day. The "fast food" alternatives available in most workplaces and schools really should not be options for you during the fast—or after the fast if you're pursuing the Daniel Cure healthy lifestyle approach.

However you decide to do it, plan ahead and make a commitment to have the food you need when you need it. That means if you leave home each morning and won't return until evening, you need to have all of your food with you when you leave for the day. Keep it in the refrigerator at work until it's time to eat. If you don't have a refrigerator or your vehicle is your workplace, carry your food inside a small cooler. Whatever it takes, do it. We cannot stress enough the importance of having your food with you throughout the day, during the Daniel Fast and afterward. Without it, you're left to rely on meals prepared by restaurants or food manufacturers, which typically means expensive, noncompliant meals of poor nutritional quality.

4. Stock the Pantry

To help you maintain the fast, you'll want to have a variety of shelf-stable foods on hand. The following list of Daniel Fast–friendly foods are at most supermarkets. You may need to visit a health-food store for some products. Read the labels of prepared foods to make sure the ingredients comply with the Daniel Fast guidelines.*

Fruits and vegetables (fresh, frozen, canned)	Yams, sweet potatoes
	Squash
Pasta sauce	Brown rice
Beans of any variety (dried or canned)	Pearl barley
	Quinoa
Unsweetened applesauce	Old-fashioned rolled oats
Vegetable stock	Whole-wheat durum pasta
Potatoes	Whole-wheat flour

---

*If you have completed the Daniel Fast and have adopted a modified approach using the Daniel Cure as your model, feel free to add other items to your grocery list that might meet the criteria of the healthy plan that you have constructed for yourself—such as lean meats, fish, and low-fat dairy products (milk, yogurt, cottage cheese).

Dried fruit

Nuts of any variety (raw preferred)

Nut butters (natural only with
no additives except salt)

Rice cakes (plain, lightly salted)

Plant-based milks (unsweetened
soy, coconut, almond, rice,
hemp, oat, etc.)

Apple juice (unsweetened)

Orange juice (unsweetened)

Hot sauce (such as Tabasco)

Unsweetened vinegar

Olive oil

Protein powder (see chapter 11,
page 123)

5. Identify Your Core Recipes

Studies show that families typically have a set of six or seven core recipes they repeat over a seven- to ten-day period. To help you be successful on your Daniel Fast and Daniel Cure plans, we encourage you to select a set of core recipes. Of course, this core may expand somewhat once you enter into the Daniel Cure stage and have increased options. Regardless of the plan you are following, be willing to experiment with a few different recipes, making adjustments to suit your taste or eliminating those you don't like. Keep trying new recipes until you have your core set and then rotate them over time. If you are following a twenty-one-day Daniel Fast, it's likely that you will want to retain these recipes after your fast is completed. You'll come to enjoy them that much. Identify recipes for meals and snacks as follows:

> *Breakfast:* three recipes
> *Lunch:* three recipes
> *Dinner:* six recipes
> *Snacks:* three options

Your dinner and lunch options might be very similar. In fact, one thing we strongly recommend is to prepare extra food at dinnertime to allow for leftovers you can eat for lunch the next day. Simply package a portion in a container, refrigerate, and take it with you in the morning as you head out to work. This will greatly reduce your food preparation time and stress—and it's a good plan whether you are following the Daniel Fast or not.

MEAL TIPS

For you to ensure success on the Daniel Cure plan, it's important to have lots of options for meals and snacks. Equally important is making certain that many of these options are simple to prepare and could be easily packaged and transported if needed (if you spend a good deal of time away from home).

Determine whether meals you enjoy comply with the program guidelines. If they do, consider adding these to your list. If not, either modify these meals so that they do fit into your plan or consider alternative meals and snacks. Planning ahead and making certain that you include in your overall plan meals that you truly enjoy is vital to your long-term success. In the following sections we provide ideas for meals and snacks for your consideration.

Breakfast

My favorite breakfast during the Daniel Fast is cooked muesli with unsweetened soy milk. I measure the muesli and water into a pan, cover it, and cook over low heat for 5 minutes. I often warm the milk for about 20 seconds in the microwave while the muesli is cooking and use the time to empty the dishwasher or do some other kitchen task.

Rick uses a similar staple for his breakfast. He cooks old-fashioned rolled oats, a ripe banana, raisins, almonds, and cinnamon for about ten minutes. He then removes this mix from the pan and adds unsweetened applesauce and protein powder to make a tasty, and incredibly well-balanced, meal.

Eating whole grains such as muesli or oats for breakfast will keep you satisfied for many hours—possibly until lunch but preferably until you consume a mid-morning snack. As an alternative to a standard breakfast cereal, you might opt for a meal-replacement shake (see chapter 13). These work great for breakfast, especially if you are pressed for time and need to grab something and run out the door. Remember, skipping meals is an unhealthy choice.

Lunch

If you're away from home each day for work or school, it's important to prepare your lunch and take it with you. If you're following the traditional Daniel Fast, finding compliant meals in restaurants can be difficult. As noted earlier, a simple option for lunch is to have leftovers from dinner the night before. Add a snack of fruit, vegetables, or nuts and you're set.

You might also use very simple, easy-to-prepare meals. One of Rick's staples is black beans, brown rice, sweet corn, and hot sauce. This can be made one to two days ahead. He steams the rice and rinses a can of cooked black beans and then portions them out in containers to which he adds frozen corn and hot sauce. The corn defrosts overnight in the refrigerator and the meal is easily reheated in the microwave when he's ready to eat. It doesn't get much easier than that! He also finds that a nutritious meal-replacement shake works well for an occasional lunch meal.

Dinner

Use your dinner preparation time to fix meals other than the one you are about to consume. For example, double or triple the recipe so you have food remaining to use for lunch or dinner over the next day or two. Or freeze a portion of the meal for next week or the week after. This is particularly important if you have a family and are preparing a separate meal for those not following the Daniel Fast (assuming you are). This can be one of the more frustrating experiences with fasting. (One option is to serve "meat on the side" for the others along with your Daniel Fast meal.) You feel as though you are doing more work now that you are on the fast. Having several days of prepared meals helps. Crockpot meals are also easy and minimize preparation time. A steamer for rice or vegetables is a great tool when following the Daniel Fast guidelines.

Snacks

Having snacks on hand is important to help maintain your fast. Make snack bags at the start of each week and pack them in the refrigerator. These bags might contain carrot sticks, sliced bell peppers, or edamame (soybeans). You could also make snack bags with mixed nuts or a homemade trail mix. Whatever you prefer, make sure you have something prepared. Then when it's time to walk out of the house, just grab the pre-packed bags and go. Pre-packing your snacks is a good idea even if you don't routinely leave the home during the day—the snacks are already portioned out and ready to eat. You don't need to spend time thinking about what to eat or preparing anything. Just grab a snack bag and get back to what you're doing.

As with breakfast and lunch, you can always consider a meal-replacement shake for a mid-morning or mid-afternoon snack/meal. Rick has been doing this for years, and it works incredibly well. Make a few of these ahead of time and just place them in shaker bottles in the refrigerator. When needed, remove the bottle from the fridge, shake it for a few seconds, and consume. No thinking and no waiting. Instant nutrition!

Whatever you choose, having snacks available can help you to keep on track, avoid the temptation to binge when you get to that next meal, and prevent you from stopping the fast. Remember, when you're hungry, you are much more prone to be tempted by foods you should not be eating. Set yourself up for success by not getting to that point. Plan ahead and eat regular, nutritious meals and snacks throughout the day so you can maintain focus and stay on track.

GROCERY SHOPPING TIPS

When most people think about following a healthy eating plan, they focus their attention solely on the food. But before eating the food we have to shop for it — and it's important to be as deliberate in our shopping strategy as we are in our food selection strategy.

- *Do not shop hungry.* Hungry shoppers are much more likely to buy foods that are not conducive to optimal health.
- *Shop once a week for major items.* Save time by making a weekly grocery list and purchasing everything you need in one trip to the store. You may need a second trip for perishable items such as fresh fruits and vegetables.
- *Shop the perimeter of the store, with an occasional trip down the center aisles.* Most quality foods are located in the outer aisles — fresh fruits and vegetables, fresh meat, poultry, fish, milk, eggs, and other dairy products (assuming you decide to include meat and dairy in your dietary plan). The center aisles do contain some quality foods, such as oats, beans, barley, and rice, but have mostly processed foods that are able to sit on supermarket shelves for weeks and months at a time. Let them remain there.
- *Purchase certain foods in bulk quantities.* These may include oatmeal, rice, potatoes, onions, meats (after the fast), frozen fruits and vegetables (which are close in taste and nutritional value to fresh varieties) to assure that quality food is always available. Warehouse stores sometimes offer large bags of whole grains and legumes at deep discounts, including brown rice, quinoa, dried beans, whole-wheat cereals, and oatmeal.

Although fresh foods are generally preferred over frozen or canned, the latter have a much longer shelf life, can be of excellent quality, and are often offered at a lower price than fresh varieties. Just be sure to read the list of ingredients on the labels of the frozen and canned goods to make sure they all comply with the Daniel Fast or Daniel Cure guidelines for healthy eating. With regard to canned varieties, more and more food companies are offering products that are free of added sugar, chemicals, and artificial flavorings. If you want to use canned fruit, consider the "lite" varieties as they are often free of added sugar and canned in natural fruit juices. Avoid products that are packed in heavy syrup. If using canned vegetables, look for options with no added sodium.

Although many packaged foods contain ingredients that are not allowed on the Daniel Fast, you may find some prepared foods that are acceptable.

Since this is an ever-changing list, visit our website for regular updates (*www .DanielCure.com*). I keep bottles of pasta sauce in my cupboard to use when I need a quick meal. I like mixing the prepared sauce with brown rice and green olives for a quick lunch or dinner. I also use boxed vegetable broth for soups and stews. The broth keeps for a long time and is also great to braise vegetables so I can eliminate the need for oil and its calories. Rice cakes, crackers, nut butters, and soy products may also be acceptable prepared foods as you plan your weekly meals. Just read the labels to be certain that all ingredients are allowed.

TIME-SAVING TIPS

We already mentioned some time-saving tips such as washing, trimming, and cutting fruits and vegetables as soon as you return from the market. This enables you to quickly prepare a colorful and nutritious snack or salad in just a few minutes. This practice also makes it easy for family members to help you prepare salads or snacks, or for you to quickly put together a soup or stew for dinner. You will be amazed at the amount of time you can save during busy days by investing in a little up-front food preparation time. Here are a few other time savers:

Cook Ahead. For example, if you decide to include meat in your long-term plan, cook portions of fresh chicken, turkey, and other meats, slice into serving portions, and keep available in the refrigerator for easy access during the week. Note that a suggested serving size of meat is generally 3 to 4 ounces (about the size of a deck of cards). While this may be adequate for some individuals, if you are very active and/or have a large amount of muscle mass, you may require or desire a slightly larger portion.

Double Up. When preparing main dishes such as soup, chili, casseroles, etc., consider making a double or triple batch. Portion out leftovers into serving-size containers and freeze for later use. For example, let's say you prepare a large recipe of dried beans or rice using your favorite method. When the food is cooled, spoon single-serve or recipe-sized portions into food storage bags and freeze. To use, merely run the bag under warm water and then transfer the food to a microwave-safe dish and reheat or add the food to your recipe. I like to freeze my rice in one-cup portions since that's the amount called for in most of the recipes I prepare. Cooked beans can be frozen in larger amounts. I take out just the amount I need, reseal the bag, and return it to the freezer. Not only does this technique save time, but dried beans cost a fraction of what canned beans cost. So I cook a large pot of beans and then they are always available.

Cook Once and Eat Twice. I like to cook large batches of curried lentils, vegetable stews, and rice-and-bean dishes and then freeze them for later. I also do the same with thicker soups. A great way to save space in your freezer is to freeze the meals in gallon-sized food storage bags. Here's how I do it:

1. Mark a gallon-sized storage bag with the name and date of the contents. Stand the open bag in a large bowl or a four-cup liquid measuring cup. Ladle the cooled food into the bag.
2. Carefully close the bag except for about one inch on one of the top corners.
3. Holding the top of the bag and using both hands, carefully lift the bag from the bowl and lay it on the counter, keeping the opening slightly upright so nothing spills out.
4. Expel as much of the air as possible from the bag as you lay it on the counter (or you can use a straw and suck the air from the bag). When all or most of the air is gone, seal the bag and lay it on a large piece of firm cardboard. Place it in the freezer and, when frozen, position the bag in the freezer in whatever spot is most efficient.

Mix It Up. Mix protein and carbohydrate foods in small easy-to-carry containers the night before you need them. For example, cut up 4 ounces of cooked, marinated chicken breast (assuming you are including meat in your plan) and add this to 1 cup of cooked corn and peas and 1 cup of cooked quinoa. Add seasoning and ½ tablespoon of olive oil to perfect the taste and meal balance. A nutritional powerhouse ready to be eaten for lunch the next day.

Blend or Shake It. If you're pressed for time, consider using meal-replacement shakes during the day (see chapter 13). These work remarkably well for many people.

TIPS FOR EATING WHEN YOU'RE AWAY FROM HOME

If you spend several hours each day away from the home, it's essential that you have food and water with you at all times. When you know you will be spending many hours in your car, working outdoors, or on a college campus — put a small icepack in a cooler or a backpack and carry all your meals and snacks. You'll also want to include your water, utensils, and napkins. I sometimes make homemade granola bars and carry them with me if I know I'll be away from home for a while. I also pack a small sharp knife in a sheath in case I want to cut a piece of fruit. I have smaller plastic bags to use for garbage so everything can be quickly disposed of when I return home or stop at a rest stop. Whatever you decide, plan ahead and make it a habit to always have healthy food available when you're away from home.

When I travel out of town, the most difficult meal to have for the Daniel Fast is breakfast since most restaurant offerings include animal products. So I carry what I need with me. I have a small plastic bowl and a set of plastic utensils that I slip into my suitcase. I also use a large Ziploc bag to hold packets of oatmeal, small boxes of raisins, organic microwave popcorn, and snack bags filled with nuts. I can make the hot cereal in my room, heating the hot water in the coffeemaker. If I know the hotel doesn't offer a coffee maker in the room, I bring my own one-quart electric water heater. I add the raisins to the oatmeal for a naturally sweetened breakfast that's fast, easy, inexpensive, and nutritious. Rick actually does something very similar. He mixes vanilla protein powder in warm water, and then adds this to a bowl of dried oats and raisins—a quick and nutritious breakfast. If the room has a microwave, popcorn serves as a nice snack later in the day.

Restaurants are accustomed to special dietary requests from their guests. So when you eat other meals, ask your server to modify the menu items to meet your needs. For example, ask for oil and vinegar for the salad dressing or a baked potato topped with steamed vegetables and olive oil on the side for the main course. Doing so will allow you to remain on track with your dietary goals when following the Daniel Fast and beyond.

■■■■■■■■■ TURN YOUR THOUGHTS INTO ACTIONS ■■■■■■■■■

1 Skim through the recipes in part 5 and identify three breakfast recipes, three lunch recipes, three snack recipes, and six dinner recipes to use during the first week of your fast. Write down a shopping list of ingredients you'll need.

2 Use your food preparation time to pray, listen to teachings or worship music, and to involve family members in meal preparation.

CHAPTER 13

meal-replacement shakes

Over the last twenty years or so, I (Rick) have consulted with several hundred individuals about what they eat. Most people really do want to eat healthier. Some already know exactly what to do and have the discipline to make it happen. But many people I've worked with struggle. Among the biggest obstacles people have to overcome is making the time to prepare and consume nutritious meals.

A meal-replacement shake is one solution that's helped many of the people I've worked with. I know that the very mention of meal-replacement shakes will make some people nervous, especially dietitians who often have a problem with people consuming liquids rather than whole foods. I understand the concerns, but I have also seen the value of this nutritional tool, and I am convinced that incorporating shakes into a well-balanced meal plan is an effective option to help people with limited time stay on track with nutritional goals.

MEAL-REPLACEMENT SHAKES VERSUS DIETARY SUPPLEMENTS

Given the hectic pace at which most of us live our lives, devoting time to meal planning and preparation is often a challenge. In the rush to keep up, good dietary habits are too often exchanged for meals that are quick and cheap. To help compensate for nutrient-poor meals, many people turn to dietary supplements — typically in the form of tablets and capsules.*

Having studied the health impact of dietary supplements for more than ten years, and having served as a consultant to multiple dietary ingredient

---

*Protein powders are technically referred to as dietary supplements and can be used alone and in meal-replacement shakes. See "What's the Difference between Protein Shakes and Meal-Replacement Shakes?" on page 157.

and supplement companies, I can state the following with confidence: Certain dietary supplements absolutely can provide health benefits (see *www.DanielCure.com/supplements*). However, dietary supplements can never compensate for a poor diet. We all need to start with food first—solid or liquid—and use dietary supplements to further improve an already well-balanced and complete diet. This is the main distinction between dietary supplements and meal-replacement shakes. Dietary supplements can function to enhance a well-balanced nutrition program. Meal-replacement shakes are in fact part of the well-balanced nutrition program.

WHAT ARE YOU LOOKING FOR?

Whether you are obtaining your nutrients exclusively from solid food or from a combination of solid and liquid nutrition, you likely desire a meal plan that enables you to consume healthy foods that are:

- Easy to prepare
- Affordable
- Enjoyable and tasty
- Compatible with the demands of a busy lifestyle*

Meal-replacement shakes meet all of these characteristics. Shakes generally contain an excellent balance of protein and carbohydrate and are relatively low

---

* See "Meal-Replacement Shakes and the Traveler" on page 160.

WHAT'S THE DIFFERENCE BETWEEN PROTEIN SHAKES AND MEAL-REPLACEMENT SHAKES?

Protein shakes are just that—protein powder mixed in water. They sometimes are fortified with vitamins and minerals (about what you would get with a typical multi-vitamin/mineral supplement). They are not designed for complete nutrition. They are meant to provide only additional protein. These are most popular in the bodybuilding and fitness communities.

In contrast, meal-replacement shakes provide protein along with carbohydrate and fat as well as vitamins and minerals. They are meant to serve as a complete meal replacement, providing all three macronutrients and an array of micronutrients.

Both protein and meal replacements can be purchased as powders and mixed into your favorite beverage, or you can purchase ready-to-drink protein and meal-replacement supplements. If you make your own meal-replacement shakes, you might use protein powder as the foundation (or a protein-rich beverage such as skim milk in place of the powder) and then add a variety of other ingredients such as fruit and oats.

in fat and calories. Most meal-replacement shakes contain from 300 to 500 calories and an abundance of quality nutrients. Many people, including myself, find that consuming two to three shakes per day along with two to three whole-food meals is the perfect combination of nutrition and time savings that both satisfies hunger and maintains energy levels. I have used such a regimen for close to twenty years, and I highly recommend the use of meal-replacement shakes to complement your whole food meals. Shakes are particularly helpful if you plan to adopt the small and frequent meal pattern recommended in chapter 11.

READY-MADE VERSUS HOMEMADE SHAKES

You have the option of purchasing ready-made meal-replacement shakes or making your own. For example, some people opt for powdered meal-replacement products that can be mixed into a beverage of choice. Others prefer the convenience of ready-to-drink meal-replacement shakes — simply shake, pop the top, and consume. However, we encourage you to start by making homemade shakes that you can customize to suit your own tastes. (See "Tips for Making Great Shakes" below.)

From a pure quality, convenience, and economic point of view, you absolutely cannot go wrong with homemade shakes. They're easy to make, fresher

TIPS FOR MAKING GREAT SHAKES

- Use cold liquids (water, juice, milks, etc.).
- Increase or decrease the amount of liquid to make your shake thinner or thicker. A good starting point is 1½ to 2 cups (12 to 16 ounces) of liquid per shake. Use less liquid to create a shake that can be eaten with a spoon.
- For thicker, colder shakes, add five to six ice cubes.
- Use frozen fruit to make shakes that have the thick consistency of a frozen dessert. Bananas, berries, pineapple, and peaches are great fruit options to freeze for use in shakes.
- For additional carbohydrate and fiber, add ½ to 1 cup of rolled oats (old-fashioned or quick) to each shake recipe. Oats also increase thickness.
- When not on the Daniel Fast, add 1 tablespoon of honey (or other sweetener) for added flavor and sweetness.
- Add ½ to 1 tablespoon of flax oil (or another essential fatty acid rich oil, such as borage oil) to add quality fatty acids — something that may be missing in many shakes.
- Blend ingredients thoroughly — 10 to 15 seconds is usually adequate.
- Rinse out the blender immediately after use. The longer it sits, the more difficult it is to clean.

than ready-made shakes, and less expensive. A typical homemade shake costs about $1.25. Think about it ... where else can you find a tasty, macronutrient-balanced, nutritious, high-protein, 300- to-500-calorie "meal" for $1.25? The answer is simple. Nowhere else.

Shakes can be easily customized for any taste preference and are nutritionally equal to or even nutritionally superior to many whole food meals. After all, they are simply whole foods blended into a liquid meal. The only thing you miss with a shake is the chewing. (See "Are Meal-Replacement Shakes Really Satisfying?" on page 165.) Because shakes typically contain only a few ingredients, you are guaranteed a super-healthy meal—with no guesswork or empty calories. Shakes can be blended the night before, dispensed into bottles, and refrigerated. In the morning, pack them along with your whole-food lunch meal and you're ready to start the day in no time.

CUSTOMIZE YOUR SHAKE INGREDIENTS

Like any other meal planning, designing your own meal-replacement shakes is based largely on personal preference. I've used everything from shredded wheat to canned pumpkin in customizing my shakes—and a bodybuilder friend once told me he knew of someone who used canned tuna in his shakes. I don't recommend that.

My shake staples over the past several years (both on and off the Daniel Fast) include four kinds of ingredients:

- *Liquids:* water, skim milk (when not on the Daniel Fast), plain soy milk (or other non-dairy milk), orange juice, apple juice, pineapple juice
- *Fruit:* bananas, pineapple, peaches, apples, grapes, berries, etc.
- *Texture, flavor, and nutritional ingredients:* for example, old-fashioned rolled oats,* flaxseed oil, peanut butter, non-fat yogurt (or "CARBmaster"†)
- *Protein powders:* When on the Daniel Fast, I use a plain, unsweetened soy protein powder. If you plan to use a plant-based protein powder such as soy or pea, you must identify a product that is unflavored

---

*Old-fashioned rolled oats are a great carbohydrate source and very inexpensive. "Quick" oats, which are essentially larger oats chopped up into smaller pieces for faster cooking, are an acceptable option as long as the package contains only oats—some oatmeal products are a packet of sugar with a few oats thrown in. This is unacceptable.

†CARBmaster is a Kroger grocery store product that is higher in protein and lower in carbohydrate than most other yogurts; you might also try Greek yogurt, which has a higher protein content than traditional yogurt.

and unsweetened (see *www.DanielCure.com/supplements*). Almost all commercial protein powders are flavored and sweetened and are not suitable for a traditional Daniel Fast. Plain soy powder does not taste very good when mixed with water only. However, the flavor of soy powder is masked quite well when mixed with fruit, oats, soymilk, and/or peanut butter in a blender drink.

When not on the Daniel Fast, I prefer a high-quality whey protein isolate over soy powder. The quality of whey protein isolate is superior to soy, with the overall protein quality meeting or exceeding that of most whole-food protein sources. (See "Which Is a Better Source of Protein — Shakes and Powders or Whole Foods?" on page 162.) The powder I use also tastes great if I decide to simply stir it into my favorite beverage. I find that vanilla flavor is most

---

MEAL-REPLACEMENT SHAKES AND THE TRAVELER

I (Rick) do not like to travel unless I am going on vacation with my family, preferably to the beach. Travel disrupts my routine — and I am a very structured, routine-oriented guy. My workout schedule, meal schedule, and sleep schedule are all challenged by travel. But if I plan ahead, I can still achieve my goals.

In terms of food intake, the problem starts at the airport (assuming air travel). The food is generally of poor quality and extremely overpriced. (Did I really just pay $18.00 for a chicken sandwich and a bottle of water?) You board the plane and things don't get any better. At your destination, you have the options of room service (also insanely overpriced) or a local restaurant. Now, to opt for these choices sparingly does not present a major problem. But to do so for every meal during a trip should be a concern.

I travel with my shake powder, whether a complete meal-replacement powder or a simple protein powder. If it's a meal-replacement powder, I simply take the number of single-serving packets I need and throw them in my carry-on (in case my luggage gets lost, I still have my food). If it's a protein powder, I place as many servings as I need inside a double zip-locked food storage bag (you do not want powder to break open in your carry-on: I know from experience). I also bring a shaker bottle that I use to mix the powder with water or whatever beverage I choose. Just dump the powder into the liquid (in that order) and shake vigorously for fifteen to twenty seconds. I often have three to four shakes a day when traveling. I typically buy a bottle of orange juice or other beverage to mix my powder in. I also sometimes fill my shaker bottle with juice at the continental breakfast bar and add my powder.

Along with my few shakes per day, I usually have a quality lunch and dinner. I start with lean protein and add a steamed vegetable and a small portion of starch, such as potato or rice. This is simple eating that allows me to stay on course with my meal program and socialize with friends or clients over lunch and dinner. Remember, eating clean and getting in great physical health is important, but you do not want to divorce yourself from everyday life. Perfection is not necessary, but progress is.

versatile and the powder can be added to just about any shake recipe with excellent results. I also routinely stir it into my cooked oatmeal for a more macronutrient-balanced meal.* Chocolate-flavored powder is also very good and versatile, as is strawberry.

A FEW SHAKE RECIPES TO GET YOU STARTED

If you include meal-replacement shakes in your Daniel Fast plan, use the following four shakes to get started. Each meets all the criteria of a traditional plant-based Daniel Fast. The only modification you may want is to make half of a recipe to get one serving rather than two, or adjusting the portion size to make a shake the appropriate size for you in terms of calories. You can include any combination of fruit, juice, plain and unsweetened soy milk, or any plain and unsweetened variety of nut milk, plant-based protein powder, and other natural ingredients to produce excellent Daniel Fast–compliant shakes.

PINEAPPLE-ORANGE SHAKE

Makes 2 Servings (serving size: 3–4 cups)

    1 (20-ounce) can pineapple in natural juice or water (not in syrup)
    1 (10-ounce) can mandarin oranges in natural juice or water (not in syrup)
    1½ cups rolled oats (old-fashioned or quick)
    2½ cups (20 ounces) cold water
    20 grams (about 2½ tablespoons) soy protein powder

Puree all ingredients in a blender until smooth.

> **Nutrition** (per serving): **calories** 475; **fat** 5g (saturated 0g); **protein** 19g; **carbohydrate** 90g; **fiber** 9g; **sodium** 30mg

Variation: Instead of soy protein powder, use 30 grams (about 4 tablespoons) of vanilla protein powder. This is typically a whey protein isolate or a whey/casein blend, which offers a better quality of protein than soy. Note: this variety is *not* Daniel Fast compliant due to the use of whey/casein powder.

> **Nutrition** (per serving): **calories** 500; **fat** 4g (saturated 0g); **protein** 24g; **carbohydrate** 92g; **fiber** 9g; **sodium** 30mg

---

* See *www.DanielCure.com/supplements* for important information related to protein powder and other dietary supplements.

PEANUT BUTTER AND BANANA SHAKE

Makes 2 Servings (serving size: 2½ cups)

2 large bananas, sliced
1 cup rolled oats (old-fashioned or quick)
2 cups (16 ounces) plain, unsweetened soy milk
2 tablespoons natural peanut butter

Puree all ingredients in a blender until smooth.

Nutrition (per serving): **calories** 435; **fat** 15g (saturated 1.5g); **protein** 18g; **carbohydrate** 58g; **fiber** 8g; **sodium** 130mg

WHICH IS A BETTER SOURCE OF PROTEIN — SHAKES AND POWDERS OR WHOLE FOODS?

This has been a topic of continued study and debate. It really depends on which whole food sources you are talking about and which protein is being used for comparison. For example, whole food sources of high quality and complete protein include egg whites (or whole egg — if you don't mind the fat and cholesterol content of the yolk), milk, cottage cheese, white-meat poultry, fish, and lean beef. Protein powders vary considerably in type and quality, but in general, whey (isolate is preferred) and casein are popular and of high quality, with certain specialty proteins offered by some companies likely of even better quality. However, for the overall retail price of a quality whey or casein powder (about $12 per pound), these two seem most attractive to consumers. Gram for gram they are of similar quality compared with whole-food protein sources, much more convenient, and more economical.

Consider the following: One pound of protein powder (about 454 grams) will deliver about twenty servings, each containing approximately 21 grams of protein, 1 gram of fat, and 1 gram of carbohydrate. That is essentially 100 percent pure protein — only egg whites are comparable from a whole food perspective. That's a cost of about $0.60 per serving (at 21 grams of protein) or less if you decide to use less than 21 grams (which many people will choose to do). Compare that to most whole food sources on a gram-for-gram basis and you are clearly better off economically purchasing and using a powder as your protein source. Moreover, you have a protein that is pure and of excellent quality, without the added fat and carbohydrate found in many whole food sources. Of course, you are not getting vitamins and minerals by using the powder, two nutrients that you likely would be getting by consuming whole food. We address this concern by using the powder in a meal-replacement shake with many other ingredients rich in vitamins and minerals.

If you are considering including meal-replacement shakes as one component of your overall nutrition plan but are concerned about the use of protein powders, don't be. The powders of today can be of excellent quality and superb taste, quite economical, and extremely convenient. This latter point is of vital importance to so many of us who lead busy lives but still desire to maintain optimum nutritional practices. The use of a good-quality protein powder (as a component of meal-replacement shakes) can help you tremendously.

APPLE-BERRY SHAKE

This is a thick shake that can be eaten with a spoon. Thin with ½ to 1 cup of water if you'd prefer to drink it rather than eat it.

Makes 1 Serving (serving size: 1½ cups)

1 cup (8 ounces) apple juice
1 cup frozen berries
10 grams (about 1¼ tablespoons) soy protein powder

Puree all ingredients in a blender until smooth.

Nutrition (per serving): **calories** 260; **fat** 2g (saturated 0g); **protein** 12g; **carbohydrate** 47g; **fiber** 5g; **sodium** 20mg

BANANA-BERRY SHAKE

Makes 1 Serving (serving size: 2 cups)

1 cup (8 ounces) plain, unsweetened soy milk
1 cup frozen berries
1 large banana, sliced
10 grams (about 1¼ tablespoons) soy protein powder

Puree all ingredients in a blender until smooth.

Nutrition (per serving): **calories** 320; **fat** 5g (saturated 1g); **protein** 18g; **carbohydrate** 49g; **fiber** 8g; **sodium** 70mg

MORE SHAKE RECIPES

The six shake recipes that follow are not Daniel Fast compliant, but they are excellent options for the Daniel Cure healthy lifestyle once you've completed your fast. They can also easily be modified to make them Daniel Fast compliant. Mix and match any combination of liquids, fruits, texture/flavor ingredients, and protein powder to suit your taste and add variety to your meals. The options are limitless.

LOW-CALORIE, PRE-WORKOUT SHAKE

This refreshing shake tastes like an Orange Julius—especially with the addition of a few ice cubes.

Makes 1 Serving (serving size: 1 cup)

1 cup (8 ounces) orange juice
15 grams (about 2 tablespoons) vanilla protein powder

Puree ingredients in a blender until smooth or simply shake in a bottle.

Nutrition (per serving): **calories** 190; **fat** 1g (saturated 0g); **protein** 15g; **carbohydrate** 30g; **fiber** 0g; **sodium** 0mg

HIGHER-CALORIE, POST-WORKOUT SHAKE

This is a great shake to replenish nutrients depleted by a strenuous workout.

Makes 1 Serving (serving size: 3 – 4 cups)

1½ cups (12 ounces) cold water
1 (6-ounce) container "CARBmaster" yogurt (or low-sugar [<10 grams]
  yogurt; Greek yogurt is a good option)
2 large bananas, sliced
1 cup rolled oats (old-fashioned or quick)
20 grams (about 2½ tablespoons) vanilla protein powder

Puree all ingredients in a blender until smooth.

Nutrition (per serving): **calories** 675; **fat** 8g (saturated 2g); **protein** 42g; **carbohydrate** 110g; **fiber** 12g; **sodium** 120mg

SIMPLE BANANA SHAKE (NO PROTEIN POWDER)

Makes 1 Serving (serving size: 3 cups)

2 cups (16 ounces) skim milk
1 large banana, sliced
1 teaspoon cocoa powder

Puree all ingredients in a blender until smooth.

Nutrition (per serving): **calories** 250; **fat** 0g (saturated 0g); **protein** 16g; **carbohydrate** 46g; **fiber** 2g; **sodium** 240mg

SIMPLE STRAWBERRY SHAKE (NO PROTEIN POWDER)

Makes 1 Serving (serving size: 4 cups)

2 cups (16 ounces) skim milk
1 (6-ounce) container "CARBmaster" yogurt (or low-sugar Greek yogurt)
1 cup sliced strawberries (or other soft berries/fruit such as blueberries,
  peaches, etc.)

Puree all ingredients in a blender until smooth.

Nutrition (per serving): **calories** 320; **fat** 1g (saturated 0.5g); **protein** 24g; **carbohydrate** 55g; **fiber** 4g; **sodium** 340mg

ARE MEAL-REPLACEMENT SHAKES REALLY SATISFYING?

They can be. I (Rick) have used many different types of shakes over the past twenty years. But how satisfied I feel depends on the size of the shake—the amount of calories—and the ingredients—whether or not it contains fat and fiber, which both help to keep me from feeling hungry longer.* For example, a shake consisting of 20 grams of protein powder mixed into 8 ounces of orange juice will contain only around 220 calories. You should expect to be as satisfied as 220 calories will allow—whether eating whole foods or a shake—which is likely in the one- to two-hour range. But if you have a 500-calorie shake, you will likely be satisfied for two to four hours, similar to the expected timeframe if you had 500 calories of whole foods. The issue here is not the delivery system—liquid shake versus solid whole food. The issue is calorie level and what nutrients are contained in the shake or whole food meal.

Most people consume many more calories when they eat a whole food meal. That's because it's largely uncontrolled and most people have no idea how many calories are in the foods they eat. They also consume much more fat in the meal, which provides for slower digestion and longer satiety. This is why critics of meal-replacement shakes claim shakes don't satisfy hunger like whole foods do. But shakes are not meant to satisfy hunger for four hours or more. To do so, you'd need to generate a shake that contains a very high amount of calories, likely including a significant amount of dietary fat. Those of us who use and design these shakes know better; we never want to dump that number of calories into our bodies at any one time. It simply is not wise.

Excess calories lead to gains in body weight and body fat. Excess calorie intake at an individual meal can lead to fatigue, decreased motivation, and reduced productivity. This is one of the main reasons why so many people rely on stimulants to get them through a typical day. They overfeed themselves at lunch and are wiped out an hour or two later. By incorporating small meal-replacement shakes in your overall nutrition plan (one mid-morning shake and one mid-afternoon shake, sandwiched between whole food meals of breakfast, lunch, and dinner), you will feel satisfied throughout the day, be constantly charged with healthy fuel, and have the energy you need to perform at your very best.

---

* Both dietary fat and fiber slow the digestion of food, resulting in a greater feeling of fullness after eating a meal. However, be careful not to add too much fat to a meal, as calorie intake will increase significantly. This is not the case for fiber, and you should strive to add high quantities of fiber to your diet, as indicated in chapter 11.

SIMPLE BANANA-ORANGE SHAKE (WITH PROTEIN POWDER)

Makes 1 Serving (serving size: 3 cups)

1 cup (8 ounces) cold water
1 cup (8 ounces) orange juice
1 large banana, sliced
20 grams (about 2½ tablespoons) vanilla protein powder

Puree all ingredients in a blender until smooth.

Nutrition (per serving): **calories** 300; **fat** 1g (saturated 0.5g); **protein** 21g; **carbohydrate** 50g; **fiber** 2g; **sodium** 20mg

Variation: Add 1 container (6 ounces) of fat-free yogurt for additional protein, flavor, and thickness.

> **Nutrition** (per serving): **calories** 370; **fat** 2g (saturated 1g); **protein** 28g; **carbohydrate** 60g; **fiber** 2g; **sodium** 120mg

SIMPLE PINEAPPLE-BANANA SHAKE (WITH PROTEIN POWDER)

Makes 1 Serving (serving size: 3 cups)

  1 cup (8 ounces) cold water
  1¼ cups (10 ounces) fresh or canned pineapple (if canned, in water or juice, not syrup)
  1 large banana, sliced
  20 grams (about 2½ tablespoons) vanilla protein powder

Puree all ingredients in a blender until smooth.

> **Nutrition** (per serving): **calories** 320; **fat** 1g (saturated 0.5g); **protein** 21g; **carbohydrate** 55g; **fiber** 4g; **sodium** 20mg

▬▬▬▬▬ TURN YOUR THOUGHTS INTO ACTIONS ▬▬▬▬▬

1 Make two to three different meal-replacement shake recipes in the next two days. Choose your favorite ingredients and experiment until you find a shake you really enjoy.

2 Use a meal-replacement shake as your breakfast or lunch meal. Compare your experience of preparing and eating the shake with your typical breakfast or lunch experience. What differences do you notice?

CHAPTER 14

breakfast

All recipes provided in this book are Daniel Fast compliant. In addition, for all recipes, the total number of servings is indicated, as well as the nutrition facts per serving. We have also done our best to provide serving size information for recipes. While we were able to be precise with some, others include a degree of variability based on the fact that fluid volume and other factors (such as cooking time) influence the exact portion size for each serving. To closely approximate the actual size of one serving, simply divide the total amount of the prepared recipe by the number of servings indicated. For example, if a recipe produces six servings, each serving size would be one-sixth of the total amount of prepared food.

If a food item is listed as optional in a recipe (or it is included as a separate recipe that should be added to the main recipe; for example, Herbed Crumbs), it is not included as part of the nutrition facts. If you opt to use such items, simply add the relevant nutrient information to what is already provided for the recipe.

If you are not following a traditional Daniel Fast and would like to modify the recipes by adding items such as meat, milk, and cheese, feel free to do so. Many recipes may be enhanced from both a nutritional perspective and a taste perspective with the addition of certain non-plant-based ingredients.

APPLE PIE OATMEAL

Oatmeal is one of the best fiber-rich foods you can eat to help reduce cholesterol. Apple Pie Oatmeal is an excellent healthy alternative to sugary boxed cereals, pastries, or other sweet breakfast foods. The natural sweetness of the fruit and juice make the healthy recipe tasty and enjoyable. Plus, oatmeal will leave you with a sense of fullness throughout the morning.

Makes 4 Servings (serving size: 1 cup)

    1 tablespoon sunflower oil

    1 apple (sweet variety), peeled (optional), cored, and finely diced

    1 teaspoon ground cinnamon

    ¼ teaspoon ground nutmeg

    ½ teaspoon salt

    1½ cups old-fashioned rolled oats (not instant)

    1½ cups apple juice

    1½ cups water

    ½ cup unsweetened plant-based milk (soy, almond, rice, coconut, etc.) for serving (optional)

    Nuts, seeds, fresh fruit, extra cinnamon for serving (optional)

1. In a heavy saucepan over medium heat, add oil, apple, cinnamon, nutmeg, and salt. Cook, stirring frequently, for about 4 minutes.

2. Stir in oats and cook 2 minutes until liquid is absorbed. Increase heat to medium-high, add apple juice and water and bring to a boil.

3. Reduce heat to simmer, cover, and cook for 7 to 10 minutes until oatmeal thickens and apples are soft.

4. Remove from heat, cover, and let stand for 2 minutes.

5. Serve in individual bowls accompanied by chopped nuts, fresh fruit, and plant-based milk (soy, almond, rice, coconut, etc.).

Nutrition (per serving): **calories** 320; **fat** 8g (saturated 1g); **protein** 10g; **carbohydrate** 54g; **sodium** 585mg

BAKED APPLE AND PORRIDGE

This recipe conveniently makes applesauce in the apple itself while retaining nutrients from both the skin and the core.

Makes 1 Serving (serving size: 1 stuffed apple)

    1 apple, any sweet variety, cored and bottom sliced off so apple stands upright

    ¼ cup water

    1 recipe Porridge Pot, prepared (page 211; add the nutritional information for Porridge Pot to the totals provided)

    ¼ cup plant-based milk (soy, almond, rice, coconut, etc.) for serving (optional)

    Dash of cinnamon for serving (optional)

1. Preheat oven to 350°.
2. Cut off the top quarter of the apple. Using a small knife, carve the interior of the apple to form a bowl (about 2 inches in diameter). Chop the top and remove portion of the apple and set aside.
3. Place apple and water in a small lidded casserole or tightly covered oven-safe bowl. Bake for 20 minutes, or until apple skin just begins to wilt (differing varieties bake at varying times).
4. While the apple is baking, prepare the oatmeal porridge. Stir in the reserved chopped apple.
5. Remove the baked apple from the oven and place in a bowl. Fill the apple with porridge and serve with milk and a sprinkle of cinnamon, to taste.

Nutrition (per serving): **calories** 100; **fat** 1g (saturated 0g); **protein** 0g; **carbohydrate** 26g; **sodium** 0mg

BLUEBERRY-APRICOT OATMEAL

This piping hot breakfast meal is rich in flavor, fruity sweetness, and nutrients.

Makes 2 Servings (serving size: 1 cup)

¾ cup old-fashioned rolled oats (not instant)

1 cup water

½ cup apricot nectar (available in the juice section of most grocery stores)

½ banana, sliced

½ cup fresh or frozen blueberries

Unsweetened, plant-based milk (soy, almond, rice, coconut, etc.) or fruit juice for serving (optional)

Nuts or seeds for serving (optional)

1. In a saucepan over medium heat, mix all ingredients; cover and gently simmer 8 to 10 minutes, until oatmeal is tender.
2. Serve in individual bowls accompanied by chopped nuts and plant-based milk or juice.

Nutrition (per serving): **calories** 335; **fat** 5g (saturated 1g); **protein** 11g; **carbohydrate** 66g; **sodium** 6mg

GRANOLA MIX

Add your own creative touch and expand this mixture with dried fruits, such as apricots, prunes, or dates. You can also supplement the flavors with additional seeds and nuts, such as pumpkin seeds, hazelnuts, or almonds.

Makes 14 Servings (serving size: ½ cup)

1 cup wheat germ
5 cups old-fashioned rolled oats (not instant)
1 cup unsweetened shredded coconut
½ cup raw sunflower seeds
¼ cup sesame seeds
½ cup walnuts, chopped
8 tablespoons sunflower oil
1 teaspoon vanilla extract
1 cup raisins
¼ cup water

1. Preheat oven to 350°.

2. On a rimmed baking sheet, spread wheat germ in a thin layer and bake 5 to 10 minutes, or until lightly browned. Check and stir frequently for even toasting. Remove from oven.

3. In a large bowl, combine toasted wheat germ, oats, coconut, sunflower seeds, sesame seeds, and walnuts.

4. In a separate bowl, whisk sunflower oil, water, and vanilla to combine. Pour over oat mixture and mix thoroughly.

5. On three large, rimmed baking sheets, spread the granola in even, thin layers, and bake for 25 to 30 minutes, stirring frequently until oats and coconut are crispy and golden.

6. Remove from oven and let cool before transferring to a large bowl. Add raisins and mix to combine.

7. Store in airtight container up to three weeks.

Nutrition (per serving): **calories** 523; **fat** 29g (saturated 12g); **protein** 17g; **carbohydrate** 55g; **sodium** 11mg

POTATO-AND-MORE PANCAKES

Vegetable cakes give a hearty start to cold-weather days. Shred and season the vegetables the night before, cover with a paper towel, and store in the refrigerator. Complete remaining steps the following morning.

Makes 6 Servings (serving size: 2–3 pancakes)

1 large carrot, trimmed, peeled, and sliced crosswise into 2 or 3 pieces

1 zucchini, ends trimmed and halved lengthwise

¾ pound russet potatoes (peeled and diced)

3 tablespoons Herbed Crumbs (page 211; add the nutritional information for Herbed Crumbs to the totals provided)

½ teaspoon salt

¼ teaspoon pepper

¼ teaspoon cayenne pepper (optional)

¼ cup water

1 teaspoon olive oil

3 tablespoons brown-rice flour

olive oil cooking spray (or 2 teaspoons olive oil)

1½ cups unsweetened applesauce, warmed, for serving (optional)

1½ cups grated soy cheese for serving (optional)

1. Preheat oven to 400°. Mist a rimmed baking sheet with cooking spray and set aside.

2. Using a food processor (or large-hole box grater), shred carrot, zucchini, and potatoes. Place in large bowl. Add crumbs and seasonings to vegetables and mix thoroughly.

3. In a small bowl, mix ¼ cup water, 1 teaspoon olive oil, and 3 tablespoons flour until smooth and slightly runny (add extra water, 1 teaspoon at a time, if necessary). Add to potato mixture and mix thoroughly.

4. Heat a large skillet misted with cooking spray (or 2 teaspoons olive oil) over medium heat. Scoop 2 heaping tablespoons of potato mixture (per pancake), drop in skillet, and flatten to ¼-inch thick. Cook, turning once, until golden on both sides (about 5 minutes per side). Repeat until all vegetable mixture is used. Transfer pancakes to prepared baking sheet and bake until vegetables soften, about 12 to 14 minutes. Top with applesauce and serve.

Nutrition (per serving): **calories** 85; **fat** 1g (saturated 0g); **protein** 3g; **carbohydrate** 14g; **sodium** 205mg

main dishes

ACORN SQUASH BOATS

Colorful and full of flavor, these self-contained main-dish servings are a pleasant focus for your meal. Serve with a green vegetable, soup, or a salad for a full meal packed with nutrition and enjoyable tastes.

Makes 6 Servings (serving size: ½ squash)

    3 acorn squash, halved and seeded
    4 tablespoons olive oil, divided
    Salt and pepper
    2 cups green cabbage, coarsely sliced
    1 red bell pepper, seeded and coarsely chopped
    ½ large onion (about ½ cup), thinly sliced and cut into short lengths
    1 cup fresh or frozen corn kernels, cooked
    1 cup fresh or frozen green beans, cooked and cut in short lengths
    1 tablespoon minced garlic
    2 teaspoons fresh thyme
    1 teaspoon fresh sage
    ¼ teaspoon cayenne pepper
    1 cup grated carrots for garnish
    2 tablespoons flat-leaf parsley, stemmed and chopped, for garnish

1. Preheat oven to 375°.
2. Place squash halves on a baking sheet (cut side up). Brush insides with 2 tablespoons oil. Season each with a dash of salt and pepper. Bake 30 to 35 minutes or until edges are roasted golden and flesh is soft. Transfer baking sheet to a wire rack and loosely cover with foil. Reduce oven to 300°.

3. Heat 1 tablespoon oil in a large skillet over medium heat and cook cabbage until tender and nearly translucent (about 4 minutes), stirring often. Add bell pepper and onion and cook, stirring occasionally, 6 to 8 minutes or until pepper is tender-crisp and onion is soft.

4. Reduce heat to low and add corn, beans, garlic, thyme, sage, and cayenne. Mix well, season with salt and pepper, if desired, and cook 2 to 4 minutes. Remove from heat, stir well, cover, and let stand 5 minutes.

5. With a spoon, fill squash halves with skillet mixture, garnish with carrot and parsley, and return to oven. Turn off heat and allow squash to reheat by warming for about 15 minutes.

Nutrition (per serving): **calories** 192; **fat** 10g (saturated 1g); **protein** 3g; **carbohydrate** 27g; **sodium** 21mg

ASPARAGUS AND SWEET CORN CASSEROLE

This recipe is quick to make, but if you have the extra time and local fresh vegetables are in season, consider using fresh asparagus and corn.

Makes 4 Servings (serving size: about 1 cup)

2 tablespoons olive oil
1 small onion, chopped (about ½ cup)
1 green bell pepper, seeded and chopped
1 (16-ounce) can whole-kernel sweet corn (or frozen and thawed corn kernels)
1 (10-ounce) can asparagus tips
1 (7-ounce) can pimientos, finely sliced
1 cup grated soy cheese
Salt and pepper, to taste

1. Preheat oven to 300°.

2. Heat oil in a stovetop-safe casserole dish or Dutch oven over medium heat. Sauté onion and bell pepper until tender. Add corn, asparagus, pimiento, salt, and pepper, stirring until all ingredients are well warmed. Remove from heat, sprinkle with cheese, and transfer to oven for 30 minutes until cheese lightly browns.

Nutrition (per serving): **calories** 286; **fat** 11g (saturated 1g); **protein** 7g; **carbohydrate** 40g; **sodium** 534mg

CABBAGE ROLLS

These are great little bundles of nutrition and flavor. Play around with the sauce to meet your taste preferences, exchanging the soy sauce for hot sauce or other flavors.

Makes 4 Servings (serving size: 2 cabbage rolls)

    8 cabbage leaves
    2 tablespoons olive oil
    ½ medium onion (about ⅓ cup), finely chopped
    1 small bell pepper (about ½ cup), seeded and finely chopped
    3 green onions, white and green parts, finely chopped
    2 large tomatoes (about 2 cups), trimmed, seeded, and coarsely chopped
    4 cups cooked brown rice
    1 cup fresh green beans, cooked and finely sliced
    Salt and pepper, to taste

Sauce:

    1 tablespoon olive oil
    ½ small onion (about ¼ cup), finely chopped
    1 (15-ounce) can tomato sauce
    1 tablespoon soy sauce or tamari
    2 bay leaves
    Salt and pepper, to taste

1. To prepare sauce, heat oil in a saucepan over medium heat and add onion. Sauté until golden. Add all remaining ingredients and simmer for 10 minutes. Set aside.
2. Pour boiling water over cabbage leaves until softened (about 2 to 3 minutes). Drain and set aside on paper towels to dry.
3. Heat oil in a saucepan over medium heat; add onion, pepper, green onions, and tomatoes and cook until tender (6 to 8 minutes). Add brown rice and green beans; mix thoroughly and season to taste with salt and pepper.
4. Divide mixture into eight portions and place on each cabbage leaf. Roll up, fold in leaf ends, and secure with fine string or wooden toothpicks.
5. Place rolls in a large saucepan and pour sauce over them; gently simmer for 20 to 30 minutes. Remove bay leaves and serve.

Nutrition (per serving): **calories** 317; **fat** 13g (saturated 3g); **protein** 7g; **carbohydrate** 45g; **sodium** 370mg

CAULIFLOWER STEAKS WITH BELLS

Using cauliflower as a faux steak is a creative way to make a delicious meatless dinner. The "steaks" are slices of the nutritious vegetable served in a bed of rice, quinoa, or couscous.

Makes 4 Servings (serving size: 1 slice with toppings)

1 head cauliflower (about 3 pounds), trimmed

4 tablespoons olive oil, divided

2 to 4 cups grape, cherry, or small Roma tomatoes

Salt and pepper (optional during cooking)

2 large bell peppers

1 tablespoon rice or red wine vinegar

2 tablespoons fresh parsley, stemmed and coarsely chopped

1 cup pitted Kalamata or green olives, rinsed, drained, and halved

2 garlic cloves, minced and divided into two portions

2 to 4 cups cooked grain (couscous, quinoa, rice), for serving

1. Preheat oven to 375°.

2. Place the whole cauliflower stem down on a cutting board. In the same way you would slice a loaf of bread, start from the center of the cauliflower and use a sharp knife to make four slices to create the steaks (¾-inch to 1-inch thick); set aside.

3. Cut the remaining pieces of cauliflower into florets and mix in a bowl with about 1 teaspoon of the divided oil; place on one side of a rimmed baking sheet. Toss the tomatoes with about 1 additional teaspoon of the divided oil and arrange on the opposite side of the baking sheet. Season with salt and pepper and place in preheated oven. Roast vegetables for 15 to 25 minutes or until florets begin to brown and tomatoes begin to collapse. Check after 10 minutes and reposition, if necessary. Remove baking sheet to a wire rack and reduce oven to lowest heat setting. Spoon precooked grain (couscous, quinoa, or rice) into a covered casserole dish; place in oven to warm.

4. Meanwhile, roast bell peppers over a high gas flame or under a broiler, turning frequently, until the sides are all charred, about 10 minutes. Place the hot, charred peppers in a medium bowl and cover with plastic wrap; set aside to steam for 10 minutes. Then rub the peppers with a paper towel to remove the skin. Remove the stem and seeds; chop coarsely.

5. In a large non-stick skillet over medium heat, heat 1 tablespoon oil

and briefly cook 1 clove minced garlic until fragrant (about 1 minute). Add two cauliflower steaks, cover, and cook 5 minutes until underside is lightly brown. Flip, season with salt and pepper, cover, and cook 10 minutes or until tender. Place cooked steaks in oven on baking sheet under aluminum foil tent. Repeat process for remaining steaks, adding 1 tablespoon oil and 1 clove minced garlic.

6. When cauliflower steaks are tender and still hot, serve on a bed of warm grain, topped with roasted peppers and tomatoes.

Nutrition (per serving): **calories** 390; **fat** 18g (saturated 3g); **protein** 8g; **carbohydrate** 54g; **sodium** 540mg

CURRIED HEARTY VEGETABLES

Using herbs and spices to flavor your vegetables makes them very satisfying and enjoyable. Curry is a good choice and pairs with many vegetables.

Makes 4 Servings (serving size: about 1½ cups)

3 tablespoons olive oil
2 teaspoons dried mustard
2 teaspoons ground cumin
2 teaspoons fenugreek seeds*
1 medium onion, sliced (about ¾ cup)
2 garlic cloves, minced
2-inch piece fresh ginger, peeled and minced
1 teaspoon ground turmeric
1 teaspoon ground cumin
4 teaspoons ground coriander
1 cup water
3 cups fresh tomato, chopped
2 cups peeled potato, cubed
1 cup carrots, sliced (cut in rounds)
3 cups green cabbage, shredded
½ cup fresh peas (or 1 cup pea pods, trimmed)
Juice of ½ lemon
Salt, to taste
Fresh cilantro, finely chopped, for garnish

---

*Fenugreek seeds are a common ingredient in Indian cuisine and can be found in the natural foods section of most supermarkets or in health-food stores.

1. Heat oil in a large skillet over medium heat. Sauté mustard, cumin, and fenugreek seeds; immediately cover with a lid until seeds stop popping. Add onion, garlic, and ginger and sauté until onion is soft. Add turmeric, cumin, and coriander and sauté for 1 minute. Remove skillet from heat and let cool.

2. In a blender, puree skillet mixture with the water. Return to skillet and stir in tomatoes, potatoes, and carrots. Cover and simmer for 8 minutes. Add cabbage, cover, and simmer for 20 minutes. Add peas, lemon juice, and salt and mix well. Serve hot with cilantro garnish.

Nutrition (per serving): **calories** 258; **fat** 12g (saturated 2g); **protein** 6g; **carbohydrate** 36g; **sodium** 43mg

VEGETABLE MEDLEY PAELLA

Paella has its origins in Spain, and there are as many varieties as there are hamlets that prepare it. This all-vegetable paella is a filling and satisfying meal for your Daniel Fast.

Makes 4 Servings (serving size: about 1½ cups)

3 tablespoons olive oil
½ medium sweet onion, finely chopped (about ½ cup)
1 medium red bell pepper, seeded and cut into bite-sized pieces
1 medium yellow or orange bell pepper, seeded and cut into bite-sized pieces
½ fennel bulb, trimmed and cut into strips
2 cloves garlic, minced
2 bay leaves
¼ teaspoon smoked paprika
¼ teaspoon cayenne pepper
½ teaspoon ground turmeric
1 cup short-grain brown rice
1 teaspoon saffron threads
½ teaspoon salt
2 cups Basic Vegetable Broth (page 185)
¾ cup frozen lima beans, thawed
12 medium plum tomatoes, halved
5 artichoke hearts, canned in oil, cut into quarters
¼ cup pitted Kalamata olives, halved lengthwise
2 tablespoons chopped fresh parsley
1 fresh lemon, cut into wedges

1. Heat the oil in a paella pan or large skillet over medium heat. Sauté onions for about 5 minutes; add bell peppers and fennel. Continue to cook for about 6 minutes or until onion and bell peppers are softened. Add garlic and cook for 1 more minute.

2. Add bay leaves, paprika, cayenne, and turmeric to the vegetables and gently blend. Add rice and stir well for about 2 minutes and then add saffron and vegetable stock.

3. Reduce heat to low, add ½ teaspoon salt, and simmer very gently undisturbed in the uncovered pan for about 20 minutes or until the rice has absorbed most of the liquid.

4. Remove the rice from the heat and scatter the lima beans, tomatoes, artichokes, and olives over the top. Cover tightly with foil and allow to rest for 10 minutes.

5. Serve in pan after sprinkling the parsley over the top and arranging the lemon wedges around the sides.

Nutrition (per serving): **calories** 423; **fat** 15g (saturated 2g); **protein** 11g; **carbohydrate** 68g; **sodium** 442mg

CURRIED VEGETABLE STEW

You might want to double this recipe to serve one for dinner and then freeze the second portion for later. It's a thick stew with lots of vegetables and thickened with split peas.

Makes 4 Servings (serving size: about 1½ cups)

½ cup dried yellow split peas

3 cups water

1 chopped cup yellow onion

2 cups Basic Vegetable Broth (page 185)

2 cloves garlic, crushed or minced

¼ teaspoon ground turmeric

1 to 2 tablespoons finely minced fresh garlic

1 (14.5-ounce) can diced tomatoes

1 cup large cauliflower florets, cut into bite-sized pieces

1 cup diced carrots

1 cup large broccoli florets, cut into bite-sized pieces

1 cup diced red bell pepper

2 teaspoons ground cumin

2 teaspoons ground coriander

½ teaspoon freshly ground pepper

Dash of cayenne pepper

Salt, to taste

2 tablespoons coarsely chopped fresh cilantro for garnish (optional)

1. Rinse the split peas under running water. Place in a large stock pot and cover with 3 cups water. Bring to a boil and then reduce heat to simmer the peas for about 40 minutes or until they are tender.

2. Puree the peas using an immersion blender, food processor, or blender and set aside.

3. While the peas are cooking, braise the onions in 1 cup vegetable stock in a 3- to 4-quart sauce pan over medium heat until just tender. Add the garlic, turmeric, and ginger. Continue to cook for about 5 more minutes. Add the tomatoes, cauliflower, and carrots.

4. Meanwhile, blanch the broccoli in boiling water for 60 to 90 seconds and then run it under cold water so it retains its bright green color. Drain and set aside.

5. When the carrots are just tender, add the red bell pepper, cumin, coriander, pepper, and cayenne. Continue to gently simmer until all the vegetables are cooked.

6. Add the split pea puree to the pot along with the broccoli. Add additional vegetable stock until the stew reaches the consistency you desire.

7. Season to taste with salt, serve in individual serving bowls, and garnish with cilantro.

Nutrition (per serving): **calories** 191; **fat** 1g (saturated 0g); **protein** 11g; **carbohydrate** 37g; **sodium** 172mg

LENTIL PATTIES WITH FRESH TOMATOES

Pleasant flavors, color, and texture all combine to make these patties a delicious option for your dinner meals. You can also make extra patties and serve them for lunch along with a green salad and a piece of fruit.

Makes 4 Servings (serving size: 1 patty)

1½ cups brown lentils, cooked and drained

1 small red onion (about ½ cup), finely diced

1 tablespoon Italian seasoning

1 cup water, divided

3 teaspoons olive oil, divided

3 heaping tablespoons brown-rice flour

2 ounces frozen spinach, thawed

3 garlic cloves, minced

Salt and pepper, to taste

1 to 2 medium tomatoes (about 1 cup) diced, for serving

1. In a bowl, mash cooked lentils. Add onion and Italian seasoning, mix well, and set aside.

2. In another bowl, mix ¼ cup water, 1 teaspoon oil, and 3 tablespoons flour until smooth; set aside.

3. In a saucepan over medium-high heat, bring ¾ cup water to a boil and add spinach and garlic; immediately reduce heat to low. Cook 5 to 7 minutes, stirring occasionally; remove from heat. Transfer spinach to a colander placed over a bowl; press mixture with a rubber spatula to remove excess water; let cool.

4. Combine drained spinach with lentil mixture and stir well. Add 1 to 3 tablespoons of flour mixture to lentil-spinach mixture, 1 tablespoon at a time, stirring well, until patties hold together. Shape ½-inch- to 1-inch-thick patties using wet hands.

5. Heat 2 teaspoons oil in skillet over medium heat; cook patties until underside begins to toast. Lightly season with salt and pepper, if desired, and flip. Continue cooking and turning until patties are evenly toasted.

6. Remove from skillet, top with fresh tomatoes, and serve.

Nutrition (per serving): **calories** 184; **fat** 4g (saturated 1g); **protein** 9g; **carbohydrate** 30g; **sodium** 22mg

QUICK VEGGIE FAJITAS

Fajitas are so fun to eat and packed with color, flavors, and nutrition. If following the Daniel Fast, you may need to search for whole-grain tortillas at your local health-food store, as most traditional tortillas have added leavening or food additives and will not be Daniel Fast compliant.

Makes 4 Servings (serving size: 2 fajitas)

8 (6-inch) brown-rice or whole-grain tortillas

1 (15-ounce) can refried beans

2 tablespoons olive oil

1 large white onion (about 1 cup), halved and cut into ½-inch slices

2 large poblano chilies (about ½ cup), halved, seeded, and cut crosswise into ½-inch slices

2 medium zucchini (about 2–3 cups), ends trimmed, and cut into ½-inch half circles

2 cups corn kernels (thawed, if frozen)

Salt and pepper, to taste

½ cup Salsa Sauce (page 225)

Lime wedges, for serving (optional)

1. Preheat oven to 275°.

2. Wrap tortillas in parchment-lined aluminum foil and place in oven to warm, about 15 minutes. In a small saucepan, warm the beans over low heat.

3. In a large skillet, heat oil over medium-high. Add onion and chilies and cook until softened, 12 to 15 minutes. Add zucchini and cook until tender-crisp, about 6 minutes. Add corn and cook until warmed, about 3 minutes. Season with salt and pepper. Spread beans on tortillas, top with vegetables, and serve with salsa and lime wedges.

Nutrition (per serving): **calories** 513; **fat** 14g (saturated 2g); **protein** 16g; **carbohydrate** 81g; **sodium** 1,279mg (possibly less depending on how much salt is added)

TOFU PATTY SAUTÉ WITH SPICY TOMATO SAUCE

Tofu is like a flavor chameleon, picking up the flavors of the foods it's served with. That's what happens with this meal, making the patties delicious.

Makes 4 Servings (serving size: 1 patty)

1 recipe Spicy Tomato Sauce (page 226)

1 cup (8 ounces) firm tofu, rinsed, drained, dried, and cut into ½-inch-thick slabs

½ cup soy sauce or tamari mixed with ¼ cup water

½ cup brown-rice flour

1 teaspoon curry powder

⅛ teaspoon cayenne pepper

1 tablespoon olive oil

½ medium onion (about ⅓ cup), finely sliced

1. In a 9-by-13-inch glass casserole dish, place tofu patties in a single layer

and drizzle with soy sauce or tamari. Turn with a spatula until both sides are coated. Set aside, turning occasionally until tofu absorbs all liquid.

2. On a large platter, mix together flour, curry powder, and cayenne pepper. Dredge tofu patties until well coated.

3. In a skillet over medium heat, add oil and sauté onion until softened. Add tofu patties and sauté until both sides are browned and some of the onion is lightly crisped. Reduce heat to prevent overcooking.

Nutrition (per serving): **calories** 247; **fat** 11g (saturated 2g); **protein** 16g; **carbohydrate** 24g; **sodium** 2071mg

TORTILLAS WITH ZUCCHINI AND GUACAMOLE

These wraps pair nicely with a green salad or cup of chili. Satisfying flavors plus filling and nutritious, the tortillas are sure to delight you.

Makes 4 Servings (serving size: 2 tortillas)

    1 zucchini, ends trimmed, sliced lengthwise into spears and spears halved

    ½ red bell pepper, seeded and sliced julienne lengthwise into slivers

    1 cup (8 ounces) firm tofu, cubed

    1 garlic clove, minced

    1 tablespoon olive oil

    ½ teaspoon ground cumin

    ¾ cup green onions, whites and greens, thinly sliced

    1 recipe Guacamole (page 227)

    8 brown-rice or whole-grain tortillas, wrapped in parchment paper and aluminum foil

1. Preheat oven to 200° or lowest warm setting. Place wrapped tortillas in oven to warm.

2. In a bowl, mix zucchini, bell pepper, and tofu with 1 tablespoon oil; stir until well coated.

3. In a large skillet over medium-high, sauté zucchini, bell pepper, tofu, and garlic. Drizzle with excess oil from bowl and sprinkle with cumin. Reduce heat to medium-low, add onion, and stir fry 3 to 5 minutes. Remove from heat and set aside, covered with kitchen towel to absorb excess moisture.

4. On a baking sheet, lightly spread guacamole on a tortilla; add 1 to 2 tablespoons of skillet mixture, and roll tortilla to contain filling. Position

on baking sheet and repeat until all tortillas are filled. Loosely cover with aluminum foil, place baking sheet in oven 10 to 15 minutes until warmed through, and serve.

Nutrition (per serving): **calories** 370; **fat** 14g (saturated 2g); **protein** 17g; **carbohydrate** 46g; **sodium** 346mg

STUFFED POTATO CUPS WITH SAUTÉED KALE

Bypassing the meat counter while you're on the Daniel Fast saves you money, and you'll soon find new life in a lot of your standards like these potatoes.

Makes 4 Servings (serving size: 1 stuffed potato)

    4 small sweet potatoes, yams, or thick-skinned baking potatoes
    1 pound fresh kale greens, stem removed and coarsely chopped
    ½ tablespoon olive oil
    ½ cup walnuts, whole and halved, soaked in a small amount of water
    ⅔ cup soy cheese, cubed
    1 cup (8 ounces) tofu, crumbled
    4 green onions, whites and greens, finely sliced

1. Preheat oven to 400°.

2. Scrub potatoes and puncture with a fork in a number of places. Place in the center of oven rack and bake 45 minutes or until flesh is soft when pierced.

3. In a large skillet over medium-high heat, add oil and kale and stir fry for 2 minutes; reduce heat to medium-low, cover, and cook for 10 minutes, stirring occasionally. Remove from heat and set aside, covered.

4. Reduce oven to 375° and remove baked potatoes; let cool on a wire rack for 5 to 10 minutes. On a cutting board, gently cut potatoes lengthwise into halves. Scoop flesh from each half into a large bowl with care not to scrape skins. Mash potato flesh thoroughly and add walnuts, soy cheese, and tofu; mix thoroughly. Spoon mixture into each potato cup, top with grated cheese, and transfer to a casserole dish and bake for 20 minutes or until cheese begins to turn golden. Remove and garnish with green onions. Serve with kale and vinaigrette dressing.

Nutrition (per serving): **calories** 522; **fat** 19g (saturated 2g); **protein** 21g; **carbohydrate** 69g; **sodium** 384mg

ZUCCHINI AND CHICKPEA PASTA WITH ASPARAGUS

Make your meatless dishes lip-smacking favorites by adding two or three complex flavors to the recipe. This one uses cumin, roasted red peppers, and olives to make this wholesome dish a bowl full of flavor.

Makes 4 Servings (serving size: about 2 cups)

8 ounces whole-grain penne pasta, cooked al dente according to package instructions

1 scant teaspoon cumin seeds

1 (7-ounce) jar roasted red peppers, drained and rinsed

1 cup tomatoes, chopped

Olive oil cooking spray

3 zucchini, quartered lengthwise and sliced ¼-inch thick

1 bunch fresh asparagus, trimmed and cooked tender-crisp in a steamer

Pinch pepper, or to taste

2 cups chickpeas, cooked

12 green olives, pitted

3 ounces soy cheese, grated, for garnish (optional)

1 tablespoon parsley or cilantro, for garnish (optional)

1. In a medium saucepan over medium-low heat, add cumin and toast, until fragrant, shaking pan occasionally, 1 to 2 minutes. Add and stir together red peppers and tomatoes. Increase heat to medium; bring to a simmer and cook, stirring occasionally, until slightly thickened, about 7 minutes. Remove from heat and cool slightly. Purée in a blender into slightly chunky sauce and return saucepan to low heat. Add pasta and stir occasionally.

2. On a rimmed baking sheet lined with aluminum foil lightly sprayed with oil, spread zucchini in a single layer; mist with oil, sprinkle with pepper, and roast on top oven rack under broiler about 5 to 7 minutes, tossing once, until barely tender and lightly browned.

3. Add chickpeas and olives to pasta mixture, stirring ingredients together, then occasionally, until warmed through. Add zucchini, gently toss, and remove from heat. Place in individual serving bowls; garnish with cheese and parsley and serve with asparagus.

Nutrition (per serving): **calories** 360; **fat** 5g (saturated 0g); **protein** 17g; **carbohydrate** 71g; **sodium** 695mg

soups and stews

BASIC VEGETABLE BROTH

Homemade vegetable broth is easy, rich in flavor, and less expensive than the canned or boxed varieties. It's easy to prepare a big pot of stock and either store in jars in the refrigerator or in Ziploc bags in the freezer.

Makes 12 Servings (serving size: 1 cup)

3 tablespoons olive oil
3 carrots, peeled and cut into sticks
5 celery stalks, sliced into 3-inch pieces
1 large yellow onion (about 1 cup), unpeeled and quartered
1 small celery root (about ½ cup), peeled and chopped in large pieces
7 garlic cloves, peeled
2 small bunches of fresh parsley
5 sprigs fresh thyme
12 black peppercorns
3 fresh or dried bay leaves
8 whole pitted prunes
Salt, to taste

1. Warm the olive oil in a large stock pot over medium heat. Add carrots, celery, onion, celery root, and garlic, stirring to coat in the olive oil. Sauté the vegetables, stirring occasionally, until golden brown, about 10 minutes.

2. Make an herb bundle by wrapping the bay leaves and thyme sprigs in the parsley bunches and then securing the whole bundle with kitchen string. Add the herb bundle to the pot along with peppercorns and prunes. Add enough cold water to cover the contents of the pot (about 16 cups).

3. Bring the broth to a boil and then reduce the heat to the lowest temperature on your range and simmer for about 90 minutes. Do not stir during this slow simmering time.

4. Remove the vegetables from the broth and use for another meal. Strain the broth using a strainer and then again through a fine sieve or cheesecloth.

5. Cool the broth quickly by placing the bowl in a sink filled with ice and water. Gently stir the stock until chilled. Cover and store in the refrigerator for up to one week or in the freezer for six months.

Nutrition (per serving): **calories** 35; **fat** 2g (saturated 0g); **protein** 0g; **carbohydrate** 4g; **sodium** 495mg

BARLEY CORN SOUP

Soup with a garden salad and a few crackers is a great way to have an easy and balanced meal come together when you're short on time. This soup can also be a great first course with heavier entrees.

Makes 4 Servings (serving size: about 2 cups)

6½ cups water or Basic Vegetable Broth (page 185)
1 cup pearl barley, white or black
1½ cups onion, coarsely chopped
½ cup celery, thinly sliced
½ cup Shitake mushrooms, sliced
½ cup carrots, thinly sliced
½ red bell pepper, sliced
1½ cups corn kernels, fresh or frozen
3 tablespoons soy sauce, to taste
2 teaspoons garlic cloves, minced
1 tablespoon miso paste
1 teaspoon minced fresh thyme
Salt and pepper, to taste

1. In a small pot over high heat, combine 4 cups water or broth and bring to a boil. Reduce heat to medium, cover, and simmer until barley plumps, about 50 minutes. Drain and set aside.

2. In a large kettle over medium heat, add 6½ cups water or broth, onion, celery, mushrooms, and carrots; cook for 20 minutes, stirring

occasionally. Add bell pepper and corn; cook for 10 minutes, stirring occasionally. Reduce heat to low. Extract 1 cup of the clear soup broth.

3. In a small bowl, combine miso with the 1 cup soup broth and mix until smooth. Return miso mixture to kettle and add all remaining ingredients, including cooked barley; stir well. Cover and cook over lowest heat for 10 to 20 minutes and serve.

Nutrition (per serving): **calories** 153; **fat** 1g (saturated 0g); **protein** 5g; **carbohydrate** 33g; **sodium** 959mg

CREAM OF BROCCOLI-BEAN SOUP

Creamy soup without the cream! White beans and a blender do the trick, making this a pleasant addition to your soup recipe collection.

Makes 4 Servings (serving size: about 1½ cups)

1 medium onion, chopped (about ¾ cup)
1 tablespoon olive oil
2 cups Basic Vegetable Broth (page 185)
4 cups broccoli florets
1 cup dried white beans, cooked according to package directions
¼ teaspoon ground allspice

1. In a soup kettle, sauté onions in oil until tender. Add vegetable broth, broccoli, beans, bay leaf, and allspice. Bring to a boil, reduce heat, and simmer for about 20 minutes. Cool and remove bay leaf.

2. In a blender, puree the soup and reheat in the kettle before serving. Store leftovers 1 to 2 days in tightly lidded container in refrigerator. This soup does not freeze well.

Nutrition (per serving): **calories** 238; **fat** 4g (saturated 1g); **protein** 15g; **carbohydrate** 39g; **sodium** 33mg

CREAM OF ZUCCHINI SOUP

Along with being a deliciously light soup, this flavorful concoction can be used as a sauce for steamed vegetables or in hot rice and pasta dishes.

Makes 2 Servings (serving size: about 1½ cups)

3 small zucchini, ends trimmed, chopped (broccoli or other summer squash can be substituted)

½ cup green onion, green tops, finely chopped (reserve white portion
   for another use)
2 tablespoons olive oil
2 tablespoons whole-wheat or brown-rice flour
½ teaspoon salt
1½ cups rice milk
Fresh chives, finely chopped, for garnish

1. In a skillet over medium heat, sauté zucchini in 1 tablespoon oil until
   tender.
2. In a blender or food processor, puree zucchini, green onion, milk, and
   salt.
3. In the skillet over medium-low heat, mix and cook remaining 1 tablespoon
   oil and flour for 2 to 3 minutes, stirring with a fork until flour is lightly
   browned. Reduce heat to low, add zucchini mixture, and stir until hot
   and well blended with flour mixture (do not boil). Immediately cover
   and remove from heat; let stand to thicken, stirring occasionally. Add
   additional rice milk, 1 tablespoon at a time, until desired consistency is
   achieved.
4. Garnish individual serving with chives. Store leftovers in tightly lidded
   container in refrigerator for 1 to 2 days. Do not freeze.

Nutrition (per serving): **calories** 198; **fat** 14g (saturated 2g); **protein** 4g; **carbohydrate** 17g;
sodium 589mg

NOODLE SOUP

*Keeping a pot of noodle soup around is a perfect way to fill in for lunch or to
supplement a dinner menu. This recipe is easy to make and it's packed with
vegetable flavor, color, and nutrition.*

Makes 10 Servings (serving size: about 1½ cups)

8 cups water or Basic Vegetable Broth (page 185)
1½ cups onion, chopped
¾ cup celery, thinly sliced
¾ cup carrot, thinly sliced
¾ cup parsnip, thinly sliced
2 tablespoons garlic cloves, minced
1½ cups (12 ounces) extra-firm tofu, cubed
6 ounces uncooked whole-grain pasta

2 tablespoons soy sauce or tamari

1½ tablespoons fresh parsley, minced

1 tablespoon fresh dill, minced

½ tablespoon olive oil

Salt and pepper, to taste

1. In a large kettle over medium heat, combine water or broth, onion, carrot, parsnip, celery, and garlic; cook for 20 minutes, stirring occasionally.

2. Add tofu and cook 5 minutes, stirring. Reduce heat to low, add remaining ingredients, and cook, stirring frequently, until pasta is tender, about 8 to 10 minutes.

Nutrition (per serving): **calories** 134; **fat** 4g (saturated 1g); **protein** 9g; **carbohydrate** 16g; **sodium** 258mg

POTATO SOUP

Potato soup has been a standby recipe for centuries. It's easy to make and is good plain or as a base for other flavors you might want to add. Plus, potatoes are one of the best vegetable bargains around!

Makes 6 Servings (serving size: about 1½ cups)

2 pounds white potatoes, unpeeled, steamed until tender, chopped into small cubes

2 teaspoons olive oil

1 medium onion (about ¾ cup), finely chopped

2 to 3 garlic cloves, minced

1 cup Basic Vegetable Broth (page 185)

2½ cups rice or soy milk

1 teaspoon salt

½ teaspoon paprika

Cayenne pepper, several dashes (optional)

Dry (ground) mustard, several dashes (optional)

Green onions or fresh chives, finely chopped, for garnish

1. Warm 2 teaspoons oil in a small kettle over medium heat and sauté onion and garlic until tender. Add broth; simmer and occasionally stir.

2. In a blender, purée 3 cups potatoes with milk, salt, paprika, cayenne, and mustard. Add to kettle, stir, and add reserved potatoes. Simmer over low

heat 10 minutes, remove, and let rest 5 minutes. Serve with onion or chive garnish. Refrigerate for 1 to 2 days; do not freeze.

Nutrition (per serving): **calories** 147; **fat** 4g (saturated 1g); **protein** 7g; **carbohydrate** 23g; **sodium** 415mg

ROASTED SQUASH SOUP

With a rich color, sweet flavor, and a smooth texture, roasted squash soup is a perfect recipe to serve in a cup as a starter or by the bowl as the main course!

Makes 8 Servings (serving size: about 1½ cups)

    1 small winter squash, halved and seeded
    1 large yam
    1 medium onion (about ¾ cup), chopped
    1 cup celery, thinly sliced
    2 tablespoons garlic, minced
    4½ cups Basic Vegetable Broth (page 185)
    2½ cups rice or soy milk
    3 tablespoons soy sauce
    ½ teaspoon curry powder
    1 small cinnamon stick
    Salt and pepper, to taste (optional)
    Sesame seeds, for garnish (optional)
    Fresh mint or cilantro, chopped, for garnish (optional)

1. Preheat oven to 375°.
2. On an oiled baking sheet, place squash facedown and cook until tender, about 30 to 35 minutes. Remove and let cool. Scoop squash flesh into a blender and set aside; discard skin.
3. In a 3-quart kettle over medium heat, combine yam, onion, celery, garlic, milk, broth, and cinnamon; cook until yam is tender (about 30 minutes), stirring occasionally. Remove from heat and cool.
4. Remove cinnamon stick, add soy sauce, and stir. Add kettle mixture to blender and puree. Return to kettle over low heat, season to taste, and serve with sesame seed and mint or cilantro garnish.

Nutrition (per serving): **calories** 89; **fat** 2g (saturated 0g); **protein** 4g; **carbohydrate** 17g; **sodium** 412mg

SPLIT PEA–PARSNIP SOUP

Even without the ham that is traditionally part of split pea soup, this soup hits the spot. It's especially good for a cold winter's night.

Makes 12 Servings (serving size: about 1½ cups)

2 cups parsnips (about 1 pound), cubed
4 teaspoons olive oil, divided
1½ cups onion, diced
¼ cup celery, diced
¾ cup carrot, cubed
2 tablespoons garlic cloves, minced
1 cup dried green or yellow split peas
8 to 10 cups water and/or Basic Vegetable Broth (page 185)
3 tablespoons soy sauce
1 tablespoon fresh parsley, minced
1 teaspoon salt (optional)
½ teaspoon pepper (optional)
¼ teaspoon red pepper flakes, crushed (optional)

1. Preheat oven to 375°.

2. On an oiled rimmed baking sheet, place parsnips and drizzle with 2 teaspoons oil. Mix well and bake until parsnips are barely soft, about 20 minutes, stirring occasionally to uniformly roast.

3. In a 5-quart kettle over medium heat, add 2 teaspoons oil, onion, celery, carrot, and garlic, and cook 5 minutes, stirring occasionally. Add 6 cups liquid and split peas and cook 20 minutes or until peas are soft. Add remaining liquid slowly; allow mixture to retain heat and peas to absorb moisture.

4. Add all remaining ingredients, including parsnips, and gently simmer over medium-low heat, stirring occasionally for 10 minutes. Reduce heat to low, taste test, and correct seasoning. Serve hot.

Nutrition (per serving): **calories** 100; **fat** 2g (saturated 0g); **protein** 5g; **carbohydrate** 17g; **sodium** 267mg

BARLEY-VEGETABLE STEW

This Barley-Vegetable Stew recipe is easy to follow and assembles quickly. Serve for supper one day and use leftovers for lunch the next day.

Makes 8 Servings (serving size: about 1½ cups)

    1 tablespoon olive oil

    2 cups onion or leeks, chopped

    2 cups potato, diced

    1½ cups carrots, diced

    1½ cups turnip, diced

    3 cups Basic Vegetable Broth (page 185), divided

    1½ cups raw winter squash, diced

    1 bay leaf

    2 teaspoons fresh savory, minced

    1 teaspoon fresh thyme, minced

    1½ cups cauliflower florets

    2 cups fresh or frozen green peas

    2 cups pearl barley, cooked according to package directions

    Fresh parsley, finely chopped for garnish

    Salt, pepper, soy sauce, to taste

1. Warm oil in a skillet over medium heat and sauté onions or leeks until tender. Add potato, carrot, turnip, and 1 cup broth, and bring to a simmer. Reduce heat to low and cook 10 minutes.

2. Add squash, bay leaf, savory, and thyme, and cook for 5 minutes.

3. Stir in cauliflower and 2 cups broth, and cook for 10 minutes.

4. Add peas and barley, and cook for 5 minutes.

5. Remove from heat and let rest for 10 minutes. Serve with parsley garnish and season to taste. Refrigerate, tightly lidded, for 2 to 3 days; does not freeze well.

Nutrition (per serving): **calories** 296; **fat** 3g (saturated 0g); **protein** 9g; **carbohydrate** 62g; **sodium** 79mg

KIDNEY BEAN STEW

This stew can be refrigerated up to seven days and freezes well.

Makes 12 Servings (serving size: about 1½ cups)

    2½ cups dried kidney beans, cooked

    1 pound fresh carrots, peeled, steam cooked tender, and sliced into bite-size chunks (about 4 cups)

    2 to 4 cups water

    3 to 5 cups button mushrooms, halved

8 to 10 celery stalks, sliced in bite-size chunks (about 4 cups)

6 medium potatoes (non-baker variety), steam cooked tender, and sliced into bite-size chunks (about 4 cups)

3 cups yellow onion, chopped

3 small zucchini squash, cut in chunks (about 3 cups)

1 cup frozen peas

1 cup frozen corn

2 tablespoons soy sauce

2 tablespoons vegetable broth powder*

3 tablespoons dried parsley (or 6 tablespoons fresh, stemmed and chopped)

1½ teaspoons salt

1 teaspoon dried basil

½ teaspoon paprika

⅛ teaspoon each cayenne pepper, ground cumin, and dried thyme

1. In a large kettle over high heat, bring one-half of water to a boil, reduce heat to medium, and add all other ingredients.

2. Stir occasionally and simmer for 30 minutes, adding more water ½ cup at a time to achieve desired consistency. Serve hot.

Nutrition (per serving): **calories** 175; **fat** 1g (saturated 0g); **protein** 8g; **carbohydrate** 37g; **sodium** 518mg

POTTER STEW

This one-pot meal is so easy it almost cooks itself!

Makes 2 Servings (serving size: 1½ cups)

¾ pound small yellow potatoes (such as Yukon Gold), peeled and cut lengthwise into quarters (about 1¾ cups)

¾ pound red bell peppers, seeded and cut into pieces the size of potato quarters (about 1–2 cups)

2 tablespoons olive oil

1 medium onion, peeled and sliced (about ¾ cup)

3 garlic cloves, sliced

1 bay leaf

3 slender strips of lemon peel

1 cup Basic Vegetable Broth (page 185)

2 teaspoons jalapeño pepper, finely diced

*A natural bouillon powder found in the natural foods section of most supermarkets.

Cilantro, chopped, for garnish

½ cup almonds (blanched or toasted), chopped for garnish

1. Preheat oven to 350°.

2. In an ovenproof kettle, heat oil over medium-low heat and add onion. Cook until barely soft. Add potatoes, peppers, garlic, bay, and lemon; blend well.

3. Add broth and increase heat to medium; cover and simmer for 15 minutes.

4. Transfer to oven for 40 minutes or until potatoes are tender and the peppers are soft. Remove from oven and stir in the jalapeño pepper.

5. Sprinkle cilantro over surface. Serve hot, garnished with almonds.

Nutrition (per serving): **calories** 550; **fat** 33g (saturated 4g); **protein** 14g; **carbohydrate** 57g; **sodium** 62mg

salads and dressings

BEET SALAD

If you are a fan of beets, then this salad will please your soon-to-be-red palette. The dill adds a little spark of flavor to harmonize with the red root vegetable.

Makes 4 Servings (serving size: about 1 cup)

6 medium beets, cooked, peeled, and diced (about 4 cups)

2 green onions, chopped

2 tablespoons soynnaise (see Homemade Vegan Mayonnaise, page 198)

2 teaspoons lemon juice

2 tablespoons minced fresh dill

Dash pepper

1. In a bowl, mix beets, onions, and soynnaise.
2. Add lemon juice, pepper, and dill. Serve warm or cold.

Nutrition (per serving): **calories** 118; **fat** 6g (saturated 1g); **protein** 3g; **carbohydrate** 15g; **sodium** 137mg

CARROT AND CUCUMBER SALAD WITH BALSAMIC VINAIGRETTE

The ultimate convenient salad mix. Use 4 cups here and store the rest in the refrigerator and use within a few days.

Makes 4 Servings (serving size: about 2 cups)

Mixed Salad Greens

1 head butter lettuce, such as Bibb or Boston, trimmed

1 head crisp long-leaved lettuce, such as romaine, trimmed

1 head loose-leaf lettuce, such as red leaf, trimmed

2 cups arugula

1. Wash all ingredients well and pat dry with paper towels.
2. In a large bowl, tear leaves into bite-size pieces and toss to mix. Transfer to food storage bags or a container lined with paper towels or loosely roll greens in a clean kitchen towel before placing in a container. When refrigerating, loosely seal the storage bags or container lids, which allows greens to get air and remain fresh.

Salad

4 cups mixed salad greens
1 English cucumber or other varieties, thinly sliced
1 large carrot, scrubbed and shredded
Balsamic Vinaigrette (see recipe on page 200)

1. Combine salad mix with cucumber and carrot.
2. Drizzle with vinaigrette and toss to coat before serving.

Nutrition (per serving): **calories** 36; **fat** 1g (saturated 0g); **protein** 3g; **carbohydrate** 7g; **sodium** 20mg

CHICKPEA MEDITERRANEAN SALAD

A hearty salad for a main course or pair it with a bowl of vegetable or squash soup.

Makes 4 Servings (serving size: about 1½ cups)

1 (15-ounce) can chickpeas, rinsed and drained
4 cups arugula
1 cup brown-rice pasta (shell-shaped), cooked and cooled
1 small red onion, thinly sliced (about ½ cup)
¼ cup red bell pepper, seeded and thinly sliced
½ cup black olives, halved
1 celery rib, sliced
1 garlic clove, minced
½ cup salad dressing of choice

1. In a medium bowl, combine all ingredients and toss.
2. Dress and serve on individual salad plates.

Nutrition (per serving): **calories** 246; **fat** 5g (saturated 1g); **protein** 10g; **carbohydrate** 46g; **sodium** 635mg

PARSLEY-RICE SALAD

Bright flavors add a bright contrast to the rice in this salad. Easy to pack for work or school lunches.

Makes 6 Servings (serving size: about ½ cup)

 1 recipe Lime and Herb Vinaigrette Dressing (page 200)
 4 cloves garlic, minced
 1 tablespoon sesame oil
 2 cups cooked brown rice
 1 cup cooked wild rice
 ½ cup celery, chopped
 ½ cup red onion, chopped
 1 cup cilantro, minced
 1 cup fresh parsley, minced
 Salt and pepper, to taste

1. In a skillet over low heat, sauté garlic in sesame oil until tender.

2. In a large bowl, mix together brown rice and wild rice; add celery, onion, cilantro, and parsley. Pour Lime and Herb Vinaigrette over salad and serve. Season with salt and pepper, to taste, if desired.

Nutrition (per serving): **calories** 138; **fat** 3g (saturated 1g); **protein** 4g; **carbohydrate** 25g; **sodium** 22mg

SPINACH MUSHROOM SALAD

Leafy green vegetables are rich in protein, micronutrients, and fiber. Spinach has a pleasant flavor and nice texture and is readily available already washed and ready to use.

Makes 4 Servings (serving size: about 1 cup)

 ½ pound fresh spinach (about 3 cups), washed, stemmed, patted dry, and chilled
 8 large fresh white mushrooms (any variety), washed and patted dry
 2 green onions, sliced
 4 radishes, sliced
 ½ cup Lemon Mustard Dressing (page 202)
 1 tablespoon soy sauce or tamari

1. Cut off mushroom stem tips, discard, and chop remaining caps and stems. Stem the spinach and chop coarsely. In a medium bowl, combine mushrooms, spinach, scallions, and radishes, and toss to mix.

2. In a small bowl or dressing bottle, combine Lemon Mustard Dressing and soy sauce or tamari; whisk or shake to mix. Pour dressing over salad. Season with salt and pepper, if desired, and serve.

Nutrition (per serving): **calories** 22; **fat** 0g (saturated 0g); **protein** 2g; **carbohydrate** 4g; **sodium** 304mg

WAYSIDE INN SALAD

This salad is an alternative to a Waldorf salad and uses a soy-based dressing instead of mayonnaise. Soynnaise is available in most supermarkets' natural-foods section or in health-food stores. You can also make your own (see Homemade Vegan Mayonnaise, below).

Makes 4 Servings (serving size: about 1 cup)

4 celery ribs, diced (about 1½ cups)
2 medium apples (tart variety), cored and diced (about 2 cups)
1 tablespoon walnuts, coarsely chopped
¼ cup soynnaise (see Homemade Vegan Mayonnaise, below)
2 tablespoons apple juice
2 tablespoons lemon juice
¼ teaspoon tarragon (fresh preferred)
4 romaine lettuce leaves, hard spine removed, coarsely chopped

1. In a medium bowl, toss celery, apples, and walnuts.
2. In a small bowl, combine soynnaise, fruit juices, and tarragon. Add to celery mixture and mix well.
3. Serve on individual salad plate on a bed of romaine lettuce.

Nutrition (per serving): **calories** 163; **fat** 12g (saturated 2g); **protein** 1g; **carbohydrate** 13g; **sodium** 91mg

HOMEMADE VEGAN MAYONNAISE (SOYNNAISE)

Makes 24 Servings (serving size: 1 tablespoon)

1 cup canola oil
½ cup unsweetened soy milk (or other plant-based milk)
¾ teaspoon salt, to taste
1 to 1½ teaspoons lemon juice
Pinch dry mustard

1. Combine the oil, soy milk, and salt in the food processor or blender. Blend until smooth.

2. Slowly add the lemon juice until the mixture thickens and tastes as desired. Adjust flavor by adding salt and mustard to taste.

Nutrition (per serving): **calories** 79; **fat** 9g (saturated 1g); **protein** 0g; **carbohydrate** 0g; **sodium** 70mg

ASIAN DRESSING

Use just a little of this dressing—only enough to make the lettuce leaves glisten.

Makes 3 Servings (serving size: 2 tablespoons)

2 tablespoons soy sauce or tamari
3 tablespoons rice wine vinegar
2 tablespoons sesame oil

In a bowl, combine all ingredients and whisk to mix. Serve immediately or store in refrigerator in a tightly capped bottle. Shake well before using.

Nutrition (per serving): **calories** 89; **fat** 9g (saturated 1g); **protein** 1g; **carbohydrate** 2g; **sodium** 656mg

BASIL AND CITRUS VINAIGRETTE

This dressing is a delicious classic when served with the mixed-greens salad recipe or with fresh arugula and red onions.

Makes 4 Servings (serving size: 2 tablespoons)

2 tablespoons fresh basil, minced
1 to 2 teaspoons grated lemon or lime zest
1 clove garlic, minced
¼ cup olive oil
3 tablespoons balsamic vinegar
Salt, to taste (optional)
⅛ teaspoon pepper (optional)

In a small bowl, combine basil, zest, and garlic. In a separate bowl, whisk together oil and vinegar. Stir in basil mixture and whisk. Add salt and pepper to taste, if desired.

Nutrition (per serving): **calories** 122; **fat** 14g (saturated 2g); **protein** 0g; **carbohydrate** 1g; **sodium** 0mg

BALSAMIC VINAIGRETTE

Makes 2 Servings (serving size: 2 tablespoons)

1 tablespoon balsamic vinegar
¼ teaspoon dry mustard
3 tablespoons olive oil
1 clove garlic, minced

Nutrition (per serving): **calories** 182; **fat** 20g (saturated 3g); **protein** 0g; **carbohydrate** 1g; **sodium** 0mg

BASIL VINAIGRETTE

Makes 8 Servings (serving size: 2 tablespoons)

3 tablespoons red wine vinegar
1 garlic clove, crushed
½ cup olive oil
¼ teaspoon dry mustard
¼ cup fresh basil leaves

Nutrition (per serving): **calories** 121; **fat** 14g (saturated 2g); **protein** 0g; **carbohydrate** 0.5g; **sodium** 0mg

LIME AND HERB VINAIGRETTE

Makes 6 Servings (serving size: 2 tablespoons)

½ cup olive oil
juice of 1 large lime (about 2 tablespoons)
2 tablespoons balsamic vinegar
fresh chopped leaves of mint, basil, thyme, or other herbs, minced red chili peppers to taste (optional)

Nutrition (per serving): **calories** 163; **fat** 18g (saturated 2g); **protein** 0g; **carbohydrate** 1g; **sodium** 0mg

CREAMY HERB DRESSING

A basil-and-chive-flavored dressing suitable for salads, as a dipping sauce for raw or cooked vegetables, or to garnish main and side dishes.

Makes 8 Servings (serving size: 2 tablespoons)

½ to ¾ cup soy milk (or other plant-based milk)
3 tablespoons soynnaise (see Homemade Vegan Mayonnaise, page 198)

2 teaspoons white wine vinegar

2 tablespoons fresh basil leaves, chopped

1 tablespoon fresh chives, coarsely chopped

¼ teaspoon dried tarragon

¼ teaspoon dried thyme

Salt and pepper, to taste

1. In a small bowl, whisk together milk, soynnaise, and vinegar. Stir in basil, chives, tarragon, and thyme.

2. Allow to sit 15 to 30 minutes before serving. Season with salt and pepper, if desired.

Nutrition (per serving): **calories** 43; **fat** 4g (saturated 1g); **protein** 1g; **carbohydrate** 0g; **sodium** 30mg

FRENCH DRESSING

This may not be quite as sweet as you'll find in bottled dressings, but the flavor is bright and fresh, plus so few calories per serving.

Makes 12 Servings (serving size: 2 tablespoons)

½ cup fresh tomatoes, chopped, seeded

1 clove garlic

½ cup green onions, chopped

½ to 1 teaspoon dry mustard

3 tablespoons red wine vinegar

2 teaspoons fresh oregano, minced

¼ teaspoon salt

⅛ teaspoon cayenne pepper

⅛ teaspoon pepper

¾ cup unsweetened tomato juice

1 tablespoon fresh parsley, minced

1. In a blender, puree tomato, garlic, and onion. Add mustard, vinegar, oregano, salt, pepper, and cayenne pepper, and mix well.

2. Add tomato juice slowly and blend thoroughly. Add parsley and mix with a rubber spatula.

3. Transfer to glass bottle with tight-fitting lid and store in refrigerator.

Nutrition (per serving): **calories** 8; **fat** 1g (saturated 0g); **protein** 0g; **carbohydrate** 2g; **sodium** 146mg

LEMON MUSTARD DRESSING

*This recipe is designed to accompany the Spinach Mushroom Salad
(see recipe on page 197).*

Makes 8 Servings (serving size: 2 tablespoons)

¾ cup French Dressing (page 201)
2 tablespoons lemon juice, freshly squeezed
¼ teaspoon dry mustard
½ teaspoon lemon zest, freshly grated

In a lidded jar, combine all ingredients, shake well to mix, and serve
immediately or refrigerate.

Nutrition (per serving): **calories** 19; **fat** 0g (saturated 0g); **protein** 1g; **carbohydrate** 5g;
sodium 146mg

NUT BUTTER DRESSING

A surprise flavor in this mixture and a great way to add interest to your greens.

Makes 2 Servings (serving size: 2 tablespoons)

3 tablespoons water
1½ tablespoons almond butter
1 tablespoon olive oil
1 tablespoon apple cider vinegar
Salt and pepper, to taste

1. Whisk ingredients and drizzle over salad greens garnished with grated soy
   cheese.
2. Serve immediately or transfer to a bottle with a tight-fitting lid and store
   2 to 3 days in refrigerator. Shake before using.

Nutrition (per serving): **calories** 91; **fat** 9g (saturated 1g); **protein** 1g; **carbohydrate** 2g;
sodium 36mg

OIL-FREE DRESSING

*Not only is this recipe oil-free, but it's almost free of calories. The good news
is that it's packed with pleasant flavors for your next salad.*

Makes 8 Servings (serving size: 2 tablespoons)

¾ cup tomato juice
2 tablespoons fresh green bell pepper, seeded and diced

1 teaspoon fresh parsley, chopped

1 thin slice of fresh onion

½ teaspoon paprika

¼ teaspoon pepper

⅛ teaspoon dry (ground) mustard

1. In a blender, puree all ingredients until smooth.
2. Transfer to glass dressing bottle with a tight-fitting lid and store in refrigerator. Shake well before serving.

Nutrition (per serving): **calories** 7; **fat** 0g (saturated 0g); **protein** 0g; **carbohydrate** 1g; **sodium** 42mg

rice and grains

BRIGHT RICE AND GREENS

This recipe includes everything wanted in a nice side dish: great colors, good food value, and great flavors.

Makes 6 Servings (serving size: about 1½ cups)

    2 tablespoons olive oil
    1 small red onion, finely diced (about ½ cup)
    ½ red bell pepper, seeded and finely chopped
    1 jalapeño pepper, seeded and diced
    1½ cups long-grain brown rice
    1 teaspoon salt
    2 teaspoons fresh thyme, minced
    2 cups Basic Vegetable Broth (page 185)
    2 cups frozen peas, thawed
    2 cups (packed) collard, mustard, or turnip greens, chopped
    8 fresh basil leaves (about 2 tablespoons), minced
    Pepper
    2 medium tomatoes, cored and chopped, for serving
    2 green onions, whites and greens, chopped, for serving

1. Heat oil in saucepan over medium heat. Add onion, red pepper, and jalapeño pepper; sauté 5 minutes.
2. Add rice, salt, and thyme and stir until rice is coated. Add broth. Reduce heat to low, cover, and simmer about 10 minutes.
3. Add peas and greens and continue to cook, covered, for 10 minutes, until all liquid is absorbed and peas are tender and rice is fluffy. Remove from heat and stir in basil and pepper.

4. Serve warm topped with tomatoes and green onions.

Nutrition (per serving): **calories** 285; **fat** 6g (saturated 1g); **protein** 8g; **carbohydrate** 50g; **sodium** 408mg

CAJUN RICE AND COLLARD GREENS

The Cajun spice gives this side dish a nice kick of flavor while the rice and collard greens provide lots of vitamins and other nutrients.

Makes 8 Servings (serving size: about 1½ cups)

2 bell peppers of any color (about 2½ cups), seeded and diced

1 medium onion, chopped (about ¾ cup)

1 tablespoon olive oil

1 cup brown rice, uncooked

1 (10-ounce) package frozen collard greens, thawed

1¾ cups Basic Vegetable Broth (page 185)

1 cup water

1 teaspoon Cajun seasoning

¼ teaspoon salt

2 tablespoons white wine vinegar

1. In a large non-stick skillet over medium-high heat, cook peppers and onion in oil, stirring occasionally, for 8 minutes or until softened and browned.

2. Add rice, collard greens, broth, water, Cajun seasoning, and salt. Bring mixture to a boil; reduce heat to medium-low, cover, and cook 20 minutes or until rice and vegetables are tender.

3. Remove from heat; stir in vinegar and serve.

Nutrition (per serving): **calories** 124; **fat** 3g (saturated 0g); **protein** 3g; **carbohydrate** 23g; **sodium** 103mg

FRIED RICE

Adapt this recipe for what you have on hand or in the fridge. It's a great way to use up little bits of ingredients you have available.

Makes 4 Servings (serving size: about 1½ cups)

1½ cups uncooked brown rice

4 tablespoons peanut oil

6 to 8 green onions, whites and greens, coarsely chopped

1 green or red bell pepper, seeded and coarsely chopped

2 carrots, halved and chopped into half-rounds (about 1 – 2 cups)

½ cup green peas, thawed, if frozen

1 tablespoon soy sauce or tamari

Salt and pepper, to taste

1. Cook brown rice in salted boiling water according to package directions. Set aside.

2. Heat oil in a large skillet over medium heat and sauté onion, pepper, carrots, and peas until tender.

3. Add cooked rice and soy sauce or tamari, season if desired, and mix ingredients with a fork.

4. Serve when hot.

Nutrition (per serving): **calories** 434; **fat** 16g (saturated 3g); **protein** 8g; **carbohydrate** 67g; **sodium** 281mg

JASMINE SPICY FRY

Serve this spicy dish along with an Asian salad and you'll have a complementary meal packed with pleasing flavors.

Makes 4 Servings (serving size: 1½ cups)

2 fresh red hot chili peppers, seeded and minced (about ⅓ cup)

3 tablespoons soy sauce or tamari

2 tablespoons peanut oil

1½ tablespoons fresh garlic, minced

1 tablespoon fresh ginger (peeled first), minced

1½ cups jasmine rice, cooked

1½ cups (12 ounces) firm tofu, drained, patted dry, and crumbled

¼ cup pineapple, chopped

¼ cup pea pods

¼ cup green onion, chopped

2 shallots, quartered and thinly sliced, for serving

5 sprigs fresh cilantro, coarsely chopped, for serving

5 sprigs fresh mint, coarsely chopped, for serving

½ cup mung bean sprouts, for serving

1 lime, cut in wedges, for serving garnish

1. In a small bowl, mix chilies and soy sauce or tamari and set aside.

2. In a wok over high heat (or large skillet over medium-high heat), sauté garlic and ginger in oil for a scant few seconds, taking care not to burn the mixture. Reduce heat immediately to medium-high; add jasmine rice and tofu; cook for 1 minute, stirring constantly until rice is thoroughly heated.

3. Add pineapple, pea pods, and green onions, mixing and stir frying until heated through.

4. Place into a pre-warmed serving dish and garnish with scallions, cilantro, mint, and bean sprouts. Serve with chili sauce and lime wedges.

Nutrition (per serving): **calories** 451; **fat** 16g (saturated 2g); **protein** 26g; **carbohydrate** 58g; **sodium** 793mg

RICE DUET WITH MUSHROOMS AND APRICOTS

Filling and flavorful with the mushrooms and apricots, this recipe also works well for leftovers. You might want to double the recipe and serve it another night or pack for lunches.

Makes 4 Servings (serving size: 1½ cups)

   1 tablespoon olive oil
   1 medium onion, chopped (about ¾ cup)
   4 stalks celery, chopped (about 2 cups)
   2 garlic cloves, minced
   ½ cup wild rice, rinsed and drained
   ½ cup brown rice, rinsed and drained
   1 cup (8 ounces) fresh mushrooms, washed clean, dried, and diced
   2 cups Basic Vegetable Broth (page 185)
   1 tablespoon balsamic vinegar
   ¼ cup dried apricots, chopped
   Salt and pepper, to taste

1. Preheat slow cooker on warm.

2. In a skillet over medium heat, add oil and cook onion and celery about 5 minutes or until softened. Add garlic and rice and stir to combine. Mix in mushrooms, and then add broth and vinegar. Increase heat to high and bring mixture to a boil. Remove from heat; transfer to the slow cooker and add apricots.

3. Place two clean, folded kitchen towels (4 layers) over slow cooker top (accumulated moisture interferes with rice consistency and fabric absorbs excess moisture from cooking). Cook for 7 to 8 hours on low or 4 hours on high or until rice is tender and liquid has been absorbed.

Nutrition (per serving): **calories** 231; **fat** 4g (saturated 1g); **protein** 6g; **carbohydrate** 44g; **sodium** 18mg

RICE AND LENTILS WITH THYME

Rice and lentils are packed with protein, and when served together you have an amino-acid-rich dish that's great for your health.

Makes 2 Servings (serving size: 1½ cups)

    2 teaspoons olive oil
    ½ cup cooked carrots, sliced
    ¾ cup onions, chopped
    ¼ cup celery, chopped
    1 teaspoon sage, ground or flakes
    1 teaspoon thyme, ground or flakes
    1 teaspoon garlic cloves, chopped
    1 cup lentils, cooked
    1 cup long-grain brown rice, cooked
    Salt, pepper, soy sauce or tamari, for serving (optional)

1. In a bowl, combine vegetables and herbs and mix until herbs are evenly distributed. In a separate bowl, combine lentils and rice.
2. In a large saucepan or skillet over medium heat, briefly sauté garlic in oil; then add herbed vegetables and cook until the onions are translucent. Add lentil mixture. Cook until uniformly warm and serve.

Nutrition (per serving): **calories** 195; **fat** 5g (saturated 1g); **protein** 10g; **carbohydrate** 30g; **sodium** 27mg

RICE AND BEANS

These companions form a hearty source of vegetarian protein when united at mealtime. This recipe provides a basic component of many flavorful, nutritious main dishes.

Makes 4 Servings (serving size: 1½ cups)

2 cups dried black beans (dried lentils or chickpeas can be substituted)
1 clove garlic, minced
1 medium yellow onion, halved (about ¾ cup)
Salt and pepper
2 to 4 tablespoons olive oil
4 cups cooked brown rice
½ cup parsley, chopped

1. Preheat oven to 350°.

2. Soak beans in cold water overnight. Drain and place in a large saucepan of about 6 to 8 cups of boiling water, with garlic, onion, salt, pepper, and dash of oil. Cover and simmer gently until beans are tender. Remove from heat and drain.

3. In a large lidded casserole dish, mix rice with parsley, and then add bean mixture. Drizzle with remaining oil and transfer to oven for 15 minutes or until warmed through. Serve immediately.

Nutrition (per serving): **calories** 659; **fat** 13g (saturated 2g); **protein** 26g; **carbohydrate** 111g; **sodium** 12mg

CURRIED COUSCOUS

A nice side to go along with roasted vegetables or bean burgers. The curry flavor is a little pungent and the currants or raisins add a bit of sweetness; a nice addition to the little pasta nuggets.

Makes 4 Servings (serving size: about ½ cup)

1 tablespoon olive oil
3 green onions, sliced
½ cinnamon stick
½ teaspoon ground turmeric
½ teaspoon ground cumin
¼ teaspoon ground coriander
⅛ teaspoon ground ginger
⅛ teaspoon ground cloves
⅛ teaspoon cayenne pepper
½ cup dried currants or raisins
1½ cups Basic Vegetable Broth (page 185)
1 cup whole-grain couscous, uncooked
¼ cup flat-leaf parsley or cilantro, chopped, for serving

1. In a saucepan over medium heat, warm the oil and add scallions; cook a few minutes until lightly browned. Add cinnamon stick and all other seasonings and cook, stirring, for 1 to 2 minutes to toast spices and coat the scallions.

2. Add currants and stir to coat; add broth, increase heat to high, and cook until mixture begins to boil. Remove from heat, add couscous, stir well to mix ingredients, cover, and let stand for 5 minutes.

3. Fluff with a fork, remove cinnamon stick, and add parsley or cilantro, stirring to combine with other ingredients.

Nutrition (per serving): **calories** 268; **fat** 4g (saturated 1g); **protein** 7g; **carbohydrate** 52g; **sodium** 11mg

COUSCOUS CON DIOS

A simple variation for your couscous dish, and a great canvas for adding your favorite fresh, frozen, or canned vegetables.

Makes 4 Servings (serving size: about ½ cup)

½ teaspoon peanut oil
¼ cup green onions, sliced
¼ cup water
½ cup Basic Vegetable Broth (page 185)
½ cup couscous, uncooked
2 teaspoons soy sauce
⅓ cup fresh tomato, peeled, seeded, and chopped
1 tablespoon fresh parsley, chopped
¼ to ½ teaspoon pepper

1. In a saucepan over medium-high heat, heat oil and add onions, and reduce heat to simmer; sauté onions until tender. Increase heat to high, add water and broth, and bring to a boil; remove from heat.

2. Add couscous and soy sauce; cover and let stand about 5 minutes. Add tomato and parsley and toss with a fork until well mixed.

3. Season with pepper, if desired, and serve hot.

Nutrition (per serving): **calories** 104; **fat** 1g (saturated 0g); **protein** 4g; **carbohydrate** 21g; **sodium** 177mg

HERBED CRUMBS

This flavorful mixture is suitable for recipes calling for bread crumbs or as a simple garnish for soups, steamed vegetables, and green salads.

Makes 1 cup

⅓ cup fresh herbs, such as thyme, oregano, basil, garlic, shallots, chives, parsley, and dill

1 cup unleavened whole-wheat bread, crackers, or tortilla crumbs

1. Place broken pieces of bread, crackers, or tortillas into a blender; add fresh herbs, garlic, and shallots.
2. Process until crumbly and herbs are evenly distributed.
3. Store small portions in sealed containers in the freezer. Thaw to room temperature before use.

Nutrition (per serving): **calories** 91; **fat** 1g (saturated 0g); **protein** 3g; **carbohydrate** 18g; **sodium** 325mg

PORRIDGE POT

A nice side dish with whole-grain goodness. Consider adding other ingredients as you plan your meal, including seeds, nuts, or vegetables.

Makes 6 Servings (serving size: 1 cup)

½ cup cracked wheat
1½ cups steel-cut oats
½ cup rye flakes
½ cup brown rice
¼ cup wheat germ
6½ cups liquid in any combination of plant-based milks or water
½ cup raisins
½ cup dates, chopped
1½ tablespoons vanilla
Pinch ground nutmeg

In a 3-quart or larger slow cooker, combine and stir all ingredients. Select lowest heat setting and longest time setting; let cook overnight and serve hot the following morning.

Nutrition (per serving): **calories** 400; **fat** 5g (saturated 1g); **protein** 13g; **carbohydrate** 80g; **sodium** 106mg

PRISTINE QUINOA

This recipe yields 4 cups of finished grain, actually a seed, that gives both a satisfying source of vegetable protein and a delicious, slightly nutlike flavor. Quinoa is tasty served either hot or cold.

Makes 3 Servings (serving size: about ½ cup)

> 1 cup quinoa
> Pinch salt
> 1 teaspoon olive oil
> 2 cups water or Basic Vegetable Broth (page 185)

1. In a medium-size saucepan over high heat, bring water, salt, and oil to a boil. Add quinoa and stir until water returns to a hard boil. Reduce heat to low, cover, and cook for about 15 minutes or until liquid is absorbed and most of the quinoa has begun showing a circle-shaped halo.

2. Remove from heat and fluff with a fork. Cover and let stand 5 minutes. Serve plain or refrigerate for future use.

Nutrition (per serving): **calories** 225; **fat** 5g (saturated 1g); **protein** 7g; **carbohydrate** 39g; **sodium** 12mg

QUINOA PILAF

This recipe enhances the naturally nutlike flavor of quinoa. The addition of ground cardamom, if desired, creates a sweet-flavored spicy effect that goes well with salad side dishes.

Makes 6 Servings (serving size: about ½ cup)

> 2 tablespoons olive oil
> ½ medium onion, diced (about ⅓ cup)
> 3 garlic cloves, minced
> 1 carrot, finely chopped (about ½ cup)
> 1 cup quinoa
> ½ teaspoon pepper
> 1 teaspoon ground cardamom (optional)
> ½ teaspoon ground sage
> 2 cups Basic Vegetable Broth (page 185)
> 1 teaspoon salt
> ¼ cup raisins
> ¼ cup pine nuts, almonds, or pecans, lightly toasted, if desired

1. Heat oil in a saucepan over medium-high and add onions. Cook, stirring, until barely browned, about 3 minutes. Reduce heat to medium, add garlic and carrots, and cook, stirring, for 1 to 2 minutes.
2. Add quinoa, pepper, cardamom, and sage and cook, stirring constantly, for 2 to 3 minutes to coat and toast the quinoa.
3. Add broth and salt and bring mixture to a boil. Reduce heat to low, cover, and simmer 15 minutes or until all liquid is absorbed and the quinoa is tender.
4. Add raisins and stir gently. Cover and let stand for 2 to 3 minutes.
5. Add nuts, fluff with a fork, and serve warm.

Nutrition (per serving): **calories** 210; **fat** 10g (saturated 1g); **protein** 6g; **carbohydrate** 28g; **sodium** 398mg

side dishes

ASPARAGUS Á LA CARTE

Asparagus is a tasty green vegetable to add to your dinner menu as a nutritious and attractive complement. Do not overcook to retain the bright green color and pleasant texture.

Makes 4 Servings (serving size: 5 spears)

    20 fresh asparagus spears, tough ends trimmed and cut into equal lengths
    1 teaspoon olive oil
    ½ teaspoon sesame oil
    Dash of soy sauce or tamari
    Pepper, to taste
    Toasted sesame seeds, for garnish
    Lemon or lime wedges, for garnish

1. Combine oils in a skillet over medium heat until hot; add asparagus, soy sauce or tamari, and pepper. Adjust heat to high, cover, and cook for about 4 minutes, constantly swirling and shaking skillet. Do not overcook.

2. When asparagus is tender, immediately remove from heat, sprinkle with sesame seeds, and serve with lemon or lime wedges. Can also be served cold or at room temperature.

Nutrition (per serving): **calories** 30; **fat** 2g (saturated 0g); **protein** 2g; **carbohydrate** 3g; **sodium** 1mg

BREADED CAULIFLOWER SPRIGS

This crunchy dish doubles as a healthy snack or lunch bag item. Broccoli florets also work for this recipe.

Makes 4 Servings (serving size: 1½ cups)

1 cup brown-rice flour
¾ cup soy or rice milk
Salt and pepper
1 cauliflower, broken into florets
2 teaspoons caraway seeds
Juice of ½ lemon (about 1 tablespoon)
1 to 3 tablespoons olive oil

1. To prepare batter, sieve flour into a mixing bowl. Stirring continuously, gradually add milk until a smooth batter forms. Add a dash each of salt and pepper. Let stand for 30 minutes before using.

2. Prepare a large saucepan of boiling, salted water. Add cauliflower, caraway seeds, and lemon juice and cook until barely tender; drain and cool.

3. Dip cauliflower in batter and stir fry in well-oiled skillet over medium heat until golden brown. Place on paper-towel-covered baking sheet in warm (200°) oven to retain heat until serving.

Nutrition (per serving): **calories** 235; **fat** 9g (saturated 1g); **protein** 5g; **carbohydrate** 35g; **sodium** 27mg

BROCCOLI WITH PINE NUTS

This side dish will bring color to your dinner table and liven up any meal. You can leave out the pine nuts, if you like. However, they add a pleasant flavor and texture to the dish.

Makes 4 Servings (serving size: 1 cup)

4 cups fresh broccoli, floret and stem, coarsely chopped
1½ tablespoons olive oil
Juice of ½ lemon (about 1 tablespoon)
⅓ cup pine nuts, lightly toasted

1. In a vegetable steamer, cook broccoli until barely tender when pierced with a fork.

2. In a dry skillet over medium heat, toast pine nuts, stirring constantly, until slightly browned. Remove to small bowl and set aside. Heat oil and lemon juice in the skillet over medium heat, add broccoli, and sauté for 3 minutes. Stir in pine nuts, reduce heat to low, and continue cooking for 2 minutes.

3. Serve warm.

Nutrition (per serving): **calories** 133; **fat** 12g (saturated 2g); **protein** 5g; **carbohydrate** 7g; **sodium** 24mg

CARROTS JULIENNE

There are countless ways to prepare carrots, but this variation will become a favorite as you enjoy the kick of ginger and herbs.

Makes 4 Servings (serving size: 1 cup)

4 cups fresh carrots, peeled and sliced julienne

¼ cup water or Basic Vegetable Broth (page 185)

½ cup soynnaise (see Homemade Vegan Mayonnaise, page 198)

2 tablespoons onion, finely minced

1 tablespoon fresh ginger (peeled first), grated

Salt and pepper, to taste

¼ cup Herbed Crumbs (page 211; add the nutritional information for Herbed Crumbs to the totals provided)

1½ tablespoons olive oil

¼ cup fresh parsley, chopped

Paprika, for garnish

1. Preheat oven to 375°.

2. In a covered saucepan over medium heat, steam carrots until barely tender, about 3 minutes. Reserve ¼ cup carrot-cooking liquid. Arrange carrots in an 8-inch oiled baking dish and set aside.

3. In a small bowl, mix reserved carrot liquid with soynnaise, onion, and ginger, and salt and pepper, to taste; pour over carrots.

4. In a separate bowl, mix Herbed Crumbs, olive oil, and parsley. Spread evenly over carrots, garnish with paprika, and bake, uncovered, for 10 to 15 minutes or until top is lightly toasted. Serve hot.

Nutrition (per serving): **calories** 296; **fat** 27g (saturated 4g); **protein** 1g; **carbohydrate** 12g; **sodium** 191mg

COLESLAW MOMENT OF TRUTH

We've added this recipe in the "side dish" section because it's so versatile with vegan entrees.

Makes 12 Servings (serving size: about 1 cup)

1 small cabbage, trimmed and shredded
1½ cups corn kernels, thawed, if frozen
1 cup red onion, diced
1 cup carrot, shredded
1 cup red bell pepper, diced
½ cup white vinegar
2½ tablespoons olive oil
2 tablespoons water
1 teaspoon salt
1 teaspoon celery seeds
¼ teaspoon mustard seeds
¼ teaspoon white pepper
Dash of hot sauce

1. In a large bowl, add and toss cabbage, corn, onion, carrot, and bell pepper; set aside.
2. In a large saucepan over medium-high heat, combine vinegar, oil, water, salt, celery seeds, mustard seeds, white pepper, and a dash of hot sauce, stirring frequently. Bring to a boil and remove from heat. Pour over cabbage mixture; gently toss until all ingredients are coated with saucepan dressing. Cover.
3. Transfer to refrigerator and chill for 2 hours or more. Gently toss before serving.

Nutrition (per serving): **calories** 62; **fat** 3g (saturated 0g); **protein** 1g; **carbohydrate** 9g; **sodium** 206mg

GINGERY GREEN BEANS

Add some tang to fresh green beans with just a simple grating of fresh ginger. It sends a simple vegetable to a place of delight for all who enjoy them.

Makes 4 Servings (serving size: about 1 cup)

1 tablespoon olive oil
1 small onion, very thinly sliced (about ½ cup)

2 teaspoons fresh ginger (peeled first), grated
2 tablespoons fresh fennel, minced
Salt, to taste
1 pound fresh green beans, trimmed and whole
¼ cup Basic Vegetable Broth (page 185)

1. Heat olive oil in a large skillet over medium heat. Add onion, ginger, fennel, and salt. Sauté 8 to 10 minutes or until onions are translucent.

2. Add beans and broth, cover, and cook until beans are tender.

Nutrition (per serving): **calories** 84; **fat** 4g (saturated 1g); **protein** 3g; **carbohydrate** 12g; **sodium** 6mg

HERBED TOMATOES

Another way to take the "plain" out of vegetables, this recipe adds fresh herbs that please the eye and the palette.

Makes 6 Servings

6 tomatoes, large and firm
4 tablespoons fresh basil, minced
1 cup fresh parsley, minced
2 green onions, chopped
3 garlic cloves, minced
1 teaspoon fresh thyme, minced
Salt, to taste
Freshly ground pepper, to taste
¾ cup Herbed Crumbs (page 211; add the nutritional information
    for Herbed Crumbs to the totals provided)
1 tablespoon olive oil
Lemon wedges, for garnish

1. Preheat oven to 350°.

2. Trim stems and tomato eyes. Scoop out pulp and place in a sieve over a bowl to drain juice (reserve juice for another use).

3. Combine tomato pulp with basil, parsley, onion, garlic, and thyme. Add salt and pepper, to taste, and add Herbed Crumbs. Moisten the mixture with oil, stirring well. Spoon filling into the tomatoes.

4. Bake upright in an oiled, covered casserole dish for 15 minutes and then

uncover and bake at 400° for 5 minutes more to firm and brown the tomatoes. Serve hot with lemon wedges.

Nutrition (per serving): **calories** 55; **fat** 3g (saturated 0g); **protein** 2g; **carbohydrate** 8g; **sodium** 18mg

GINGER SPINACH

Enjoy the Asian influence of this dish of dark-green nutritional goodness. Adding sliced water chestnuts makes for an extra color and texture contrast.

Makes 4 Servings (serving size: ½ cup)

4 cups fresh spinach, coarsely chopped
1 tablespoon sesame oil
1 garlic clove, minced
¼ teaspoon fresh ginger (peeled first), grated
1 tablespoon soy sauce or tamari
1 (8-ounce) can sliced water chestnuts, drained
1 tablespoon water

1. Wash spinach thoroughly and set aside in colander to drain.
2. Heat oil in a large skillet over medium heat; add garlic and ginger and cook until lightly brown. Add spinach, soy sauce or tamari, and water. Cover and steam 1 to 3 minutes; stir once or twice. Remove lid, increase heat to high and cook until all liquid has evaporated.
3. Serve immediately.

Nutrition (per serving): **calories** 77; **fat** 4g (saturated 1g); **protein** 2g; **carbohydrate** 10g; **sodium** 306mg

PIE OF THE SHEPHERD

A little twist on the traditional shepherd's pie, this recipe adds vegetable protein in the soy cheese and the added peas. Nice color and texture will make this recipe a favorite for your dinner table.

Makes 6 Servings (serving size: 1½ cups)

1½ cups frozen peas, thawed
1½ cups carrot, diced
1 medium onion, chopped (about ¾ cup)

1 cup green bell pepper, chopped

2 teaspoons dried thyme

2 teaspoons paprika, plus more for garnish

Olive oil, for oiling casserole dish

4 cups frozen hash browns, thawed

Water, for cooking hash browns

⅔ cup soy cheese, grated

¼ teaspoon salt

2 cups dried black-eye peas, cooked and drained

1 (14.5-ounce) can diced tomatoes, drained

1 (8-ounce) can salt-free tomato sauce

2 teaspoons soy sauce

1. Preheat oven to 400°.

2. In a bowl, add and thoroughly stir peas, carrot, onion, bell pepper, thyme, and paprika. Transfer to well-oiled casserole dish (2½ quarts or larger) and bake, uncovered, for 10 minutes. Stir mixture and bake for 10 minutes more. Remove from oven and add black-eyed peas, diced and drained tomatoes, and soy sauce. Stir well and set aside. Reduce oven setting to 350°.

3. In a saucepan of boiling water, cook hash browns until tender according to package instructions. Remove from heat, drain, and mash until smooth. Add cheese and salt and mix well.

4. Using a large spoon and rubber spatula, place and form hash brown mixture into a border around edges of vegetable mixture; place a scoop of hash browns in the center of vegetables. Sprinkle extra paprika on hash brown border and centerpiece. Return to oven and bake, uncovered, for 20 minutes.

Nutrition (per serving): **calories** 264; **fat** 2g (saturated 0g); **protein** 1g; **carbohydrate** 50g; **sodium** 904mg

POTATO CRISPS

Hot or cold, these potatoes add crunch and a nice side for soups, salads, vegetable hot dishes, and health-friendly dips and sauces.

Makes 4 Servings (serving size: 3–4 crisps)

1½ pounds small yellow potatoes, non-baking variety

3 tablespoons olive oil
Salt

1. Preheat oven to 450°.

2. In a large pot, bring potatoes to a boil in salted water; reduce heat and simmer until barely tender when pierced, about 15 minutes.

3. Drain and transfer to a baking sheet. Let cool 5 minutes, and then lightly crush each potato with the heel of your hand or the bottom of a drinking glass.

4. Drizzle with olive oil and season with salt. Place in preheated oven and roast until golden brown and crisp, about 35 minutes, turning once so both sides brown.

5. Serve hot as a healthy replacement for french fries!

Nutrition (per serving): **calories** 224; **fat** 10g (saturated 1g); **protein** 4g; **carbohydrate** 31g; **sodium** 10mg

ROASTED BEETS

The mild sweetness of beets offers a pleasant flavor for your meal, plus the pretty vegetable adds a nice complement to your dinner table.

Makes 6 Servings (serving size: ¾ cup)

6 to 8 medium yellow or red beets, trimmed and scrubbed
Olive oil
4 garlic cloves, minced
⅛ to ¼ cup Italian parsley, finely chopped, for garnish

1. Preheat oven to 350°. Line a rimmed baking sheet with parchment paper.

2. Arrange beets on baking sheet, drizzle with oil, and sprinkle with garlic. Cover with aluminum foil and tightly seal all edges. Place in oven for 1 hour.

3. Remove baking sheet and reduce oven heat to warm. Uncover beets and let cool until skins can be easily removed.

4. Quarter the beets, place in serving dish, and sprinkle with parsley; return to oven until warm enough to serve. Serve warm.

Nutrition (per serving): **calories** 43; **fat** 0g (saturated 0g); **protein** 2g; **carbohydrate** 10g; **sodium** 72mg

STUFFED MUSHROOMS

This dish is nicely complemented by a dressed green salad and freshly sliced tomatoes.

Makes 4 Servings

8 large (2½-inch-diameter) white mushrooms, stemmed

2 tablespoons olive oil, divided

1 medium onion, peeled and minced (about ¾ cup)

1 large celery stalk, peeled and minced (about ½ cup)

1 large lemon, completely zested and juiced (about 2 tablespoons)

1¼ cups Herbed Crumbs (page 211; add the nutritional information for Herbed Crumbs to the totals provided)

2 tablespoons parsley, stemmed and finely chopped

1 teaspoon minced fresh thyme leaves

2 garlic cloves, minced

1 cup grated soy cheese

Salt and pepper, to taste

Lemon wedges, for serving

1. Preheat oven to 350°.

2. Remove stems from mushroom and set caps aside. Mince the stems and set aside in a small bowl.

3. Heat 1 tablespoon oil in a deep skillet over medium heat; add onion, celery, and mushroom stems; lightly season with salt and pepper; stir fry until mixture begins to brown, about 3 to 5 minutes. Transfer mixture to a bowl and add lemon zest, crumbs, parsley, thyme, and garlic. Mix and toss thoroughly with a fork without compacting ingredients; set aside.

4. On stovetop in an oven-safe casserole dish, heat 1 tablespoon oil over medium heat. With open sides down, place mushroom caps in a single snug layer. Allow mushrooms to gently sizzle for 1 to 2 minutes, turn, and cook for 1 to 2 minutes.

5. Remove from heat and sprinkle with lemon juice. Fill mushrooms with stuffing mixture without patting down. Transfer casserole dish to oven and bake 25 to 30 minutes, reducing heat to 300° to 325° if stuffing begins to brown too much. Test tenderness with a skewer stick or small knife. Add cheese garnish during last 5 to 7 minutes of baking.

6. Remove from oven when the mushrooms are tender. Serve immediately with lemon wedges.

Nutrition (per serving): **calories** 88; **fat** 7g (saturated 1g); **protein** 1g; **carbohydrate** 7g; **sodium** 12mg

VEGGIE-STUFFED TOMATOES

Mix and match familiar beet, collard, and spinach greens with exotic arugula, sorrel, radicchio, and cress flavors. Leftover stuffed tomatoes in soup or stew are tasty and healthful additions.

Makes 4 Servings (serving size: 1 stuffed tomato)

4 garlic cloves, minced

1 medium onion (about ¾ cup), chopped

2 tablespoons olive oil

3 cups greens, trimmed and spines removed, finely chopped

4 large tomatoes, whole and firm

⅛ teaspoon pepper

1 tablespoon red wine vinegar

1 cup Herbed Crumbs (page 211; add the nutritional information for Herbed Crumbs to the totals provided)

½ cup walnuts, coarsely chopped

3 tablespoons fresh parsley, stemmed and finely chopped, for garnish

1. Preheat oven to 325°.

2. In a large skillet over medium heat, sauté garlic and onions in oil until tender. Add greens, stir, and remove from heat.

3. Hollow out the tomatoes by removing seeds, pulp, and juice with a spoon. Add the pulp, pepper, and vinegar to the skillet mixture. Return to heat and simmer until tomato juice evaporates. Remove from heat and stir in Herbed Crumbs and nuts. Fill tomatoes with warm stuffing and place in an oiled 8-by-8-inch baking pan and bake for 15 to 20 minutes. Garnish with parsley and serve.

Nutrition (per serving): **calories** 213; **fat** 16g (saturated 2g); **protein** 6g; **carbohydrate** 15g; **sodium** 31mg

gravies, sauces, and dips

MUSHROOM GRAVY

Full of flavor, our mushroom gravy goes well with bean burgers, rice, or other grains. It's also a nice way to dress up steamed vegetables.

Makes 4 Servings (serving size: ½ cup)

½ cup olive oil
6 garlic cloves, minced
½ yellow onion (about ¾ cup), finely chopped
6 fresh button mushrooms, stems and caps coarsely chopped
½ cup brown-rice flour
4 tablespoons soy sauce
2 cups Basic Vegetable Broth (page 185), room temperature
½ teaspoon ground sage
¼ teaspoon pepper
½ teaspoon salt

1. Heat oil in a skillet over medium heat; add garlic and onion, and sauté 3 to 5 minutes until onion is tender and begins to brown. Reduce heat to low and add mushrooms.

2. Cook until mushrooms begin to release juice. Sprinkle flour across surface, slowly add soy sauce, and stir constantly with a fork or whisk. Add broth gradually and stir constantly as gravy thickens.

3. Add seasonings, remove from heat, cover, and let stand for 5 to 10 minutes while flavors blend. Taste test and correct consistency by adding broth or flour, just a bit at a time.

4. If needed, return to heat and serve warm.

Nutrition (per serving): **calories** 338; **fat** 28g (saturated 4g); **protein** 3g; **carbohydrate** 21g; **sodium** 1,323mg

BASIL-ALMOND PESTO

A great spread for flat bread and tortillas, mixed with pasta or vinaigrette, and as salad dressing or hot-dish topping.

Makes 6 Servings (serving size: ¼ cup)

½ cup parsley leaves, packed
½ cup basil leaves, packed
½ cup toasted whole almonds
2 garlic cloves, skin removed
½ cup almond or olive oil
½ cup (4 ounces) firm tofu, cubed
Salt and pepper, to taste

1. Place parsley, basil, almonds, and garlic in food processor; pulse until finely chopped.
2. Gradually mix in oil and tofu and process until puréed. Add salt and pepper, if desired.

Nutrition (per serving): **calories** 265; **fat** 25g (saturated 3g); **protein** 6g; **carbohydrate** 4g; **sodium** 30mg

SALSA SAUCE

So easy to prepare and so versatile to use as a spread over sliced tomatoes or as a garnish for entrées.

Makes 16 Servings (serving size: ¼ cup)

1½ cups fresh tomatillos, husked, rinsed, and coarsely chopped
1½ cups fresh tomatoes, firm, ripe, cored, and coarsely chopped
¾ cup onion, coarsely chopped
½ cup fresh cilantro, finely chopped
3 tablespoons fresh lime juice
2 teaspoons garlic cloves, minced
1½ to 2 tablespoons fresh jalapeño peppers, seeded and coarsely chopped
Salt, to taste (optional)

1. Mix tomatillos and tomatoes in a bowl. Add onion, cilantro, lime juice, garlic, jalapeños, and salt.

2. Can be prepared up to 2 hours before serving. If so, place in refrigerator, covered.

Nutrition (per serving): **calories** 9; **fat** 0g (saturated 0g); **protein** 0g; **carbohydrate** 2g; **sodium** 2mg

SPICY TOMATO SAUCE

The surprise "spice" in this sauce comes from the ginger root, cloves, cardamom, caraway, cinnamon, and peppers. Great over pasta, rice, quinoa, or bean burgers.

Makes 6 Servings (serving size: about ⅓ cup)

    1 tablespoon olive oil
    2 medium onions (about 1½ cups), coarsely chopped
    2 garlic cloves, minced
    1 teaspoon fresh ginger (peeled first), grated
    1 to 2 chili peppers (any variety), seeded and coarsely chopped
    6 whole cloves
    4 pods green or white cardamom
    1 cinnamon stick, 2-inch piece
    1 teaspoon caraway seed
    1 teaspoon salt (optional)
    ½ teaspoon black peppercorns, cracked (optional)
    1 (28-ounce) can tomatoes, including juice

1. If your model requires it, preheat slow cooker on high for 15 to 20 minutes.

2. In a large skillet, heat oil over medium heat, add onion, and stir until softened. Add garlic, ginger, chili pepper, cloves, cardamom, cinnamon, caraway, salt, and pepper. Cook for 1 to 2 minutes, stirring occasionally. Add tomatoes with juice and bring to a boil.

3. Transfer sauce to the slow cooker, cover, and cook on high for 4 to 5 hours or on low for 8 to 10 hours.

4. Serve over your choice of grain, pasta, or cooked vegetables.

Nutrition (per serving): **calories** 93; **fat** 3g (saturated 1g); **protein** 2g; **carbohydrate** 17g; **sodium** 295mg

GUACAMOLE

A favorite with chips, but you can also use guacamole as a dip with raw vegetables or as a garnish. It's also a nice spread on flat bread with refried beans and salsa.

Makes 4 Servings (serving size: ½ cup)

2 ripe avocados, halved, seeded, and peeled

1 lime, grated zest and juice

1 garlic clove, minced

½ to 1 teaspoon chili powder

¼ teaspoon salt

A few sprigs Italian parsley, stemmed and leaf segments cut apart

1. In a bowl, mash avocado flesh with a fork into small chunks. Add lime zest and juice, garlic, chili powder, and salt, and mix until creamy and chunky.

2. Top with parsley and serve. Or refrigerate, tightly covered, for no more than 2 hours before serving.

Nutrition (per serving): **calories** 178; **fat** 14g (saturated 3g); **protein** 3g; **carbohydrate** 16g; **sodium** 160mg

HUMMUS

Making hummus is so easy and costs a fraction of what you find in the grocery cooler trays. The other great benefit to homemade hummus is that it's free of preservatives. Use this recipe for your base and then experiment with lemon zest, olives, extra garlic, sundried tomatoes, or herbs.

Makes 6 Servings (serving size: ¼ cup)

1 (15-ounce) can chickpeas, drained and rinsed

1 garlic clove, peeled

2 tablespoons lemon juice

¼ cup tahini (sesame paste)

1. Combine all ingredients in a blender and pulse until smooth and creamy.

2. Serve as a spread or a dip with chips.

Nutrition (per serving): **calories** 143; **fat** 6g (saturated 1g); **protein** 5g; **carbohydrate** 19g; **sodium** 224mg

SPINACH DIP

A great dip for raw vegetables sliced and cut to your liking. Packed with flavor and lower in calories than typical spinach dip.

Makes 6 Servings (serving size: ½ cup)

2 cups fresh spinach, washed, drained, and coarsely chopped

1 cup soy cheese, grated

1½ cups (12 ounces) canned artichoke hearts, drained and finely chopped

½ cup Salsa Sauce (page 225)

¼ cup water

1 garlic clove, minced

Salt and pepper, to taste

1. If desired cold and smooth, combine ingredients in a blender and pulse until smooth. Add extra milk, 1 tablespoon at a time, to achieve desired consistency. Transfer to serving bowl.

2. If preferred warm and chunky, combine ingredients in a slow cooker, cover, and cook for 2 hours on high heat until bubbling hot.

3. Transfer to a bowl and serve.

Nutrition (per serving): **calories** 86; **fat** 2g (saturated 0g); **protein** 2g; **carbohydrate** 10g; **sodium** 395mg

desserts and snacks

BERRY CRUMBLE

Dark red, blue, and purple berries are rich in antioxidants, lovely to look at, and loaded with flavor. Add the crumble to provide protein and you have a wonderful and nutritious dessert.

Makes 6 Servings (serving size: about ½ cup)

5 cups berries (blackberries, blueberries, strawberries), lightly rinsed and drained

2 tablespoons brown-rice flour

1 cup old-fashioned rolled oats, not instant

1 cup whole-wheat flour

½ cup sunflower or olive oil

1. Preheat oven to 350°.

2. Place berries in 8-by-8-inch baking dish to within 1 inch of rim. Gently stir in rice flour; set aside.

3. In a bowl, mix oats, wheat flour, and oil until crumbly. Spoon onto berries and pat into an even crust. Bake (uncovered) for 30 to 35 minutes, until berry juice bubbles at topping edges. Serve hot in individual serving bowls.

Nutrition (per serving): **calories** 408; **fat** 21g (saturated 3g); **protein** 8g; **carbohydrate** 51g; **sodium** 9mg

GLAZED APPLES

This is a simple and tasty dessert you can enjoy all year. Select a variety of apple that is naturally sweet, such as Fuji, Gala, or Honeycrisp. This is a versatile recipe, so add different spices, or make with pears, peaches, or other fruit.

Makes 4 Servings (serving size: about ¾ cup)

½ cup apple juice
1 tablespoon fresh lemon juice
¼ teaspoon ground cinnamon
1 to 2 tablespoons olive oil
4 apples, peeled, cored, and cut into ½-inch-thick rings

1. In a small bowl, whisk together apple juice, lemon juice, and cinnamon.
2. In a large skillet, heat oil over medium heat, add apples, and cook until golden, about 2 minutes each side.
3. Drizzle juice mixture on apples, cover, and cook for about 5 minutes until apple rings are glazed and tender.
4. Serve warm.

Nutrition (per serving): **calories** 76; **fat** 7g (saturated 1g); **protein** 0g; **carbohydrate** 4g; **sodium** 1mg

Variation: You can also make the crumble from the Berry Crumble recipe (page 229). Spoon the glazed apples into a small baking dish, sprinkle the crumble over the apples, and bake for about 20 minutes in a 350° preheated oven.

ROASTED PINEAPPLE

You will enjoy this easy-to-prepare dessert, which can be made with food items from your pantry. I like keeping this as a backup when I have unexpected guests and want to serve a quick and easy dessert.

Makes 6 Servings (serving size: about ½ cup)

1 fresh pineapple, whole (or canned unsweetened rounds, drained)
Vanilla bean powder, for garnish (optional)
Coconut, flaked, shredded, or freshly grated, for garnish (optional)

1. Preheat oven to 375°.
2. To prepare fresh pineapple, peel, cut lengthwise into eighths, and core. If using canned pineapple rounds, drain in a colander over a bowl; reserve juice for another use.

3. Place fruit on a rimmed baking sheet and roast for 30 minutes.

4. Remove and cool slightly. Serve warm on dessert plates and garnish with vanilla bean powder and coconut.

Nutrition (per serving): **calories** 32; **fat** 0g (saturated 0g); **protein** 0g; **carbohydrate** 8g; **sodium** 1mg

FAUX BANANA ICE CREAM

Once you try this amazing dairy-free treat, you'll never throw another over-ripe banana away! So good tasting and so good for you. Plus, you can top with berries and/or nuts and make the dessert even more delightful.

Makes 4 Servings (serving size: about ⅓ cup)

4 medium over-ripe bananas
Sliced berries, chopped nuts (optional)
Natural peanut butter (optional)

1. Slice the bananas and place on a cookie sheet lined with waxed paper; place in freezer long enough to freeze (30 to 60 minutes).

2. Transfer the frozen bananas into a blender or food processor; blend until creamy, frequently scraping down the sides.

3. You can serve now as a custard consistency, or transfer to a bowl, cover, and return to the freezer for 60 minutes and serve as a more typical ice cream consistency.

4. Top with sliced fresh berries and nuts if desired.

Nutrition (per serving): **calories** 105; **fat** 1g (saturated 0g); **protein** 1g; **carbohydrate** 27g; **sodium** 1mg

BAKED BANANAS

Another easy way to prepare dessert packed with potassium and other trace minerals that are good for your health.

Makes 1 Serving (serving size: 1 banana)

Firm ripe bananas; uniformly yellow (no green or dark spots on skin)

1. Preheat oven to 400°.

2. Place one or more bananas in a casserole dish. Cut skin tip to tip along top of fruit. Position an aluminum foil tent over the fruit and place in preheated oven. Immediately reduce heat to 300°.

3. Bake for 10 minutes or until juices begin to flow. Use spatulas to transfer
   fruit to plate, and then use forks to part skin. Spoon excess juice on fruit.
   Serve warm.

   Nutrition (per serving): **calories** 105; **fat** 0g (saturated 0g); **protein** 1g; **carbohydrate** 26g;
   sodium 1mg

Variation: You can also sprinkle the cooked banana with cinnamon or dab
with peanut butter for a little extra flavor.

APPLE CRISPS

*For a chewy or crispy snack, keep these healthy treats on hand. They're also great
for school or work snacks or even in the car as a quick and satisfying bite.*

Makes 4 Servings (serving size: ½ cup)

   3 large apples, sweet variety, stemmed and cut into ¼ inch thick strips
   Cinnamon (optional)

1. Preheat oven to 275°.
2. Place apple strips in a single layer without overlapping on two large
   baking sheets lined with parchment paper (or use stick-free or lightly
   oiled baking sheets).
3. Bake 2 hours or until apples are dry and crisp. For chewier crisps,
   remove from oven at 1½ hours.
4. Using a spatula, transfer crisps to wire rack to cool.

   Nutrition (per serving): **calories** 95; **fat** 0g (saturated 0g); **protein** 1g; **carbohydrate** 23g;
   sodium 1mg

KALE CHIPS

*Kale chips are a low-fat and satisfying alternative to potato chips. They're crunchy,
are sure to stir conversations at a party, and are a healthy way to crunch.*

Makes 2 Servings (serving size: ½ cup)

   1 bunch fresh kale (approximately 5 ounces)
   1 to 2 tablespoons olive oil
   Salt, for seasoning (omit, if using cayenne pepper to season)
   Cayenne pepper, for seasoning (omit, if using salt to season)

1. Preheat oven to 375°.
2. Wash and fully dry kale leaves. Remove stems and central veins.

3. In a bowl, tear leaves into 2- to 4-inch pieces; drizzle with olive oil and toss to assure kale is evenly coated.

4. Using tongs, arrange kale on a large baking sheet in a single layer. Sprinkle with salt or cayenne pepper and bake 10 minutes or until chips are crisp but not brittle. Remove and serve or let cool.

Nutrition (per serving): **calories** 170; **fat** 14g (saturated 2g); **protein** 3g; **carbohydrate** 10g; **sodium** 44mg

ROASTED CHICKPEAS

It's easy to prepare these nutritious legumes. Munch them for an energy boost between meals or use to garnish salads, soups, and hot dishes for a contrasting and tasty crunch. Use cayenne pepper for spicy heat or garlic salt for tangy zest. This is a nutritional superstar—high in protein and fiber.

Makes 8 Servings (serving size: ½ cup)

4 cups chickpeas, home cooked or canned (rinse first if canned)

3 tablespoons olive oil

seasoning as desired (ground coriander, ground cumin, garlic salt, chili powder, paprika, etc; add more seasoning if desired—hot sauce, such as Tabasco, works great, as does dry steak seasoning)

salt for seasoning as desired

1. Preheat oven to 375°.

2. On a paper-towel-lined rimmed baking sheet, scatter peas and let stand for about 15 minutes to allow ample draining. Once water is drained, transfer peas to a container or bowl. Add olive oil to coat peas. Then add seasoning mix.

3. Place seasoned peas on an aluminum-foil-lined rimmed baking sheet. Spread thoroughly on sheet.

4. Place peas in oven and roast about 30 minutes, stirring occasionally.

5. Remove from oven and allow to cool. Or for extra crispy peas, return to oven for an additional 5 to 10 minutes (possibly using the broiler) until peas are crisp and golden. Transfer to a bowl and mix with additional spices or salt to taste.

6. Serve. Store in airtight container.

Nutrition (per serving): **calories** 170; **fat** 6g (saturated 1g); **protein** 7g; **carbohydrate** 22g; **sodium** 500mg (or less if you decide to use less salt)

FRUITY PROTEIN SMOOTHIE

Viewed as a meal-replacement shake. See the following shakes and those in chapter 13.

Makes 1 Serving (serving size: about 1½ cups)

    1 cup almond, rice, soy, or oat milk
    1 large banana, sliced
    ½ cup cooked oatmeal
    1 tablespoon vanilla protein powder (vegan)
    1 tablespoon flaxseed

In a blender, puree ingredients until smooth. Add water or 1 to 2 ice cubes to achieve desired consistency.

Nutrition (per serving): **calories** 543; **fat** 11g (saturated 2g); **protein** 25g; **carbohydrate** 92g; **sodium** 84mg

SWEET CHERRY SMOOTHIE

Sweet and tart from the cherries, orange juice, and bananas, this healthy liquid meal will delight your taste buds.

Makes 2 Servings (serving size: about 2½ cups)

    1 cup cherries, frozen, canned, or fresh (pitted)
    2½ cups orange juice
    1 large banana, sliced
    1 cup ice cubes
    ¼ teaspoon ground cinnamon (optional)

1. In a blender, puree all ingredients until smooth.
2. Cinnamon can be omitted from blending process and added to individual servings or omitted altogether.

Nutrition (per serving): **calories** 236; **fat** 1g (saturated 0g); **protein** 3g; **carbohydrate** 56g; **sodium** 7mg

GINGERY CARROT AND AVOCADO SMOOTHIE

A little different than the fruitier smoothies, this one packs lots of nutrients in every swallow!

Makes 4 Servings (serving size: about 1½ cups)

  10 to 15 medium carrots, trimmed and chopped (steamed until barely tender, if desired)
  1 bunch Italian parsley, coarsely chopped
  1-inch piece fresh ginger, peeled and coarsely chopped
  ½ ripe avocado, peeled
  2 to 3 cups water
  Salt and pepper, to taste

1. In a blender, combine half of the carrots with parsley, ginger, and enough water to cover ingredients. Puree, and then add remaining carrots and enough water to achieve a smooth consistency.

2. Refrigerate before serving. Add salt and pepper, to taste, to individual servings.

Nutrition (per serving): **calories** 131; **fat** 4g (saturated 1g); **protein** 3g; **carbohydrate** 24g; **sodium** 78mg

sample menus

If you're eager to get started on your twenty-one-day Daniel Fast, the sample menus in this chapter will give you a strong head start. They'll also be a guide to you if you are continuing with the Daniel Cure lifestyle. The first two menus provide a breakdown of meal timing and proportions of protein, carbohydrate, and fat. They are not specific to the Daniel Fast or Daniel Cure plans. They can be used with any dietary plan aimed at optimal health. Eight others (four for the Daniel Fast and four for the Daniel Cure) include meal options you can use as a quick reference to see how you might construct a workable meal plan for yourself. One of the four Daniel Fast menus gives a lot of detail on nutrients and calories—this is an example of a personal plan that I (Rick) routinely use.

EXAMPLES OF MEAL TIMING
AND MACRONUTRIENT PROPORTIONS

These examples give you an idea of how to design your daily meals to include the right amounts of protein, carbohydrate, and fat. Notice that the daily totals are close to the recommended amounts of protein (20 percent), carbohydrate (60 percent), and fat (20 percent). (See chapter 11.) This does not mean that every meal must match these proportions.

To keep things simple, just split your plate into three equal parts with one part containing a low-fat source of protein and the other two parts for carbohydrates. Make one part vegetable and/or fruit and the other part whole grains. By following this simple step, you don't need any complex math. But if you are interested in doing the math (and some are), see "How Do I Compute the Calorie Contribution of Protein, Carbohydrate, and Fat in Foods?" on page 246.

The meal-planning examples of nutrient amounts in tables 22.1 and 22.2 apply to both the Daniel Fast and the Daniel Cure.

TABLE 22.1
Sample Diet (1,500 Calories per Day)

Meal	Time	Calories	Protein in grams (%)	Carbs in grams (%)	Fat in grams (%)
1	6:00 a.m.	100	8 (32%)	12 (48%)	2 (20%)
Exercise	7:00 a.m.				
2	8:30 a.m.	400	25 (25%)	60 (60%)	7 (15%)
3	11:00 a.m.	300	20 (26%)	40 (53%)	7 (21%)
4	2:00 p.m.	200	10 (20%)	30 (60%)	5 (20%)
5	6:00 p.m.	400	15 (15%)	58 (58%)	12 (27%)
6	8:30 p.m.	100	10 (40%)	10 (40%)	2 (20%)
Totals		**1,500**	**88 (23%)**	**210 (56%)**	**35 (21%)**

TABLE 22.2
Sample Diet (2,500 Calories per Day)

Meal	Time	Calories	Protein in grams (%)	Carbs in grams (%)	Fat in grams (%)
Exercise	5:00 a.m.				
1	7:00 a.m.	650	30 (19%)	90 (56%)	18 (25%)
2	9:30 a.m.	400	20 (20%)	60 (60%)	9 (20%)
3	12:30 a.m.	550	30 (22%)	95 (69%)	5 (9%)
4	3:30 p.m.	350	20 (23%)	45 (52%)	10 (25%)
5	6:30 p.m.	550	35 (25%)	70 (52%)	14 (23%)
Totals		**2,500**	**135 (22%)**	**360 (57%)**	**56 (21%)**

DANIEL FAST

If you are beginning a traditional Daniel Fast, an exclusively plant-based eating plan, consider the menus in tables 22.3 to 22.6.

TABLE 22.3
Sample Daniel Fast Menu 1

Time	Meal	Food	Quantity
6:00 a.m.	Breakfast (1)	Soy milk (plain) Banana	2 cups 1 large
8:30 a.m.	Breakfast (2)	Steel-cut oats Walnuts Apple Soy protein powder	1 cup uncooked ¼ cup raw 1 medium 2 tablespoons (15 grams)
11:00 a.m.	Mid-morning shake	Pineapple Quick oats Soy protein powder Water	10 ounces ½ cup uncooked 2 tablespoons (15 grams) 16 ounces
1:15 p.m.	Lunch	Brown rice Black beans Corn Red hot sauce	1 cup cooked 1 cup cooked 1 cup cooked 2 tablespoons
3:15 p.m.	Mid-afternoon shake	Pineapple Quick oats Soy protein powder Water	10 ounces ½ cup uncooked 2 tablespoons (15 grams) 16 ounces
6:00 p.m.	Dinner	Whole-wheat pasta Broccoli Tomatoes Garbanzo beans Olive oil	¼ pound cooked 1 cup steamed ½ cup fresh ½ cup roasted and seasoned 1 tablespoon

TABLE 22.4
Sample Daniel Fast Menu 2

Time	Meal	Food	Quantity
5:00 a.m.	Pre-exercise	Soy milk (plain)	1 cup
7:00 a.m.	Breakfast	Old-fashioned oats Banana Raisins Grapes Soy protein powder	1 cup uncooked 1 large ¼ cup ½ cup 2 tablespoons (15 grams)
9:30 a.m.	Mid-morning shake	Soy milk (plain) Natural peanut butter Banana	2 cups 2 tablespoons 1 large
12:30 p.m.	Lunch	Lentil soup Orange	3 cups 1 large

Time	Meal	Food	Quantity
3:30 p.m.	Mid-afternoon snack	Hummus Carrots (baby) Bell pepper	½ cup 15 pieces 1 large (sliced)
6:00 p.m.	Dinner	Pearled barley Cucumber Pine nuts	1 cup cooked and seasoned 1 medium ¼ cup (toasted)
8:00 p.m.	Dessert	Mixed berries Mandarin oranges	1 cup ½ cup

The following plan (table 22.5) is the typical menu that Susan adheres to when she is following the Daniel Fast.

TABLE 22.5
Susan's Typical Daniel Fast Menu

Time	Meal	Food	Quantity
7:00 a.m.	Breakfast	Muesli Unsweetened soy milk	½ cup ½ cup
10:00 a.m.	Snack	Almonds or walnuts Pear or apple	¼ cup 1 medium
12:30 p.m.	Lunch	Hearty vegetable soup Green salad with dressing	1½ cups 2 cups greens 1 – 2 tablespoons dressing
3:00 p.m.	Snack	Carrot sticks Homemade hummus	From 1 carrot ⅓ cup
6:00 p.m.	Dinner	Pasta sauce Whole-wheat noodles	½ cup 1½ cups cooked noodles
7:30 p.m.	Snack	Watermelon Grapes	½ cup ½ cup

Table 22.6 (see next page) is the menu that I adhere to when following the Daniel Fast, listing what I eat and when. For less than 3,000 calories, I can eat a lot of food and feel great throughout the day. I often don't eat as much food as this in one day. I typically consume more calories on exercise training days. My usual calorie intake is from 2,500 to 3,000 calories a day—true both on and off the Daniel Fast. You will need to do some experimenting to determine what is best for you.

TABLE 22.6
Rick's Sample Daniel Fast Menu

Meal (Time)	Food	Serving Size	Calories	Protein (grams)	Carbs (grams)	Fat (grams)	Fiber (grams)	Comments
Pre-Workout (4:15 a.m.)	Orange juice	8 ounces	120	0	30	0	0	Mix orange juice and powder the night before. Place in bottle in fridge for easy access in the morning.
	Soy protein powder	10 grams (½ scoop)	50	10	0	1	0	
Workout (4:30–6:10 a.m.)	Water	32 ounces	0	0	0	0	0	It is important to remain hydrated during exercise.
Breakfast (6:45 a.m.)	Oats	1 cup uncooked	300	12	54	5	8	Cook the oats with the banana and raisins. Stir in the protein powder. Add grapes.
	Banana	1 large	100	0	25	0	2	
	Raisins	¼ cup	125	1	28	0	2	
	Grapes	1 cup	125	1	30	0	2	
	Soy protein powder	10 grams (½ scoop)	50	10	0	1	0	
Mid-morning (9:15 a.m.)	Pineapple	10 ounces (in juice)	150	0	38	0	3	Mix ingredients with water in a blender to make a meal-replacement shake.
	Oranges	5 ounces (in juice)	50	0	12	0	0	
	Oats	¾ cup uncooked	225	9	40	4	6	
	Soy protein powder	10 grams (½ scoop)	50	10	0	1	0	
Lunch (11:45 a.m.)	Brown rice	¼ cup uncooked	155	4	33	1	2	This meal is inexpensive, extremely easy to prepare, and tastes great.
	Black beans	1 cup	250	16	45	1	12	
	Corn	1 cup	130	3	28	1	1	
	Hot sauce	1 tablespoon	0	0	0	0	0	

Meal (Time)	Food	Serving Size	Calories	Protein (grams)	Carbs (grams)	Fat (grams)	Fiber (grams)	Comments
Mid-afternoon (2:45 p.m.)	Pineapple	10 ounces (in juice)	150	0	38	0	3	Mix ingredients with water in a blender to make a meal-replacement shake (same as mid-morning meal).
	Oranges	5 ounces (in juice)	50	0	12	0	0	
	Oats	¾ cup uncooked	225	9	40	4	6	
	Soy protein powder	10 grams (½ scoop)	50	10	0	1	0	
Dinner (5:45 p.m.)	Wheat durum pasta	4 ounces uncooked	410	14	80	3	12	Place seasoned and baked chickpeas on top (see Roasted Chickpeas on page 233).
	Peas	1 cup	90	6	15	0	5	
	Chickpeas	½ cup	120	6	20	2	6	
Totals			2,975	121	568	25	70	
Percentages				16%	76%	8%		See "How Do I Compute the Calorie Contribution of Protein, Carbohydrate, and Fat in Foods?" on page 246.

Note: The pre-workout meal and breakfast are both consumed at home. I then bring the two shakes and lunch meal with me to work (these are prepared the night before—or sometimes two days before). These are placed in the refrigerator for easy access during the day. I then consume dinner at home. On occasion, I will have another small meal or snack after dinner.

This meal plan is only one example. On this day you can see that my protein intake is close to 16 percent (which is likely adequate based on my body mass of about 82kg, or 180 pounds). My carbohydrate intake is very high at 76 percent of calories and my fat intake is very low at only 8 percent. I may have other days when I consume less carbohydrate and more fat, placing my percentages for the week closer to 65 percent for carbohydrate and 20 percent for fat. Overall, my ratios on the Daniel Fast fall somewhere in the middle: 15 percent protein, 70 percent carbohydrate, and 15 percent fat. Considering the high fiber intake (70 grams), this diet looks very good.

While this represents a typical day for me while following the Daniel Fast, my usual non-Daniel Fast diet is very similar. In fact, after doing the Daniel Fast many times, I have adopted many of the meals into my year-long routine. The only real differences are:

1. I usually consume a higher percentage of protein (20–25%) and a lower percentage of carbohydrate (60%) when I'm not following the Daniel Fast.

2. I use whey or whey-casein protein powder rather than soy protein powder. The quality of whey and casein protein powder is typically much better than soy (despite soy being a complete protein).

3. I include lunch and dinner meals that often contain lean meat— poultry, steak, fish. An ideal meal might be 5 ounces of marinated chicken breast, 1 cup of steamed brown rice, 1 cup of steamed broccoli, and a side salad (with balsamic vinegar dressing)—nutritionally excellent and very satisfying.

4. I will occasionally include white rice, breads, and other "processed" carbohydrate—they taste great to me and I like to include these for something different.

5. I occasionally have a "cheat" meal such as pizza, burgers, a sausage roll, garlic bread, desserts, etc. But I don't do this often and I get right back on track with the next meal. In fact, to make progress and get into the best overall health that your genetics will allow, it has to be this way— consistency, consistency, consistency!

DANIEL CURE

As you begin the Daniel Cure lifestyle eating plan, note that you do not need to include animal products or "cheat meals" in your weekly menu. However, we know from working with so many over the years that most people enjoy these on occasion. We also know that permanent restrictions often result in poor overall compliance and people give up. This is typical for most dieters.

The Daniel Cure is different. We want you to enter this plan knowing that you are in it for life. Develop a plan that maintains the core principles of the Daniel Cure, but is also reasonable to adhere to. You have a great deal of flexibility. Use it.

Most menu plans shown (tables 22.7 to 22.10) include animal products and protein powder. Animal products contain several healthful nutrients and can work well with the plant-based foods you'll incorporate in your overall plan. Figure out what you enjoy eating and develop your plan around those foods.

TABLE 22.7
Sample Daniel Cure Menu 1

Time	Meal	Food	Quantity
6:30 a.m.	Breakfast	Eggs Tomato Whole-wheat bread Peach	1 whole egg and 5 egg whites 1 large (sliced) 2 slices (toasted) 1 large
9:00 a.m.	Mid-morning shake	Soy milk (plain) Almond milk (plain) Old-fashioned oats Natural peanut butter	1 cup 1 cup ½ cup uncooked 2 tablespoons
12:30 p.m.	Lunch	Brown rice Peas Chicken breast Apple	1 cup cooked ½ cup cooked 5 ounces grilled 1 large
3:30 p.m.	Mid-afternoon shake	Greek yogurt Whey protein powder Strawberries Skim milk	1 cup 2 tablespoons (15 grams) 1 cup 1 cup
6:00 p.m.	Dinner	Salmon Sweet potato Mixed-greens salad	6 ounces grilled 1 large 1 large (balsamic vinaigrette)

TABLE 22.8
Sample Daniel Cure Menu 2

Time	Meal	Food	Quantity
5:00 a.m.	Pre-exercise	Apple juice	1 cup
		Whey protein powder	2 tablespoons (15 grams)
7:15 a.m.	Breakfast	Shredded wheat	1½ cups
		Skim milk	1½ cups
		Raisins	¼ cup
		Whey protein powder	3 tablespoons (22 grams)
9:30 a.m.	Mid-morning shake	Skim milk	2 cups
		Old-fashioned oats	½ cup uncooked
		Banana	1 large
12:30 p.m.	Lunch	Lean ground turkey	5 ounces grilled
		Whole-wheat pita	1 medium
		Beans (mixed)	½ cup cooked and seasoned
		Corn	½ cup cooked
		Plumb	1 medium
3:15 p.m.	Mid-afternoon shake	Yogurt (plain)	1 cup
		Soy milk (plain)	1 cup
		Blackberries	1 cup
6:00 p.m.	Dinner	Chicken breast	6 ounces grilled
		Red potatoes	1½ cups
		Cauliflower and carrots	1½ cups cooked

TABLE 22.9
Sample Daniel Cure Menu 3

Time	Meal	Food	Quantity
8:00 a.m.	Breakfast	Cream of wheat	½ cup uncooked
		Soy milk (plain)	1½ cups
		Apple sauce	1 cup
10:30 a.m.	Mid-morning shake	Yogurt (plain)	1 cup
		Peach	1 cup frozen
		Orange juice	1 cup
		Whey protein powder	2 tablespoons (15 grams)
1:30 p.m.	Lunch	Vegetarian chili (black bean/sweet potato)	2 cups
4:15 p.m.	Mid-afternoon shake	Soy milk (plain)	1 cup
		Raspberries	½ cup
		Whey protein powder	2 tablespoons (15 grams)
7:00 p.m.	Dinner	Top sirloin	5 ounces grilled
		Quinoa	1 cup cooked
		Corn on the cob	2 ears

TABLE 22.10
Sample Daniel Cure Menu 4

Time	Meal	Food	Quantity
7:00 a.m.	Breakfast	Skim milk Wheat bread	3 cups 2 slices
10:00 a.m.	Mid-morning snack	Cottage cheese Mandarin oranges	1 cup 1 cup
12:45 p.m.	Lunch	Tilapia fillet Baked red potatoes Apple	6 ounces 6 ounces 1 medium
3:30 p.m.	Mid-afternoon shake	Apple juice Strawberries Protein powder	1 cup 1 cup 2 tablespoons (15 grams)
6:00 p.m.	Dinner	Turkey chili (with black beans and corn)	2 cups
8:30 p.m.	Snack	Greek yogurt	1 cup

SO WHAT WILL WORK FOR YOU?

The examples we have given are just that—examples. They are balanced plans that include a variety of foods and will work well for most people. But you need to determine what will work best for you and your lifestyle. Perhaps you would prefer to minimize animal products and reserve these for only once or twice per week. That's fine. Or maybe you really enjoy the meal-replacement shakes and want to replace your traditional whole food breakfast with a shake each day. Again, this is fine. What is most important is figuring out what will work best for you and then sticking with it. This includes adjusting not only your food choices and timing of meals but also the amount of food consumed. You may require more food than what is presented. Or you may require less. Spend some time experimenting and determine what works for you. Your goal is to be satisfied at the end of your meals but never overly full. Slow down when you eat. Allow yourself time to decide if you need more food. The answer usually is no.

There are no secrets to eating a healthy diet and getting into great physical health. It's just a matter of knowing a few essentials, understanding how they impact your dietary plan, developing a plan that is realistic, and then sticking to it. You're ready to make this work.

HOW DO I COMPUTE THE CALORIE CONTRIBUTION OF PROTEIN, CARBOHYDRATE, AND FAT IN FOODS?

Follow these steps to calculate the calorie contribution of macronutrients in the foods you eat:

1. There are approximately 4 calories per gram for protein and carbohydrate and 9 calories per gram for fat. There are approximately 7 calories per gram for alcohol.
2. Determine how many grams of each macronutrient are contained in the food. If it is a packaged food item, look at the nutrition facts label. If it's an unpackaged food item (such as fruits or vegetables), you'll need to search online or use a published food guide.
3. Multiply the number of grams for each nutrient by the calories per gram.

    Example: 8 (grams of protein) x 4 (calories per gram) = 32 (8 × 4 = 32).

4. To get the percentage of calories for each macronutrient in a food, divide the number of calories for each macronutrient (protein, carbohydrate, fat) by the total number of calories in the food, and then multiply this number by 100. For example, we know that one serving of skim milk contains a total of 80 calories and 8 grams of protein, which equates to 32 calories from protein.

    Example: 32 (protein calories) / 80 (total calories) × 100 = 40% of total calories are protein (32 / 80 × 100 = .40 or 40%).

We can do the same with carbohydrate in one serving (one cup) of skim milk, first figuring the number of calories from carbohydrates:

    Example: 12 (grams of carbohydrate) x 4 (calories per gram) = 48 carbohydrate calories (12 × 4 = 48).

    Example: 48 (carbohydrate calories) / 80 (total calories) × 100 = 60% of total calories are carbohydrate (48 / 80 × 100 = .60 or 60%).

The zero grams of fat in skim milk means 0% of total milk calories are from fat.

This same math works for any food, drink, or recipe. And while you don't need to calculate these often, it's a good idea to at least know how. It will help you to understand what is in the foods you eat.

twenty-one-day devotional

food for the soul

By Susan Gregory

DAY 1
An Invitation to New Life

We were therefore buried with him through baptism into death in order that, just as Christ was raised from the dead through the glory of the Father, we too may live a new life.

—Romans 6:4

Today is the first day of your new journey. You're probably feeling excited with anticipation, but also a little nervous about following the fasting guidelines and lasting all twenty-one days. The beginning of any excursion can feel daunting, especially if it's your first time. And feeling uneasy is normal when you are about to encounter a time of stretching, challenge, and growth.

But instead of focusing on the trials of fasting, set your sight on the prize —the grand reward of drawing closer to God and experiencing more of his love, grace, and presence as you focus more attention on him and his ways. The cost? Being willing to submit to him—simply accept his invitation to a life that only he can give.

When we fast, we have the opportunity to set aside our habits, desires, and wants—and choose to live a different way. It's part of dying to self so we can more fully experience the new life God wants to give us. That new life is better health for our body, improved clarity for our mind, and a deeper and closer walk with our Lord. To realize these blessings, we enter the journey, stay on the path, and keep our eyes on the prize.

Do you want to have a more intimate relationship with your Father? What can you do today to open your heart to him?

Loving Father, thank you for offering your generous invitation for the new life only you can give. Today I give myself to you. I accept your invitation for better health, clearer direction for my life, and a closer, more intimate walk with you. Amen.

DAY 2
Bought at a Price

Do you not know that your bodies are temples of the Holy Spirit, who is in you, whom you have received from God? You are not your own; you were bought at a price. Therefore honor God with your bodies.

— 1 Corinthians 6:19–20

When we begin an extended period of prayer and fasting, we often find we are paying more attention to our physical needs. You may be craving a cup of hot coffee or tea. You feel a little sluggish. Or, even worse, you're struggling with caffeine and sugar withdrawal, and your body is revolting with headaches, fatigue, and leg cramps.

When we experience a craving or hunger pang, we immediately attend to what our body wants ... even when it's not the best for our health. We crave sweets, potato chips, ice cream. And when we want it ... we go get it and satisfy the desires of our body.

During the Daniel Fast, we have the opportunity to bring order to our eating habits and develop healthy disciplines. We can realize the truth that Christ paid a high price for us. We are not our own. Our bodies are the dwelling place of God's Holy Spirit. Each one of us is the caretaker of this temple — our body.

Take a moment to consider your body. Are you willing to release it to the Lord and allow his Spirit to fill it with his grace as you continue your journey toward complete health?

Jesus, thank you for the immeasurable sacrifice you made on my behalf. Today I acknowledge that I am not my own. You bought me at a price — your life. I am thankful and I will honor you by caring for my body, the temple where the Holy Spirit takes up residence. Amen.

DAY 3
A Rewarding Experience

> On reaching Jerusalem, Jesus entered the temple courts and began driving
> out those who were buying and selling there. He overturned the tables of
> the money changers and the benches of those selling doves, and would not
> allow anyone to carry merchandise through the temple courts.
> —MARK 11:15–16

Can you imagine Jesus entering the holy temple in Jerusalem? There was no
place more holy for God's people. The temple was where almighty God was
with his people. It was his home, his dwelling place, his holy meeting hall.

When Jesus saw his Father's house being defiled, his reaction was immediate and intense. The gentle and kind Rabbi quickly transformed into a determined Mr. Clean. Nothing dishonoring would remain in the temple grounds.
Jesus drew a line—no junk in his Father's house!

Daniel, who had dedicated himself to God, had the same determination
when offered food considered unclean by Jewish standards. "But Daniel
resolved not to defile himself with the royal food and wine, and he asked the
chief official for permission not to defile himself this way" (Daniel 1:8).

As followers of Jesus, our bodies are holy, set aside for the purposes of God.
When you gave your life to Christ, your body was immediately cleansed by the
blood of Christ and transformed into a holy dwelling place where God's Spirit
could reside. You are his temple.

This is one of the most powerful lessons we can learn on the Daniel Fast.
When we acknowledge that our bodies are the home of God, we are sum-
moned to a higher calling.

Do you hear the Lord calling you like the commitment Daniel accepted …
and that Jesus modeled? Do you truly accept that you are the temple of God?
That you are holy and nothing should defile the beautiful dwelling place God
created?

*Father, I am humbled that you have chosen to live inside of me. In loving
response to you I will guard this temple and care for it in the way it
deserves. Thank you for making your home in me. Amen.*

DAY 4
God's Revelation for Your Health

> Where there is no revelation, people cast off restraint; but blessed is the one who heeds wisdom's instructions.
>
> —PROVERBS 29:18

Submitting to God's ways is always the right thing to do. And putting our trust in the Lord is at the center of the confidence and security that will see us through every situation. As we open our hearts to God and his Word, we open our minds to his revelation—that personal exposure to truth that he wants to give each of his precious children so we can live the life he desires for us.

When we close our minds to God's revelation, we choose to go without him and to subject ourselves to our own ways and the ways of the world. And as this verse says, we "cast off restraint."

Sadly, this seems to be the picture of what has happened with God's people and the frightful condition of our health. It seems we've pushed aside what the Creator says about our health and not received his revelation. Consequently the majority of Christians have lived lives with little restraint.

The good news is that God's mercies are new every morning. We can change. We can receive the revelation from our Creator and start practicing self-control and wisdom.

Are you ready to walk away from habits that don't support you and walk toward those that bring health and vitality? Are you ready to choose health over death and join the growing number of people who are saying, "Enough is enough"?

> *Lord, help me to receive the truth of your Word. Help me to receive your revelation about my health and well-being. And help me to walk away from habits that hurt me and toward those that give me life. Amen.*

DAY 5
Knowledge into Action

> Apply your heart to instruction and your ears to words of knowledge.
>
> —PROVERBS 23:12

This book is packed with a lot of information and advice about fasting and health. It serves as instruction for you to experience the Daniel Fast and use it as a launch for your healthy lifestyle.

Now you have a choice. You can use what you're learning. You can make the decision to live a lifestyle of health. And you can take the steps to reach that goal. Or you can absorb the knowledge but remain idle.

This is where the Spirit of God meets our self-will. If we believe God's Word is true, we know we are to honor our bodies and give them the care they deserve. We know that we are called to a life of discipline and self-control. We know there are good ways to treat our bodies—and ways that lead to destruction.

So for today and tomorrow and next week and forever, we decide what we will do with the instruction we've received. As we commit to the challenges of change, we can know that God is with us every step of the way. Will this be easy? No. We will face temptations and cravings. But the rewards are immense —far beyond what we can imagine.

Are you ready to turn your commitment to health into actions? Are you ready to accept God's desire for your health? What can you do today to act on your conviction?

Father, I thank you for your instruction and your guidance. Thank you for being with me, for teaching me, and for helping me to follow your ways as I submit myself to you. Amen.

DAY 6
Highly Valued and Deeply Loved

Are not two sparrows sold for a penny? Yet not one of them will fall to the ground outside your Father's care. And even the very hairs of your head are all numbered. So don't be afraid; you are worth more than many sparrows.
—MATTHEW 10:29 – 31

We know there is an important balance between healthy self-worth and pride. Arrogance, conceit, boastfulness, and vanity are against the ways of God. Instead, we are called to be humble yet still value ourselves in a wholesome way that honors our Creator. We are to honor our bodies and commit to good health.

What I discovered is that too often in the past, I didn't think much about my health—well at least not until I felt an ache or a pain. I took my body for granted, expecting it to make do with whatever I fed it or however I treated or mistreated it.

After first experiencing the great health benefits of the Daniel Fast several years ago, I started paying more attention to what the Bible says about health. I gained a better understanding of how God wants us to feel good about who we are and to respect ourselves as his precious children.

God values us. He values you. Allow this truth to stir your heart. God loves you more than you can imagine. You are precious to him.

Can you accept the Lord's immeasurable love for you? Open your heart … and receive.

Father, thank you for helping me to experience your love. You gave your one and only Son for me and for others. Thank you for loving me. Help me to receive your precious gift. Amen.

DAY 7
Made in God's Image

Then God said, "Let us make mankind in our image, in our likeness, so that they may rule over the fish in the sea and the birds in the sky, over the livestock and all the wild animals, and over all the creatures that move along the ground."

—Genesis 1:26

The fact that we are created in God's image is good to think about. In some ways, the reality is almost too much to absorb. How stunning it is that we are fashioned after the Creator of the universe. How amazing it is that he entrusted us with so much power to rule over all the earth.

This brings us to consider what this truth means for each day of our lives. First, as people of faith and followers of Jesus Christ, we each have the blessing of God to empower us and help us. The Spirit of God lives inside of us to lead and direct our steps. God's Word is packed with promises of protection, health, prosperity, goodness, and mercy. Know that all those promises are yours as you exercise your faith and walk in the Light of Christ.

Think about who you are and who God is. What do you want to do to live a life worthy of your heritage, a life that leaves a legacy to those you love? Are you so connected with your Maker that people are blessed and want to know about the One in whose image you were made? Do people you love see Christ in you?

Father, I am humbled to be made in your image. I want to live a life worthy of that high call and realize the many blessings of your care for me. Amen.

DAY 8
Be Still ... Really?

"Be still, and know that I am God; I will be exalted among the nations, I will be exalted in the earth."

—PSALM 46:10

North American culture presents ever-growing challenges to our spending quiet time alone with our Lord. Even after decades of devoting daily quiet time to study and prayer, I still find my mind wandering to my daily to-do list or the latest news headlines. And there are even times when my busy life is in such contrast with being still that entering into quiet time can be uncomfortable as it feels so inconsistent compared to most of my day. Perhaps you can relate.

When we fast, we make a decision to enter into a different way of operating in our daily lives. We choose to slow down so we can focus more of our time and attention on God. The benefits are many and, as the Word teaches, God "rewards those who earnestly seek him" (Hebrews 11:6).

We can choose to be still. In some ways, choosing to be still is like receiving treatment from your doctor, or getting your hair cut, or when you learn something from a sermon. You just sit ... and receive.

At first, five minutes of stillness feels long. But the more you practice stillness, the easier and more fulfilling it will be for you. Choose to be still for a few minutes by eliminating distractions. Create an environment that is conducive to tranquility. Then sit quietly and open your heart to receive the peace and calm the Lord provides. Be still and rest in the Lord.

Lord, open my heart to receive your gift of peace and calm so I truly can be still and know you and praise you. Help me to honor this quiet time with you and to hold it holy so we can meet and I can grow in you. Amen.

DAY 9
Ears to Hear

"Still other seed fell on good soil. It came up, grew and produced a crop, some multiplying thirty, some sixty, some a hundred times." Then Jesus said, "Whoever has ears to hear, let them hear."

—MARK 4:8–9

What is the Lord saying to you today? Will you be still and silent long enough to hear his words? Will you hear and then heed his instructions to change your life?

I know for sure that the Lord speaks to his people. And when his Word says, "Whoever has ears to hear, let them hear," he isn't talking to us about only listening and hearing. He wants us to hear what he is saying and then to act —to change, to align our lives with his ways. I also know that he wants only what is good for us and that whatever he tells us to do will be for our benefit.

I believe God is calling his church to live healthy lives. He's giving us a warning. He's shedding light on the danger we are in if we don't change and develop a lifestyle that promotes health, vitality, and longevity. But will we have ears to hear? We each are called to answer this question for ourselves.

Do you hear the Lord calling you to better health? Will you hear him and take action? As you replace unhealthy habits with those that will restore your health, are you willing to fight the temporary battle of cravings? Do you have ears to hear God calling you?

Lord, I do hear you. Help me to walk the way of health that is your desire for me and my desire for myself. Amen.

DAY 10
Walk in the Spirit

So I say, walk by the Spirit, and you will not gratify the desires of the flesh.
—GALATIANS 5:16

Walk by the Spirit ... it's a call to God's people to know the truth of his Word and to walk in his ways. And when we do this, the promise is that we won't fall prey to forces that are not aligned with God.

One way we can experience the fulfillment of this truth is with our emotions. Oh, how powerful menacing emotions can be, and when not reined in, emotional responses can cost us greatly. For example, while you are fasting one of your days might not match the blissful experience we all want to enjoy.

Perhaps you have a rough day at the office or a family member says an unkind comment to you. Ouch! That hurt! And then in your frustration, pain, or resentment ... you go for the "comfort food." I've always been stymied by the term "comfort food." I've yet to have a piece of chocolate cake hug me. Nor has a plate of lasagna shared any helpful advice. But when we're stressed or hurt or fearful ... our emotions lead our actions.

God is showing us another way. He's revealing to us that we can walk in the Spirit. We can have his truths determine our actions ... and then we will be on solid ground headed in the direction we want to go. When a sweet dessert is offering to comfort us, God invites us to stay the course and seek what we truly need from him, our true Comforter.

Think of a time when you felt "out of control" because your emotions were directing your actions. Think of what you can do to put unruly emotions in their place. Make a choice. Walk according to God's ways.

Lord, thank you for your powerful truths. You are my Rock. My Comforter. My best Friend. I accept this call to put my unhealthy emotions in their place and choose your way of the Spirit—the way that promises life, hope, and joy.

DAY 11
His Gift of Peace

"Peace I leave with you; my peace I give you. I do not give to you as the world gives. Do not let your hearts be troubled and do not be afraid."

—John 14:27

When we fast, we focus our attention on God, his ways, and our life in him. We can examine ourselves—spirit, soul, and body—and discover areas where we can come into closer alignment with our Creator's desires for us. And we can learn more of how he wants us to live as children of God.

Jesus placed in each of us his peace—not the world's type of peace—but his peace. And he tells us that because he's given his peace to us that we have no need for worry about the troubles we may encounter.

By this time in the fast, you've become more intimate with the Lord. You feel more comfortable and at ease with him. You've learned from his Word ... and your trust in God for your life has grown. God is always right ... his Word is reliable ... his love for you never ends. You can trust him. He gives you peace.

Love for the Father is our motivator. When we live in a trusting, loving relationship with our God, the beauty and power of our faith in God is realized.

On a scale of 1–10 (with 1 being never and 10 being always), to what degree do you experience the peace of Christ in your life? What is your level of trust in your Father? What can you do today to receive the peace that Christ has for you? What can you do to increase your trust and love for your Father?

Father, thank you for your faithfulness, even when I am not faithful. Thank you for your love, even when I am not loving. Thank you for your peace … and the gift Jesus has already given to me. Help me to receive this precious gift and help me to align my life with your ways. Amen.

DAY 12
The Key to Unlock Endless Love and Joy

"If you keep my commands, you will remain in my love, just as I have kept my Father's commands and remain in his love. I have told you this so that my joy may be in you and that your joy may be complete."

—JOHN 15:10–11

Jesus made this bold and awesome promise not long before he was crucified. He knew he would soon depart the world. And it seems like he was pouring his heart out to his disciples, hoping they would more fully embrace all he had been teaching them. These rich phrases capture the essence of what our Lord wants for us. He wants us to be secure in God's love. And he wants us to be overflowing with joy.

Our Lord also tells us how we can attain this brilliant and magnificent kind of life: we need only to do what he says. It's that direct and that simple. Merely embrace him and his Word, follow his instructions, and then experience more love and more joy than you can ever imagine! And not only do we receive love and joy, but so does our Lord.

You and I have this opportunity right now to get to know Jesus and then to align our thoughts, attitudes, words, actions, desires, and values with him and his Word. That is when the abundant life he promises takes root. That's when our life is secure in God's love and our joy is complete, nothing missing and nothing broken — total joy.

As you take this time to examine your heart and plan your course, what do you want to do so you can keep his commandments and remain in his love?

Lord, I know your love is immeasurable, more than I can ever fathom.
And you so love me that you want me to live in your love with you.
Help me to more fully embrace this truth and receive the love and joy
you have for me as I follow your ways.

DAY 13
Fearfully and Wonderfully Made

> I praise you because I am fearfully and wonderfully made; your works are wonderful, I know that full well.
>
> —Psalm 139:14

Men want six-pack abs and muscular arms. Women want a tiny waist and thinner thighs. I've been there … using my hula hoop to trim the middle and fast walking to expend the calories. And the sweet reward is a pound lost or an inch trimmed.

However, as I increase in years and gain more knowledge about health and my body, I realize being concerned only for my appearance is shallow thinking. Granted, weight and even a waist measurement are key indicators of health, so it's good to pay attention to both. But learning more about how our body works and how to provide the best care for this amazing instrument is central to our well-being.

Cells, organs, vessels, muscles, tendons, ligaments, and bones are just some of the components that give us life. They were all designed to work in harmony with one another to enable us to function at the highest level of all living things. Not only are we fearfully and wonderfully made, but our life—our body—is a gift to us from our Creator. And for this marvelous gift we can give honor, praise, and thanksgiving.

My friend is a gifted artist. Her paintings are breathtaking, masterful, and very valuable. If I owned one I would be sure to give it the best of care. Never would I want any kind of dirt or contamination to come near the work. And if I ever abused it, I would be ashamed for her to ever find out. We have been given a work of art by our Creator. He has given us our bodies, which are fearfully and wonderfully made. And we honor him by taking the best care of his work.

Do you see yourself as God's masterpiece? Take a couple minutes and focus on the Artist. Think of the joy and excitement he had when he created you. As you continue through this day, care for his masterpiece. Give it what it needs to function and shine as he planned.

Father, thank you for the artful way you fashioned me. I am amazed by your workmanship, and I will care for this body that you have entrusted to me. Amen.

DAY 14
The Value of Understanding

> Wisdom is the principal thing; Therefore get wisdom. And in all your
> getting, get understanding.
>
> —PROVERBS 4:7 NKJV

I am regularly taken aback by God's wisdom! Pondering his Word and his
precepts opens up powerful truths that we can use in our daily lives to be
successful and at peace.

Wisdom is defined as having experience, knowledge, and good judgment.
God's wisdom is infinite wisdom. He is always right. This verse calls us to
get wisdom, to go after the truth of God and let his wisdom become firmly
entrenched in us so that we "get it."

Then the proverb goes on to say, "and in all your getting, get understanding." Get wisdom and then understand it. Let it roll around in your thoughts
and try it out on circumstances and imagine it working out ... so that you
understand why the wisdom of God is so worthy of our trust.

Understanding is like fuel to our thinking, the driving force for our actions.
When you understand the importance of something, you are more likely to put
that truth, or that wisdom, into action.

God created your body using his incalculable wisdom. He made all the
organs, the systems, and the life forces so your body can operate in perfect
health. Do you see his wisdom in the creation of your body? Are you willing
to get more understanding so you can give your body the care it needs? Think
about the amazing creation that you are. And then determine today to do
whatever is best to give your body what it needs for good health.

Father, I value your wisdom. Thank you for sharing your truths
with me in your Word. And thank you for equipping me so I can gain
understanding and put your truths into action in my life. Amen.

DAY 15
Grow in Knowledge and Strength

> We continually ask God to fill you with the knowledge of his will through
> all the wisdom and understanding that the Spirit gives, so that you may
> live a life worthy of the Lord and please him in every way: bearing fruit in
> every good work, growing in the knowledge of God, being strengthened

with all power according to his glorious might so that you may have great endurance and patience.

—COLOSSIANS 1:9–11

"What is the Lord's will for my life?" Do you ever ask that question? You're not alone if you don't know God's purpose for your life. It's the most common question asked of pastors and certainly is why Pastor Rick Warren's book *The Purpose Driven Life* remains the best-selling book of all time except for the Bible.

It's reasonable that we want to know God's will and purpose for our life. But let me share a surprising truth with you. Most of what you will ever need to know about God's will for your life has already been written down in his Word. As our focus verse says, "fill you with the knowledge of his will through all the wisdom and understanding that the Spirit gives." The Spirit of God used people to write down the will of God, and you have ready access to it whenever you need it. And if there are specifics, such as if you should marry a certain person or if you should accept a job offer, he promises to tell you if you ask.

God's will for you is to be in "good health," even as your soul prospers (see 3 John 1:2). To "love the Lord your God with all your heart and with all your soul and with all your mind" (Matthew 22:37). To love others as yourself (see Matthew 22:39). To not gossip (see Romans 1:29). To have patience and self-control (see Galatians 5:22–23 NLT). God's will for you is in his Word. And along with his will is his promise when you follow his way of living. God told Joshua, "Keep this Book of the Law always on your lips; meditate on it day and night, so that you may be careful to do everything written in it. Then you will be prosperous and successful" (Joshua 1:8).

God's will is not a mystery. He isn't hiding it from us. We need only to open the pages of his Word along with the eyes of our heart and he will teach us all we need to know to have the great life he designed us to have.

Can you name one or two biblical principles that you know are the will of God for your life? Think about them and let the truth of God's Word sink into your heart and then act throughout the day to be in his will.

Father, thank you for your Word and for sharing so openly your desire and will for your children. I want to follow your will and be all you created me to be. Bring to my mind what you want for me ... and let your will be done in my life. Amen.

DAY 16
Let Jesus Transform You

> And we all, who with unveiled faces contemplate the Lord's glory, are being transformed into his image with ever-increasing glory, which comes from the Lord, who is the Spirit.
>
> —2 CORINTHIANS 3:18

Even now, as you experience the last week of your fast, a deep hunger remains for more of Jesus in your life. And you likely sense a barrier keeping you from deep intimacy with him. You are not alone. Most people, if they would take the time to look, can find barriers of shame, feelings of unworthiness, lack of approval, and maybe even guilt. These all create a wall that blocks Jesus from entering the deepest places in our lives.

The walls are made of unkind words from parents, teachers, an ex-spouse, or even colleagues. And then there is our own contribution when we compare ourselves to others or fill our minds with words of self-doubt and the "I'm just not good enough" kind of statements.

But let's look at Jesus and his life. He never established or recognized the hierarchy of better and worse ... pretty or ugly ... smarter or unintelligent. Jesus came as your equal—your brother—and he taught you how to fall in love with your Creator and know him so intimately that you call him Abba —Daddy.

As you continue your final days of the fast, try to replace doubts and fears with faith and trust. Meet with Jesus just as you are ... sweetly, humble like a child ... and open your heart for him to enter. You cannot change yourself, but Jesus can. He came to give you a new life, a new spirit, a new mind, a new body. Let him transform you with his love and wisdom.

Jesus, I do have doubts and fears, and I open them all to you. I ask that you remove whatever is in my heart that keeps me from being in your presence. Transform me. I open my heart to our loving Father. Amen.

DAY 17
Get to Know the Real You!

> So in Christ Jesus you are all children of God through faith.
>
> —GALATIANS 3:26

"Who are you?" Imagine that question being asked of you … and your most natural response. For most of us, we would claim our identity as what we do for a job or where we fit in a family structure, or maybe by a skill we practice. "I'm an author." "I'm Katy's husband." "I'm the owner of this company."

But how many of us think first that we are children of God? Not many, even though it's the truth. We may believe it in concept, but have we found our true identity—our primary identity—as a beloved child of the Most High?

The Bible teaches that "those who are led by the Spirit of God are the children of God" (Romans 8:14). That means that when we submit our lives and our will to the ways and will of God, then we qualify as his children. That place in God's genealogical chart becomes our identity.

Why is this so important? When you accept and embrace yourself as a child of almighty God, you can live in security and peace. And as you incorporate this identity into how you lead your life, you gain clear direction for what to do.

You are a child of God. So now that you accept this identity, how do you act? What do you do? How do you relate to your Father? To others? To yourself?

Take a few minutes to think about the truth of who you are. Then think of ways you can live out your true identity today to live the life you are destined to have.

Father, I bow in humility to you and your greatness. But I also crawl up on your lap and nestle in your strong and comforting arms. I am your child … I am precious in your sight … and because of who I am as your child, I have opportunities, responsibilities, and rights. Thank you for being my Father. Help me to more fully embrace and live out my true identity as your child. Amen.

DAY 18
Go and Bear Fruit

But the fruit of the Spirit is love, joy, peace, forbearance, kindness, goodness, faithfulness, gentleness and self-control. Against such things there is no law.

—GALATIANS 5:22–23

When we fast we are transformed. When we spend time with God and his Word, we learn more about his ways. We allow him to work in us and to mold and shape us. Along the way our worldly nature fades and a godly nature becomes who we are in Christ.

In this transformation, those around us experience the change by consuming the fruit we bear—the fruit of the spirit-led life we now have. Bit by bit, our fruit becomes sweeter and more nutritious to those who eat from what we offer.

Our transformation doesn't happen all at once. If you're like me and most other folks, there is a lot of transforming that needs to happen. But this is all part of our Christian journey and our life in Christ. We can be "confident of this, that he who began a good work in you will carry it on to completion until the day of Christ Jesus" (Philippians 1:6).

Through this experience we can be an example of Christ and his wonder for those who don't yet know his love. It's not our fruit, it's his fruit being created through us. He is the vine and we are the branches. Oh, what a joy!

As you focus your attention this week on your life in Christ and the transformation he is doing in you, what changes do you see? What fruit of the Spirit can you serve freely to people you meet today?

Father, I am blessed to be growing in you. Thank you for transforming me into a strong and deeply rooted branch that bears your fruit. I am eager to share you and your fruit with those who are still so very hungry. Amen.

DAY 19
Teach Us to Pray

One day Jesus was praying in a certain place. When he finished, one of his disciples said to him, "Lord, teach us to pray, just as John taught his disciples."

—LUKE 11:1

Your life—your spirit, soul, and body—needs adequate nourishment to stay healthy and to be ready for any call the Lord puts on your life. We nourish our body by eating a balanced diet of nutritious foods, staying adequately hydrated, exercising, and staying well rested. We feed our soul by engaging in positive activities, studying good materials that bring growth, and by living a life consistent with God's ways. Our spirit is nourished by God, and we obtain this nourishment primarily through prayer and meditation.

Prayer not only feeds our spirit but also opens us up to God's power. Answers to our prayers happen. The Bible teaches us that "[we] do not have because [we] do not ask God" (James 4:2). Our God wants us to trust him, engage with him, and communicate with him.

As you think about your life, your whole life, think about nourishing every part of who you are. Understand that you were created to work in perfect harmony with every part of your being. Stay physically healthy so you can be sharp and able. Stay emotionally and intellectually healthy and sound so you can make good decisions, do good work, and have good relationships. And be spiritually nourished so you can be strong in spirit, receive God's guidance, and walk in the light as he is in the light. Do that with prayer. Take the time to be with your Lord and in his presence.

Father, I thank you that because of Christ I can come boldly to your throne and communicate directly with you. Help me to break down any barriers that keep me from being in your presence. Help me to nourish my spirit with your amazing grace, love, and wisdom. Amen.

DAY 20
Falling Out of Love

Do not love the world or the things in the world.
— 1 John 2:15 NKJV

In today's world, where so much is offered for us to experience, I find myself having to be more selective and more intentional about my choices. There are a lot of entertaining and informative programs to watch on television. The internet offers countless articles, videos, and other material about every imaginable topic. And in the grocery stores ... the types and varieties of food continue to grow.

I expect that you're a lot like me. There is so much junk out there that never crosses our path. We don't worry about those matters. What does cause us difficulty is the multitude of good options. As a lifetime learner, I like the information I can access in books, on the internet, or on my television. And as someone who enjoys preparing and eating good food, I like making gourmet meals, baking scrumptious desserts, and making sweet and delectable candy. None of what I read or watch or eat is bad in itself. But too much of a good thing does become bad, and that's where we need to be watchful about our choices.

As we move toward completion of the Daniel Fast and then look toward the Daniel Cure way of living, we need to be diligent about making choices that are consistent with the life we want. I tease about potato chips, but they don't taste nearly as good as my good health feels. So I forgo the immediate and very short-term gratification of the fatty, salty snacks, and I choose a healthy option. Will chips ever cross my lips again? Probably. But I'll plan to have them only on occasion.

As you think about the healthy life you want to live, what choices will you make that are in line with your goals? Write them down and create a plan now so you will be ready.

Lord, help me to discern what is good for me ... and what is too much. Help me to be conscientious about how I use my time, my resources, and the foods that fuel my body. And fill me with your joy as I stay strong and on course. Amen.

DAY 21
Separate and Whole

Now may the God of peace Himself sanctify you completely; and may your whole spirit, soul, and body be preserved blameless at the coming of our Lord Jesus Christ.

— 1 Thessalonians 5:23 NKJV

Today is the final day of your twenty-one-day Daniel Fast ... and the first day of the rest of your healthy life. My sincere hope is that your heart is filled with joy and thanksgiving as you look back on your experience and look forward to the great life that awaits you.

In our Scripture for this very special day, the prayer for you is that you will be sanctified — set apart for holy worship — and not just a little bit of you, but all of you, completely. When we live in this special place — this sanctuary created by God — we are privileged — not in a haughty way, but in a blessed state that is complete and yet apart from anything that can pull us down.

As we keep our faith alive and our trust in God strong, we can be separate. We can live in an altered reality made possible by Jesus. And every day the choice is ours as to whether our spirit, soul, and body remain in God's presence ... or we choose to leave.

Today you have reached a wonderful milestone. You have completed a twenty-one-day spiritual experience that engaged all of who you are. May you carry into your future all you have learned. My hope is that you will see the Daniel Fast as your launch for the great life that awaits you. And that you will continue to grow in the love and knowledge of Jesus as you move forward. Be blessed!

> *God, through your Word, you call my whole being to agree with you and your ways. Not just part of me, but all of me ... spirit, soul, and body. You want all of me to be holy as you are holy. Father, help me to embrace the sanctified life you want for me as you continue to lead me into greater understanding. I choose you today and seek your holiness for my whole being. And I thank you for the great life that awaits me as I continue to walk in your ways. Amen.*

conclusion and resources

conclusion

THROUGH OUR WORK WITH THE DANIEL FAST OVER THE PAST SEVERAL years, we have learned that the fast not only yields great spiritual benefits but also improves multiple aspects of human health — weight loss as well as reductions in blood pressure, blood cholesterol, blood sugar, insulin levels, and systemic inflammation. Many of these benefits are linked to decreasing the risk of developing lifestyle diseases such as obesity, type 2 diabetes, and cardiovascular disease. These diseases are robbing us economically, physically, and socially, yet are diseases that are largely under our control.

Our research findings on the Daniel Fast and the latest trends in lifestyle diseases have made us more convinced than ever that the traditional or modified Daniel Fast plan is a must. Adding to the problems we see is the spiritual, physical, and economic bankruptcy that so many find themselves existing in. The Daniel Fast, coupled with daily prayer and regular exercise, can get you back on track. You can take control of your health ... and your life.

Throughout this book we have highlighted the value of Christian fasting — both from spiritual and physical perspectives. While a short-term fast should always be about growing your relationship with the Lord through a time of focused prayer, the Daniel Cure embraces both spiritual and health-specific components. First, you give yourself to the Lord during an initial twenty-one-day Daniel Fast and you seek his guidance and strength as you alter your dietary intake to favor healthy Daniel Fast–friendly choices. Second, you continue to seek him in all that you do from that day forward, asking for his grace as you embark on your newly defined healthy lifestyle — a lifestyle that will bless you richly and allow you to become all that God has created you to be.

The Daniel Cure is all about overhauling your lifestyle in favor of improved spiritual and physical health. It may not be easy at first, but it can be done. You just need help. We provide some of that in this book. But more importantly, you need God's help to infuse within you the motivation and discipline to make this new plan work ... for life.

Remember that God provides his grace to you. And his grace is more than his salvation. It's his empowerment. As his child, you are equipped to do all things through him who gives you strength. But you must come to him daily, offering praise and seeking his power. Like every loving father, he will listen to your requests and pour out his blessings and favor on your life. With regard to healthy eating, God will aid each of us in overcoming the disease-promoting lifestyles that are so prevalent in our society today. His guidance through prayer and fasting is exactly the "cure" we have been seeking all along.

the daniel cure
meal-planning worksheet

Monday	Date:
Breakfast	
Snack	
Lunch	
Snack	
Dinner	
Snack	

Tuesday	Date:
Breakfast	
Snack	
Lunch	
Snack	
Dinner	
Snack	

Wednesday	Date:
Breakfast	
Snack	
Lunch	
Snack	
Dinner	
Snack	

Thursday	Date:
Breakfast	
Snack	
Lunch	
Snack	
Dinner	
Snack	

Friday	Date:
Breakfast	
Snack	
Lunch	
Snack	
Dinner	
Snack	

Saturday	Date:
Breakfast	
Snack	
Lunch	
Snack	
Dinner	
Snack	

Sunday	Date:
Breakfast	
Snack	
Lunch	
Snack	
Dinner	
Snack	

Shopping List

☐ ☐
☐ ☐
☐ ☐
☐ ☐
☐ ☐
☐ ☐
☐ ☐
☐ ☐
☐ ☐
☐ ☐
☐ ☐
☐ ☐
☐ ☐

Personal Notes/Reminders:

NOTE: "Snack" in the planning form can mean a small meal of solid food or a meal-replacement shake, as discussed in chapter 13.

the daniel cure
health file

As you embark on the Daniel Cure lifestyle approach to health, consider using the form below and on the following page as your personal health file. Your body weight, BMI, circumference measurements, and walk time can be easily generated at home using very basic equipment (scale, tape measure, stopwatch). You may even be able to monitor your blood pressure at home using an automated device—just make sure that it is calibrated so that it provides accurate results. Other information, such as your blood cholesterol and blood sugar, will need to be gathered during your annual physical exam. Don't make the mistake of ignoring this important exam. If you want to perform any test of physical fitness as part of your health assessment (such as the one-mile walk test included on the form), make certain you first consult your physician, who will determine your physical ability to engage in such testing.

The information we believe is easily obtained and important to your overall health is included on the form. The list is by no means exhaustive, and there is space to add other variables that you believe are important to track. We included columns for three years of testing, with recordings once a year. If you desire more frequent testing, you can easily modify the table to fit your needs. You can download a copy of this table at *www.DanielCure.com*.

Consider maintaining a health file for yourself and each member of your family. This will allow you to easily and quickly track your progress on a number of key variables related to your overall health.

The Daniel Cure Health File

Name: _____

NOTE: With the exception of the one-mile walk test (which can be performed at any time of day, with or without a meal preceding it), all tests should be performed first thing in the morning, with no food or calorie-containing beverages consumed in the preceding ten to twelve hours.

Variable	Unit of Measure	Desirable Range	Year 1 Date:	Year 2 Date:	Year 3 Date:
Height	Inches	NA			
Weight	Pounds	NA			

Variable	Unit of Measure	Desirable Range	Year 1 Date:	Year 2 Date:	Year 3 Date:
Body Mass Index	BMI = 703 × Weight [pounds] ÷ (Height [inches] × Height [inches]): see table 5.3 on page 45	18.5 – 24.9			
Waist*	Inches	≤40 men			
		≤35 women			
Hip	Inches	NA			
Waist: Hip*†	NA	≤0.90 men			
		≤0.85 women			
Heart Rate‡	Beats per minute	60 – 90			
Systolic Blood Pressure	mmHg	<120			
Diastolic Blood Pressure	mmHg	<80			
Glucose	mg/dL	<100			
Total Cholesterol	mg/dL	<200			
LDL-Cholesterol	mg/dL	<100			
HDL-Cholesterol	mg/dL	>40 men			
		>50 women			
Total:HDL-C§		<4.5			
Triglycerides	mg/dL	<150			
C-Reactive Protein	mg/L	<1			
1-Mile Walk Time¶	Minutes	<15			

* Abdominal obesity is associated with risk of cardiovascular disease.

† To compute the waist:hip ratio, simply divide the waist measurement by the hip measurement. For example, if your waist measurement is 35 inches and your hip measurement is 42 inches (35/42 = 0.83), your ratio is 0.83.

‡ While 60 – 80 beats per minute is the range for most individuals, your heart rate may be lower or higher and you may be perfectly healthy. Athletes often have a lower resting heart rate. Certain medications will impact heart rate. Consult your physician.

§ To compute the total:HDL-C ratio, divide the total cholesterol by the HDL-cholesterol. For example, if your total cholesterol is 190mg/dL and your HDL-cholesterol is 60mg/dL (190/60 = 3.16), your ratio is 3.16.

¶ Find a flat area to walk on (a track is ideal) and time yourself walking one mile. Your goal is to complete the mile in fifteen minutes or less. This will be very difficult for some and very easy for others. Regardless of where you begin, your goal should be to improve. As you improve, extend the distance, and track your time for the new distance. The ultimate goal is to complete as much distance as possible in the least amount of time.

the daniel cure pledge

From this day forward,

I DO accept full responsibility for my actions related to my lifestyle choices, including my daily food intake.

I DO ask the Lord Jesus Christ to give me the strength, discipline, and motivation to make a lifestyle change that will enhance my overall health and help me to serve him in the most productive way.

I DO surrender my life, including my carnal self, to Christ as my personal Lord and Savior—as it is only by his power and his grace that I will be successful in my quest to turn my life around for better health.

I DO commit to following the essential principles of the Daniel Cure plan, including the consumption of natural, nutrient-dense, fiber-rich foods.

I WILL strive to maintain the essential principles of the Daniel Cure plan, with the understanding that perfection is not the goal—progress is.

I WILL engage in other activities known to improve my overall health aside from dietary intake, such as engaging in daily prayer and performing regular exercise.

I WILL have an annual physical exam by my physician to monitor my overall health.

I WILL teach others what I have learned and help them to develop a lifestyle of health.

I WILL commit myself in body, mind, and spirit to a lifestyle of health.

By doing these, I have the faith and assurance that

I WILL overcome all obstacles and all struggles in my pursuit of a healthy lifestyle and I will be able to do all things "through him who gives me strength" (Philippians 4:13).

_____   _____
Printed Name   Signed Name

_____
Date

_____   _____
Witness to Signature (Printed Name) Witness to Signature (Signed Name)

_____
Witness to Signature (Date)

daniel fast benefits

THROUGH OUR COLLECTIVE WORK WITH THE DANIEL FAST OVER THE PAST several years, we have noted multiple benefits in human health. The table spanning the following three pages outlines these benefits and provides information as to how they might occur and why they are important. Our ongoing research should serve to further support these findings, as well as to expand on the favorable changes observed when individuals follow the Daniel Fast.

HOW DOES IT HAPPEN AND WHY IS IT IMPORTANT?

Daniel Fast Benefit	How Does It Happen?	Why Is It Important?
Body weight/body fat reduction*	People tend to eat fewer calories due to the greater satiating effect of natural food choices (they are fuller for a longer period of time); the types of foods eaten contain more fiber, which has been shown to aid in weight loss; blood insulin levels may be lower and more stable due to stability in blood sugar (related to intake of natural, fiber-rich foods).	Improved appearance and sense of well-being—people feel better about themselves, have a greater energy level, and are more capable of performing routine activities of daily living; reduction in disease risk over time (type 2 diabetes, cardiovascular disease, certain types of cancer); improved overall quality of life.
Blood pressure reduction*	Plant-based diets have been reported to lower blood pressure; the nitrate content of the Daniel Fast dietary plan may lead to increased nitric oxide, which may allow for blood vessel relaxation and a lowering of blood pressure.	Elevated blood pressure can damage blood vessels, leading to stroke or heart attack as well as kidney disease and enlargement of the heart; high blood pressure is dangerous because it often has no warning signs or symptoms; elevated blood pressure (≥140/90 mmHg) is considered a risk factor for cardiovascular disease.
Blood cholesterol reduction*	The reduction in dietary cholesterol and saturated fat leads to a reduction in blood cholesterol; the increase in dietary fiber also leads to a reduction in blood cholesterol, as fiber helps to carry cholesterol from the circulation to the liver for removal from the body (ultimately through feces in the form of bile acids); cholesterol removal is increased with the addition to the diet of both fiber and water.	Elevated total (≥200 mgdL) and LDL (≥100 mg/dL) cholesterol are recognized risk factors for cardiovascular disease; lowering these values may reduce the risk for developing cardiovascular disease; in support of this idea, statin drugs (medicine used to lower blood cholesterol) are one of the most widely prescribed drugs in the world (note that statin use is somewhat controversial and not all physicians and scientists support their widespread use or the idea that total and LDL-cholesterol is associated with cardiovascular disease).

Daniel Fast Benefit	How Does It Happen?	Why Is It Important?
Blood sugar reduction*	Typical diets contain an abundance of processed foods and simple sugars; the Daniel Fast does not; the Daniel Fast does contain a significant amount of fiber, whole-grain products, and quality produce as well as unsaturated fatty acids, which may aid insulin sensitivity (allowing for more efficient blood glucose lowering).	Elevated fasting blood glucose is used as a diagnostic tool for pre-diabetes (≥100 mg/dL) and diabetes (≥126 mg/dL); type 2 diabetes accounts for about 95% of all diabetes cases and is strongly linked to obesity, poor dietary intake, and physical inactivity; diabetes is associated with multiple health problems, including cardiovascular disease, blindness, peripheral neuropathy, kidney failure, and amputations.
Blood antioxidant capacity increase*	The Daniel Fast includes a very rich source of dietary antioxidants in the form of whole grains, fruits, and vegetables. Dietary antioxidants can increase the blood antioxidant pool.	Antioxidants help to fight "free radicals," which have the potential to damage cells; increased production of free radicals can lead to "oxidative stress," a condition strongly associated with accelerated aging and human disease.
Blood oxidative stress reduction*	The increase in dietary antioxidants can lead to a reduction in oxidative stress biomarkers; a decrease in total calories, saturated fat, and simple sugars (observed with a Daniel Fast) has been associated with a reduction in "free radicals." Less free radical production should result in lower oxidative stress.	As indicated for antioxidants, oxidative stress is strongly associated with accelerated aging and human disease; a reduction in oxidative stress biomarkers may be associated with a reduction in disease onset and/or progression.
Blood nitric oxide increase*	The nitrate content of the Daniel Fast dietary plan may lead to increased nitric oxide, as measured by the surrogate markers nitrate + nitrite; the Daniel Fast is associated with a reduction in "free radicals." The free radical known as "superoxide" can react with nitric oxide and render it inactive (via conversion into the harmful peroxynitrite); lower superoxide generation may lead to greater availability of nitric oxide.	Nitric oxide is a molecule involved in many aspects of human health — in particular the relaxation of blood vessels; increased nitric oxide may allow for a lowering in blood pressure; increased nitric oxide is also important for male sexual function and is the main focus (via its role as a signaling molecule) of drugs targeting erectile dysfunction.

Daniel Fast Benefit	How Does It Happen?	Why Is It Important?
Blood inflammation reduction*	The reduction in processed food (and all chemicals, additives, and preservatives associated with processed food) may account for a lowering in blood inflammation; the reduction in saturated fat and calories may also be a cause for this finding; a reduction in body weight/fat may be involved as well.	Inflammation has been associated with multiple human diseases and is particularly involved in the etiology of cardiovascular disease.
Arthritic symptoms/ joint pain reduction	The reduction in body weight may be a factor in reducing joint discomfort; ingestion of wholesome foods, including a variety of micronutrients, may also aid in the alleviation of joint pain.	A reduction in joint pain equals increased mobility, leading to a more active lifestyle; a more active lifestyle should aid in weight management and associated health benefits; increased mobility also leads to improved quality of life.
Complexion improved	The reduction in processed food (and all chemicals, additives, and preservatives associated with processed food) may account for noted improvements in complexion.	Improved aesthetics; improved sense of confidence in terms of physical appearance.
Sleep quality improved	The reduction in total calories, saturated fat, and simple sugars may be associated with the noted improvements in sleep quality; this is particularly true if individuals limit high-calorie, high-fat, and high-sugar foods during the late-night hours.	Poor sleep quality (difficulty falling asleep, remaining asleep, or falling back asleep if awakened during the night) impacts millions of people worldwide; optimal dietary intake can improve sleep quality and, as a result, improve the overall quality of life.
Sense of peace improved	Providing the body with the correct fuel leads to the best results—you're now feeding your body what it needs to excel; you feel good about it; peace is now yours.	Assists in continuing with the dietary plan; reinforcement that the dietary plan can effectively impact multiple areas of your life —including spiritual and emotional peace.
Trust in God improved	Start your day on your knees; daily reading of God's Word; seeking him in all you do—he will deliver every time, and you trust in him with 100% of your mind, body, and soul; there is no stopping you now.	Easily the most important on the list—your trust in God improves due to his blessing and guidance in your life throughout the process of doing the Daniel Fast. The benefits of your growing relationship with him will exceed any physical-health-related parameter.

* Documented in peer-reviewed scientific publications of the Daniel Fast.

the science behind
the daniel fast

The purpose of this appendix is to provide you with more details regarding our research of the Daniel Fast. Although we now shift gears and discuss the health-related benefits of this fast, please keep in mind that Christian fasting is always done for the sole purpose of developing and growing your own personal relationship with the Lord through a period of fasting and prayer—not for improving your health. With this understanding, let's take a closer look at what we've discovered so far in our study of the Daniel Fast. While I (Rick) wrote this information for the "non-scientist," it is a bit more technical than other parts of this book. It may require a couple of reads to fully understand the content. Hang in there ... your full understanding of these findings will likely fuel your interest in adopting the Daniel Fast way of eating as a lifestyle.

AS ALL SCIENTISTS UNDERSTAND, RESEARCH IS AN ENDLESS PURSUIT OF answers—many of which simply raise more questions. While this can sometimes be frustrating and tedious, the job of a scientist is also one of great excitement, as new discoveries are made on a regular basis. In relation to our work with the Daniel Fast, we have noted very positive findings with regard to several components of human health, yet many questions remain. As with all areas of investigation, continued pursuit of these answers will help to support the use of this eating plan as a means to improve overall health and may provide health-care practitioners the evidence to confidently recommend this plan to clients and patients seeking improved health through dietary means. The bottom line here is that although the evidence presented in this appendix is exciting and convincing for many, the need for additional evidence remains. This includes replication of our initial findings, expansion of our findings through the use of longer-term human studies, and mechanistic studies using animal models (to understand the "why" and "how" questions). Ongoing research of the Daniel Fast is being conducted in our lab. The key points surrounding each study are explained here. Readers with additional interest should visit *www.danielfastresearch.com* to download or request the complete manuscript for each study. This will provide more detailed information in addition to a wealth of references to support the points being made. Contact information is also provided on that site.

STUDY 1: **THE DANIEL FAST AND RISK FACTORS FOR CARDIOVASCULAR AND METABOLIC DISEASE**

Background and Rationale: It is well accepted that poor dietary intake contributes greatly to disease of multiple pathologies. Diseases that have received the greatest attention in recent years are of cardiovascular (e.g., heart and vascular disease) and metabolic (e.g., obesity and diabetes) origin. Due to its elimination of animal products—in particular, the saturated fat and cholesterol contained in such foods—as well as elimination of processed foods with their additives and preservatives, and the addition of dietary fiber, fruits, and vegetables, the Daniel Fast appears as a near-optimal approach for improving cardiovascular and metabolic health. This was the general hypothesis when designing the initial Daniel Fast study, with a particular focus on known and suspected risk factors for cardiovascular and metabolic disease.

Methods: Forty-three adults ranging in age from twenty to sixty-two completed a twenty-one-day Daniel Fast. We provided detailed guidelines in addition to instruction sheets on foods that were both allowed or proscribed, as well as a basic recipe guide. All participants purchased and prepared their own food. We felt this was important in order to maintain the practical application nature of this work. That is, many studies involving food intake provide participants prepackaged food and/or prepare food in a research kitchen and have participants consume meals in the presence of an investigator. Although compliance is generally better with this approach (participants are simply told what to eat and are provided the food, and they eat it), it has little practical application. If people are going to benefit from the Daniel Fast plan, or any plan for that matter, we need to know that they can do this on their own—with some general guidance from investigators and without having their hand held throughout the twenty-one-day period. Our plan allowed for this.

After reporting to the lab for a review of all procedures, participants were given one week to prepare for the fast. On the first day of the fast, they reported to the lab for their pre-intervention assessment. After the twenty-one-day fast, they reported to the lab for their post-intervention assessment (day twenty-two). For both visits, they reported after a twelve-hour overnight fast, without performing strenuous physical activity during the preceding twenty-four to forty-eight hours. This was an important requirement, as we know that both acute eating and exercise can impact our chosen outcome measures (e.g., blood cholesterol, insulin, glucose).

At each lab visit, participants' mental and physical health, resting heart rate and blood pressure, and measurements of variables such as waist and hip circumference, body weight, and body composition were taken using a dual-energy X-ray absorptiometry device (DXA) — the same tool used for bone-density scans. Blood was collected for determination of a wide array of clinical measures, such as complete blood count, comprehensive metabolic panel, and lipid panel. These three panels are commonly included as one component of a physical examination and provide information related to the general health of numerous body systems. The variables most well-known in these panels are blood glucose (blood sugar) and blood lipids (e.g., cholesterol and triglycerides — blood fats that are thought to contribute to cardiovascular and metabolic disease). Fasting blood glucose is an indicator of how well the body processes carbohydrate and is considered clinically in the diagnosis of pre-diabetes (fasting blood glucose value 100 – 125 mg/dL) and diabetes (fasting blood glucose value >125 mg/dL). Blood lipids (total cholesterol, LDL-cholesterol, and triglycerides) are considered risk factors for cardiovascular disease. Millions of individuals worldwide are treated daily with medication (e.g., statins) for elevated blood lipids. (Note: There is some controversy surrounding the relationship between total cholesterol and LDL-cholesterol and cardiovascular disease — and the routine use of statin drugs; however, this discussion is beyond the scope of this book.)

In addition, we also measured blood insulin and C-reactive protein. Insulin is the main hormone involved in the control of blood sugar. Higher fasting insulin levels are often, but not always, associated with type 2 diabetes. C-reactive protein is considered an "acute phase protein" that serves as an indicator of systemic inflammation. Research continues to support the idea that increased inflammation may be an associated risk factor for cardiovascular disease — in particular when combined with other known risk factors.

Finally, participants' self-reported compliance, mood, and satiety (i.e., feeling of fullness and satisfaction following eating) in relation to the fast were recorded. All participants maintained diet records during the seven-day period immediately prior to the fast (representing usual intake) and during the final seven days of the fast. It should be noted that similar methods were employed in our subsequent studies of the Daniel Fast.

Results and Practical Applications: First, compliance to the fast was excellent and measured at nearly 99 percent. This is very impressive for studies of dietary manipulation — evidence that individuals can follow this plan successfully when done for a short period of time. On a ten-point scale (0 being the worst and 10 being the best), participants' mood and satiety (feeling of fullness and satisfaction with eating) were both 7.9. This is similar to most participants' pre-fast values—indicating that both mood and satiety were not negatively impacted by the Daniel Fast. Using open-ended questions, many participants reported feeling great while on the fast, with continuous energy. Others, however, did not report such findings—noting energy during the fast was similar or lower compared to before the fast. It should be noted that these individuals were generally those who failed to plan appropriately for the fast in terms of grocery shopping (i.e., they often had no food available when it was time to eat, as they typically relied on fast food prior to the fast and could not consume such food on the fast), as well as those who routinely relied on caffeine throughout the day. When eliminating caffeine, their mood suffered. These findings underscore the importance of planning prior to beginning the Daniel Fast (or any dietary plan). With appropriate planning, individuals can experience excellent results and feel great. Without planning, the Daniel Fast or any similar plan will likely prove difficult to adhere to.

One interesting finding was that many participants reported greatly improved knowledge regarding overall nutrition, in particular with regard to macro- and micronutrients, as well as additives and preservatives in foods. This has led us to believe that the Daniel Fast may serve as a nutrition education program, encouraging individuals to consume more healthy foods simply because they better understand what they are eating. In follow-up discussions with participants, it was noted that after completing the twenty-one-day fast, many altered their way of eating long-term. This finding is consistent throughout our work with the Daniel Fast—and may actually be one of the most important benefits of following the plan. When people know and understand what is in the foods they eat, they are much more likely to make better nutrition choices. This knowledge is vital if individuals are to adopt a healthier nutritional strategy as a lifestyle.

Favorable effects were noted in several variables, with those of greatest interest being the following:

Total cholesterol: A "blood fat" considered to be a major risk factor for cardiovascular disease. Healthy values are generally to be below 200 mg/dL. It is noted that elevations in total cholesterol may lead to atherosclerosis—a buildup of plaque and dead cellular debris in the artery walls. This condition has the potential to result in heart attack or stroke. (Note: Although many physicians and scientists strongly believe that blood cholesterol levels should be controlled by lifestyle factors and/or medications, not all physicians and scientists believe this to be the case. This is likely due to findings from certain studies that fail to document an association between elevated blood cholesterol [especially total cholesterol and LDL-cholesterol] and cardiovascular disease risk and mortality.) The Daniel Fast resulted in a 19 percent average reduction in total cholesterol. Although not as pronounced as with certain medications (e.g., statins) used to treat high cholesterol, the fact that a mere change in dietary intake over a period of three weeks can produce a decrease of this magnitude deserves attention. This is especially true considering that many people experienced a reduction much greater than 19 percent.

LDL-cholesterol: This so-called "bad" cholesterol is a "low-density lipoprotein" that is considered a major risk factor for cardiovascular disease. Healthy values are generally considered to be below 100 mg/dL (or 130 mg/dL, depending on the lab's reference range). Elevations in LDL-cholesterol may lead to atherosclerosis. More important than the quantity of LDL-cholesterol may be the size of the LDL-cholesterol particles—which can be determined through more sophisticated testing of the blood sample. The "small and dense" LDL-cholesterol particles appear most problematic. The susceptibility of LDL-cholesterol to undergo oxidation (chemical modification of LDL-cholesterol associated with free-radical interactions) appears important to the development of plaques in artery walls. The Daniel Fast resulted in a 23 percent reduction in LDL-cholesterol. However, in this study we did not include a breakdown of LDL-cholesterol particle size or determine the degree of LDL-cholesterol oxidation. However, measures of lipid peroxidation were determined in other Daniel Fast work presented in this appendix.

Systolic blood pressure: This is the pressure exerted on the arterial walls during the contraction phase of the cardiac cycle (i.e., each time the heart beats). Elevated systolic blood pressure is a known major risk factor for cardiovascular disease. Elevated blood pressure is associated with numerous health problems, ranging from stroke to an enlarged heart (e.g., left-ventricular hypertrophy). The Daniel Fast resulted in an 8 percent reduction in systolic blood pressure. This is impressive considering that the average pre-fast systolic blood pressure of participants was only 115 mmHg. A healthy systolic blood pressure is generally considered to be less than 120 mmHg. Participants already had "healthy" blood pressure before starting the fast and still experienced a significant reduction. It is possible that more impressive reductions may be noted in those who are hypertensive (i.e., systolic blood pressure ≥140 mmHg).

Diastolic blood pressure: The pressure exerted on the arterial walls during the relaxation phase of the cardiac cycle (i.e., the time between each heart beat).

An elevation is a known risk factor for cardiovascular disease. The Daniel Fast resulted in a 7 percent reduction in diastolic blood pressure. This is impressive since the average pre-fast diastolic blood pressure of participants was only 72 mmHg. A healthy diastolic blood pressure is generally considered to be less than 80 mmHg.

Insulin: A hormone involved in the control of blood sugar. Normally, when blood sugar becomes elevated after eating, the pancreas secretes insulin. The insulin works through a series of chemical "signals" that make it possible for the glucose in the blood to enter body cells and be used for fuel for energy or be stored as fat for future use. However, some individuals are resistant to insulin, and the same amount of insulin that once could get the job done (i.e., lower blood sugar) can no longer do so. The pancreas then secretes more insulin to accomplish the same task. A higher fasting insulin level may indicate a degree of insulin resistance, suggesting that the cells are not as responsive to the insulin that is being secreted (i.e., because glucose remains in the blood, the pancreas secretes more insulin). The Daniel Fast resulted in a 24 percent reduction in fasting insulin, indicating less resistance to insulin in response to the Daniel Fast eating plan, so less insulin was needed. This finding highlights the potential for this eating plan to improve metabolic health.

C-reactive protein: This acute-phase protein serves as a marker of systemic inflammation. Although this indicator has limitations (e.g., it can be impacted by an acute illness, leading to an elevation that may be mistaken as a normal value), its use in a clinical setting has grown considerably in recent years. It is now accepted that increased inflammation may be a risk factor for cardiovascular disease. The Daniel Fast resulted in a 49 percent reduction in C-reactive protein, which is remarkable in just twenty-one days. It is our thought that the elimination of processed foods with their additives and preservatives, coupled with the abundance of micronutrients in the fruits and vegetables in most participants' diets, is at least partially responsible for our findings.

Summary: The results indicate that a twenty-one-day period of modified dietary intake in accordance with the Daniel Fast by men and women of varying ages (1) is met with excellent compliance and is well-tolerated, (2) may serve to educate individuals regarding food choices and the composition of a variety of foods, and (3) improves several risk factors for metabolic and cardiovascular disease. These effects (as well as those noted in the following studies) are likely realized due to the significant change in dietary intake, including a reduction in total calories, protein, saturated fat, and cholesterol and an increase in dietary fiber, fruits, vegetables, and legumes.

It should be noted that body weight was also reduced considerably (>10 pounds) in many participants, with an average loss of approximately six pounds. There was some loss of lean body mass, or muscle, that coincided with this loss in body weight. It is our belief that attempts should be made to maintain lean body mass during the fasting period. One option may be additional dietary protein. Although total cholesterol and LDL-cholesterol were lowered significantly with the fast, HDL-cholesterol was also lowered—although to a lesser extent. Because HDL-cholesterol acts in a process known as reverse cholesterol transport and serves as the body's "good cholesterol," any reduction in HDL-cholesterol is not welcome. The good news is that despite this lowering in HDL-cholesterol, there was a measurable improvement in the ratio of total cholesterol to HDL-cholesterol, which is considered by many health-care providers to be the most important component in the blood lipid panel. Regardless, methods of maintaining HDL-cholesterol during the Daniel Fast need to be identified. We understand that the removal of all animal protein from the diet often results in a lowering of HDL-cholesterol (possibly due to the removal of saturated fat). This is partly our rationale for using a slightly modified Daniel Fast approach in which small amounts of lean animal protein are included in the diet. This strategy might help in both maintaining HDL-cholesterol and lean body mass during fasting.

STUDY 2: THE DANIEL FAST AND BIOMARKERS OF ANTIOXIDANT CAPACITY AND OXIDATIVE STRESS

Background and Rationale: In scientific literature, it is well-described that dietary modification via caloric and nutrient restriction is associated with multiple health benefits, including an extension of lifespan. Some of the effects are attributed to an increase in antioxidant capacity and a decrease in the production of what are known as reactive oxygen species (ROS). These ROS are also referred to as pro-oxidants and typically as "free radicals" in the lay press. Their production occurs as part of normal cell metabolism, but can be increased in the presence of certain stressful conditions such as exposure to cigarette smoke, ozone, and certain chemicals, as well as after eating high-fat meals and even after performing very strenuous and/or long-duration exercise. Related to exercise, it should be understood that your body can rapidly adapt to this increase in free radical exposure by increasing its natural production of antioxidants in an attempt to combat the free radicals, so don't use this as an excuse not to exercise.

Although not necessarily harmful (ROS are required for normal cell function), an abundance of ROS, in particular in the presence of poor antioxidant defenses, can lead to a condition known as "oxidative stress." Oxidative stress can involve oxidative modification (damage) to a variety of important molecules, such as DNA, proteins, and lipids (such as LDL-cholesterol). Excess production of ROS has been linked to various diseases as well as to the aging process. Decreasing ROS production, in particular in the presence of increased antioxidant defense, is typically viewed as beneficial.

The Daniel Fast includes fruits, vegetables, whole grains, legumes, and nuts —all considered to be healthy foods, with many rich in antioxidants. Most previous studies of plant-based diets have focused on the measurement of blood lipids. Although these plant-based diets prohibit consumption of animal products, they do allow processed and refined foods as well as foods that contain additives and preservatives—items not allowed in the Daniel Fast guidelines that may be linked to increased ROS production. We hypothesized that a twenty-one-day Daniel Fast would favorably alter biomarkers of antioxidant status and oxidative stress.

Methods: The design was similar to that described for Study 1. However, before and after the twenty-one-day fast, participants provided blood samples that were analyzed for the following variables: Trolox Equivalent Antioxidant Capacity (TEAC), Oxygen Radical Absorbance Capacity (ORAC), malondialdehyde, hydrogen peroxide, and nitrate/nitrite.

Both TEAC and ORAC provide an indication of blood antioxidant status. The higher the TEAC and ORAC values, the better the blood can protect against the damaging effects of ROS. Therefore, higher antioxidant content is viewed as positive. Malondialdehyde is a commonly used marker of lipid, or fat, oxidation and an indicator of possible damage to cellular lipids due to increased ROS. Hydrogen peroxide is often used as a surrogate marker of ROS production. Higher hydrogen peroxide in blood is often associated with increased oxidative damage to DNA, proteins, and lipids. Nitrate/nitrite is a surrogate measure of nitric oxide, a molecule that has received a great deal of attention in recent years for a variety of benefits, including the relaxation of blood vessels.

Nitric oxide was initially identified as an endothelium relaxing factor, as it was found to result in relaxation of smooth muscle in blood vessels. Brief production of nitric oxide at low (nanomolar) concentrations benefits cardiovascular health due to decreased platelet and leukocyte adhesion, decreased rapid growth of smooth muscle cells, enhanced blood flow, and improved immune defense. In general, a slight elevation in the nitric oxide level in the blood is viewed as positive for cardiovascular health. Nitric oxide has received considerable scientific attention over the last few decades, with its recognition as the "molecule of the year" by *Science* magazine in 1992 and the Nobel Prize in physiology or medicine awarded in 1998 for work related to nitric oxide signaling in the cardiovascular system. An increase in the nitric oxide metabolites nitrate and nitrite may be associated with improved blood vessel health. An increase may also be responsible for the noted lowering in blood pressure, as indicated in Study 1.

Results and Practical Applications: Following a twenty-one-day Daniel Fast, we noted lower oxidative stress in participants, shown by a decrease in both malondialdehyde (15 percent) and hydrogen peroxide (14 percent). We also demonstrated an increase in nitrate/nitrite and TEAC. Of particular interest was our finding of a 44 percent increase in nitrate/nitrite, which exceeds increases that we or other investigators have noted as a result of dietary change or nutritional supplement intake. Considering the importance of nitric oxide to human health, this finding deserves attention. The role of nitric oxide in the vascular system helps to explain our finding of decreased blood pressure, as noted in Study 1. The ability of blood vessels to "relax," which is believed to be linked with the increase in nitric oxide, reduces the pressure load on the vessel walls and lowers blood pressure.

Summary: Data from this study indicate that a twenty-one-day Daniel Fast decreases blood oxidative stress, increases antioxidant capacity (as measured by TEAC), and increases nitrate/nitrite level. Coupled with the findings for improved cardiovascular risk factors as noted in Study 1, these results indicate that this biblically based fast may be one answer to improving diet-induced morbidity and mortality in the population at large.

STUDY 3: THE DANIEL FAST, KRILL OIL, AND RISK FACTORS FOR CARDIOVASCULAR AND METABOLIC DISEASE

Background and Rationale: In our initial work with the Daniel Fast, we noted favorable effects in several health-related markers. However, we also noted a decrease in HDL-cholesterol, the so-called "good" cholesterol. Because the ideal dietary plan would reduce total cholesterol and LDL-cholesterol (the "bad" cholesterol) as well as maintain or elevate HDL-cholesterol, we sought to identify a natural nutrient that might allow for this effect on HDL-cholesterol. Although a general internet search led to several nutrients, a review of scientific literature indicated that few favorably impact HDL-cholesterol in human participants when consumed orally. One candidate was krill oil.

This oil is extracted from Antarctic krill, a small crustacean-like fish that is consumed in abundance by whales. Krill oil is rich in two health-promoting fatty acids. One of these is Docosahexaenoic acid (DHA) and the other is Eicosapentaenoic acid (EPA). In addition, krill oil contains something called phospholipids, which are thought to improve overall absorption of fatty acids, as compared to traditional fish oil. At least one published scientific report noted favorable effects of krill oil on HDL-cholesterol in humans when consuming an oral daily dose of one to three grams. We therefore believed that the addition of krill oil to the Daniel Fast plan might (1) offset the undesirable lowering in HDL-cholesterol that was observed in our initial study and (2) reduce oxidative stress, due to the inclusion of the antioxidant astaxanthin, which is found in krill.

Methods: Thirty-nine men and women completed a twenty-one-day Daniel Fast in which half of participants were assigned to consume krill oil daily and the other half were assigned to receive a placebo (a fake supplement). The krill oil was provided at a dosage of 2 grams per day, which is a common dosage recommended for fish oil.

Multiple variables were assessed both before and after the twenty-one-day fast. For example, fasting blood samples were obtained from participants before and after the fast and analyzed for a variety of clinical parameters, including serum lipids, complete blood count, comprehensive metabolic panel, insulin, and C-reactive protein. Markers of oxidative stress and antioxidant capacity were also measured. Finally, blood pressure, heart rate, and a variety of other variables, such as weight and body composition, were also included. Our test panel included the same comprehensive assessment of what had been included in prior Daniel Fast research, with the only alteration in research design the inclusion of krill oil.

Results and Practical Applications: Although we believed that the outcome measures might be improved by the addition of krill oil, this was not the case. In fact, results for both groups (krill oil and placebo) were nearly identical. The overall results were similar to our initial work with the Daniel Fast. First, participants' self-reported compliance to the fast was close to 98 percent, indicating that three weeks of pure vegan eating can be maintained with high compliance. Overall participant ratings were 8.3 for physical health and vitality and 8.6 for mental health during the fast. Satiety (feeling of fullness and satisfaction) was 8.0. These three variables were measured using a ten-point scale (1 = as low as possible; 10 = as high as possible).

The changes in the main outcome factors—blood pressure, body weight, blood lipids, insulin, C-reactive protein, and nitrate/nitrite—were similar to the changes observed in our prior Daniel Fast research. Only small reductions were noted in markers of oxidative stress (malondialdehyde and hydrogen peroxide). A decrease of approximately 10 percent was noted in fasting blood glucose. But striking reductions in fasting blood glucose (40 percent and 44 percent) were noted in two type 2 diabetic participants with poorly controlled blood glucose (pre-fast blood glucose values >250 mg/dL). This latter finding deserves attention by those with diabetes, type 2 in particular, and those who care for someone with this disease. These findings are also of relevance for those who may be "borderline" diabetic, with poorly controlled fasting blood glucose. That being said, our findings admittedly require further study using a larger sample of diabetics. If similar findings can be obtained by a larger group of type 2 diabetics, the potential for the Daniel Fast to improve fasting blood sugar will demand considerable attention. This is true considering the absolute importance of optimal blood glucose management in those with diabetes. Based on the current evidence with the Daniel Fast (in addition to other research focused on dietary plans that are similar), altering dietary intake in accordance with the Daniel Fast may have significant implications for type 2 diabetics and should be at least considered, while under the watchful eye of a qualified health-care provider. The last point requires specific attention, as alteration in dietary intake in favor of high fiber and the avoidance of processed foods (often which contain "simple" sugars which act to rapidly spike blood sugar) may require the dosage of diabetic medicine (e.g., oral hypoglycemic agents, insulin) to be adjusted accordingly. Only a qualified health-care provider should be involved in such manipulation of medication dosing for their patients.

Summary: These findings show an improvement in a variety of health-related parameters after a twenty-one-day Daniel Fast. While such documented changes do not guarantee a decrease in the onset of a disease and/or a slowing in the progression, the improvements do indeed result in risk factor reduction. The Daniel Fast eating plan does appear to be health-promoting in a variety of ways. Of course, long-term compliance to this eating plan needs to be shown. While modifying dietary intake over the course of twenty-one days appears quite manageable by most devoted individuals, the question of importance is whether individuals can maintain this plan, or one similar to it, long term. If so, we may truly have discovered a near optimal dietary plan for improving human health.

STUDY 4: THE DANIEL FAST AND POSTPRANDIAL OXIDATIVE STRESS

Background and Rationale: As briefly mentioned in the description of Study 2, ROS, or "free radicals," are important "signaling" molecules in the body that serve many beneficial physiological roles, such as insulin signaling and maintaining immune function. However, when produced in large amounts, ROS can cause problems. They can cause damage to many vital molecules, including proteins and DNA. Excessive production of ROS is usually viewed as harmful, especially when it occurs regularly.

When cells and body systems are chronically exposed to stressful stimuli, one of two things occurs: (1) the system adapts in an attempt to handle future assaults by that same stressor or (2) the system shuts down due to chronic overload and abuse. When too many ROS are produced, the body may up its own natural defense system—a family of antioxidants produced in the body that protect cells from ROS. This is why those who exercise on a regular basis usually have higher levels of blood antioxidants as compared to sedentary individuals—their exercise bouts act as low-grade stress that triggers production of ROS, and the body increases production of antioxidants (enzymatic and non-enzymatic) to combat this increase in ROS. The exercise-induced increase in ROS serves as a "trigger" for the antioxidant defense. Therefore, there should be no concern over the mild and transient increase in ROS observed after strenuous exercise. This is actually beneficial due to the improvement in antioxidant defense. The real problem arises when production of ROS is significant and prolonged, which occurs after high-calorie meals, particularly when the meals are high in saturated fat and simple sugars. Blood triglycerides (fats) and glucose (sugar) can increase significantly, resulting in the production of ROS, which is not desirable. (Note: There are many other potent stimulators of ROS—cigarette smoke is one of the greatest.)

We know that simple measurement of blood-borne variables such as triglycerides and glucose in a fasting state (as is done as part of a physical examination) fails to provide adequate information related to how an individual may metabolize nutrients. Therefore, in much of our research we expose individuals to a "stressor" by using a high-calorie, high-fat, high-sugar meal. You might think of this in the same way as you would a physical "stress test" ordered by a cardiologist to test the function of a patient's heart. Having been a technician for many such tests, I (Rick) know that in many cases, patients have no abnormalities and appear to be in good physical health when examined at rest. However, when that patient walks on a treadmill until exhaustion, abnormalities often appear. The "stressor" of walking was needed to uncover the underlying problem. The same may be true regarding the metabolism of certain nutrients — saturated fats in particular, but also simple sugars in those with poor blood glucose control (e.g., diabetics and pre-diabetics). A simple measure of fasting blood glucose and triglycerides does not tell the complete story with regard to your metabolic health.

For the past several years we have used a "test meal" to study the metabolic health of individuals. We prefer to use a milkshake as the test meal because we can precisely measure and weigh each ingredient. Blood samples obtained from test participants before and for several hours following consumption of the milkshake are then analyzed for a variety of biochemical measures, which provide us with a comprehensive indication of how the individual metabolizes the nutrient mix.

Our milkshake is made of whole milk, ice cream, and heavy whipping cream. Other scientists involved in the same line of research use whole food meals that include biscuits, eggs, cheese, and meat. Regardless of the foods consumed, one thing is clear from our work and from the work of others — ingestion of high-calorie, high-fat, sugar-rich meals induces a massive elevation in blood fat and glucose, which is strongly associated with an increase in ROS production. Therefore, minimizing the increase in blood fat (and blood glucose in those with glucose regulatory problems) may result in less ROS production, which may have important health implications. An increase in ROS — and the "oxidative stress" that results — is linked to a variety of diseases. Considering that many people eat three or more high-calorie, high-fat meals a day, they stay in prolonged periods of elevated ROS. This technically would be referred to as "postprandial oxidative stress." Postprandial refers to the time after a meal. Oxidative stress refers to the increase in ROS production that exceeds the ability of the body's antioxidant defense system to render these ROS inactive — potentially resulting in damage to cellular components. Over time, this can have major health consequences. A dietary plan in line with that of the Daniel Fast may minimize this damaging oxidative stress.

In our study, we simply wanted to know whether changing dietary intake by following the Daniel Fast for twenty-one days would improve how a person processed the same high-fat milkshake after the fast compared with before the fast. The logic for our hypothesis was based on our initial findings that fasting blood lipids and glucose as well as antioxidant status all improve after a twenty-one-day fast. Considering that individuals with higher fasting blood lipids experience a much greater increase in blood lipids and oxidative stress after meals, we hypothesized that an improvement in those blood values after a period of fasting would translate into an improvement in the body's overall response to the milkshake meal.

Methods: Both before and after the twenty-one-day fast, participants consumed a high-fat milkshake. Blood samples were taken before consuming the milkshake and at two and four hours after. We included a sample of twenty participants, and blood was analyzed for a variety of oxidative stress biomarkers.

Results and Practical Applications: After the twenty-one-day fasting period, the overall oxidative stress response to the milkshake ingestion was lower than it was before the fast. Specifically, the following variables were lower: blood triglycerides (decrease of 11 percent), malondialdehyde (decrease of 11 percent), hydrogen peroxide (decrease of 8 percent), and advanced oxidized protein products (decrease of 12 percent). It should be noted that the average decrease of 10 percent did not reach "statistical significance" and may have been limited by our relatively small sample size of only twenty subjects. However, our findings may still have clinical relevance. This is particularly true when considering the importance of measuring postprandial responses in those with increased risk for cardiovascular and metabolic disease. Our findings document that a period of Daniel fasting allows individuals to respond slightly more favorably to a high-fat meal (which is what many people consume on a regular basis). Clearly, frequent and excessive oxidative insults resulting from high-fat meals may be linked to increased development and progression of cardiovascular and metabolic disease. Abiding by a Daniel Fast eating plan may serve to enhance health by lessening the overall production of ROS, especially after high-calorie, high-fat meals. Of course, more research is needed over a prolonged period of time to determine whether slightly less oxidative stress following each meal actually improves health in the long run.

Summary: Three weeks of Daniel Fast eating may protect the body from the potentially harmful effects of free radicals as generated after high-fat meals. Providing the body with the correct fuel not only allows one to feel great but also allows the body to process nutrients more efficiently, possibly resulting in a lower overall "free radical burden," which may have implications for improved overall health.

Since these results were noted following just three weeks of modified food intake, the long-term impact of the Daniel Fast eating plan will need to be investigated to determine if more robust effects can be noted in response to ingestion of a single meal. Moreover, the long-term health implications specific to this eating plan need to be investigated. Finally, as our findings did not meet criteria for statistical significance, additional work with a larger sample of subjects is also necessary.

STUDY 5: COMPARISON OF A TRADITIONAL AND MODIFIED DANIEL FAST ON RISK FACTORS FOR CARDIOVASCULAR AND METABOLIC DISEASE

Background and Rationale: Considering our collective findings with the Daniel Fast, we are always seeking methods of improving the health-related outcomes. Although the overall results from our initial work with the Daniel Fast have been encouraging, two minor concerns remain.

First, HDL-cholesterol is lowered when switching to a diet devoid of animal protein. Although the total HDL-cholesterol ratio is improved on the Daniel Fast (due to the fact that total cholesterol decreases by about 20 percent while HDL-cholesterol decreases by only about 12 percent), which may be the variable of most importance for many clinicians, we continue to seek methods of mitigating the reduction in HDL-cholesterol.

Second, while body weight decreases from pre- to post-fast in most participants, 40–50 percent of the weight lost in some participants is lean body mass (muscle). While this is common for most diets, our aim is to minimize the amount of muscle lost.

One way to accomplish both goals is to include a small amount of lean animal protein in a typical Daniel Fast. All other components of the fast remain the same. The addition of animal protein would be one serving a day of lean meat and one serving a day of dairy (skim milk). Combining one serving of each of these foods provides an additional 30 grams of protein per day, which is an amount equal to the average decrease in dietary protein that most individuals experience when on the fast. With such a plan, we could possibly observe similar changes in outcomes as observed in our prior studies, with more favorable changes in both HDL-cholesterol and lean body mass.

Methods: We enrolled a sample of close to thirty men and women and assigned them to one of two groups: A traditional Daniel Fast or the modified Daniel Fast of one serving per day of lean meat (3 ounces of chicken, fish, beef, pork, turkey, or beef) and skim milk (8 ounces). Following all baseline assessments and the initial week of dietary recording, subjects underwent their Daniel Fast group assignment for three weeks. Numerous biochemical and body measures were taken before and after the twenty-one-day fast, as has been done in our prior work, and results were compared between the traditional and modified Daniel Fast groups.

Results and Practical Applications: Interestingly, we noted similar findings for most variables between both groups. In fact, the changes in cholesterol fractions were actually more impressive for the modified Daniel Fast, when subjects were allowed to consume small amounts of meat and dairy. These findings suggest that the inclusion of small amounts of animal products do not pose any health concern; in fact, they may provide a significant health benefit. Subjects on the modified Daniel Fast did not lose as much lean body mass as did the subjects on the traditional plan. Since many people prefer to consume at least small amounts of animal protein, the modified plan may prove more "user friendly." Even if individuals decide that consumption of animal protein is not something that they are interested in, the simple fact that individuals have the understanding that "I am allowed to eat this food if I want to" may assist greatly in long-term compliance. Freedom of choice really does matter. Although this particular modified plan does not meet the criteria of a biblical Daniel Fast done for strict spiritual purposes, it may serve as an alternative for those interested in adopting this eating plan as a lifestyle aimed at improving overall health—such as the Daniel Cure approach.

Summary: Results were similar for those who adhered to the traditional Daniel Fast and those who added small amounts of animal products. This suggests that slight deviations from the "pure" vegan-based Daniel Fast approach may be welcome in the long term as people may desire to occasionally eat animal protein.

STUDY 6: COMPLIANCE TO A TRADITIONAL AND MODIFIED DANIEL FAST OVER SIX MONTHS

Background and Rationale: While compliance to the Daniel Fast plan has been near 100 percent in our past work, it must be stressed that the fasting lasted for only three weeks. As with most dietary plans, an individual can be successful in the short term. However, if an eating program is to be adopted as a lifestyle approach, it must be something that can be done long term. We felt it important to extend the duration of the fast beyond three weeks while also making a comparison to a plan that involves some of the main food items that people tend to miss the most (e.g., meat and caffeine).

In reviewing participant comments from past studies, it was apparent that many people would like to consume an occasional piece of meat and some dairy products. Most also missed coffee and tea. These foods have potential health-enhancing properties. For example, lean meats and dairy are great sources of protein and have many vitamins and minerals that aid overall health. These foods also may help maintain HDL-cholesterol and lean body mass, as indicated in Study 5. Both coffee and tea have significant antioxidant content that potentially could result in favorable health-related effects.

Based on this evidence, we compared data from a long-term (six-month) traditional Daniel Fast (with allowable black, unsweetened coffee and tea) with a modified Daniel Fast (with allowable black, unsweetened coffee and tea; one serving [3 ounces] per day of lean meat; one serving [8 ounces] per day of skim milk).

Methods: The study design was similar to that of our prior work — in particular Study 5 (with inclusion of a variety of biochemical and body measurement variables). Subjects were assigned to either the traditional or the modified fast groups. Compliance and other outcome measurements were obtained at three weeks, three months, and six months and compared between groups.

Results and Practical Applications: The compliance for both the traditional and modified groups was similar at all times (three weeks, three months, and six months), decreasing gradually over time from close to 95 percent at three weeks, to 85 percent at three months, to 80 percent at six months for subjects who completed the entire study. These values were then compared to those of other popular diet plans and noted to be superior in those subjects who completed the study. For example, a paper published in the *Journal of the American Medical Association* compared the compliance rates of four popular diets: Atkins, Zone, Weight Watchers, and Ornish.[34] The authors presented subjects' self-reported dietary adherence scores that were far lower than what we observed for the Daniel Fast. Specifically, compliance values at three months were 50 percent or lower for all diets, and values at six months were 40 percent or lower. Compare this to the Daniel Fast compliance numbers of 85 percent (at three months) and 80 percent (at six months), and you can see clearly that the Daniel Fast (traditional or modified) may be a much more reasonable long-term strategy for dietary success.

FINAL WORD PERTAINING TO RESEARCH FINDINGS

While we believe that the research information presented on the Daniel Fast is interesting, more studies are always needed. This is necessary in order to (1) replicate existing findings and allow scientists adequate data to make informed recommendations and to (2) answer new questions that arise in ongoing studies. While we believe the Daniel Fast plan can improve many components of human health, outside of specific changes to dietary components, we still do not fully understand the specific mechanisms as to why or how this occurs. Additional studies, likely involving animal models, which allow for more detailed investigation of organ systems and mechanisms of action, are needed to extend our initial work. While the reduction in dietary protein, fat, and cholesterol appears to drive many of the health-promoting benefits, a lower protein intake may also be the reason for the lower HDL-cholesterol and lean body mass. Research is needed to identify methods of mitigating these changes.

While the traditional Daniel Fast will yield outstanding benefits in regard to many outcome measures for most individuals, the dietary plan is not perfect. Some minor modifications are needed before we can claim with confidence that this plan is "ideal" for everyone. Based on the collective body of nutrition science evidence, we feel confident in stating that the ideal would be a Daniel Fast plan that includes small quantities of animal protein (1 – 2 servings per day of lean meat or fish; 1 – 2 servings per day of low-fat dairy) in a meal pattern of small and frequent meals throughout the day and an abundance of clean water. Of course, the occasional "cheat" meal could be a component of this plan, and individuals should not feel guilty over the occasional consumption of foods that are not perfect. Perfection should not be the goal — progress is the goal. In fact, if people could adopt this dietary plan with 80 percent compliance, the health-care economy in all industrialized societies would take a rapid and dramatic turn for the better.

RELATED RESEARCH

Our work with the Daniel Fast is always evolving. Please see *www.danielfast research.com* for more information. If our work with the Daniel Fast interests you, you may also want to read about our related work, much of which can be accessed in full text PDF form by visiting PubMed (*http://www.ncbi.nlm.nih .gov/pubmed*). Simply use the search term "Bloomer and Memphis" and a list of articles will appear. When you click on each article, you will be able to view the abstract, and in many cases you will be able to print the full text PDF. Many other excellent research articles are available on PubMed by authors at other institutions. I encourage you to read the articles that interest you. (Note: the email address of the article author is often posted with the abstract title. Simply email the author and request a PDF of the article. Most authors are happy to learn that someone is interested in their work.)

The field of nutrition is constantly emerging, and many new and exciting discoveries are made annually. We encourage you to stay informed and then, and most importantly, put into practice the knowledge you have gained.

ADOPTING THE DANIEL FAST IN YOUR LIFESTYLE

This appendix has focused primarily on research findings pertaining to our work with the Daniel Fast. If interested in adopting the Daniel Fast in your daily routine, review the guidelines provided throughout this book. If not doing the fast for pure spiritual purposes, but rather as a method of improving health, consider some minor modifications that may allow overall compliance to be enhanced without sacrificing the nutritional quality of the plan (e.g., inclusion of lean meats and dairy, coffee, and tea). Certain dietary supplements may also prove helpful. For more information, see *www.DanielCure .com/supplements*.

You should also consider a structured program of exercise as an adjunct to your eating plan, as exercise not only aids in improving overall health in many ways but also helps you stay on your food plan when embarking on a new nutritional regimen. Finally and most importantly, seek the Lord's guidance in all you do. As you begin this new walk with him to enhance your overall physical and spiritual health as well as your mental outlook, ask for his blessing and favor.

notes

1. CDC Features, "Insufficient Sleep Is a Public Health Epidemic," Centers for Disease Control and Prevention, *http://www.cdc.gov/features/dssleep*.

2. "Leisure Activities in 2011," United States Department of Labor Bureau of Labor Statistics, *http://www.bls.gov/news.release/atus.nr0.htm*.

3. Finkelstein, Eric A. et al., "Obesity and Severe Obesity Forecasts through 2030," *American Journal of Preventive Medicine* 42, no. 6 (June 2012): 563–70.

4. "Lots to Lose: How America's Health and Obesity Crisis Threatens Our Economic Future" (June 5, 2012), *http://bipartisanpolicy.org/library/lotstolose*.

5. John Piper, *A Hunger for God* (Wheaton, IL: Crossway, 1997).

6. "About Glycemic Index," Human Nutrition Unit, School of Molecular Biosciences, University of Sydney, Australia, *http://www.glycemicindex.com/about.php*.

7. "Obesity Facts & Resources," Campaign to End Obesity, *http://www.obesitycampaign.org*.

8. Overweight and Obesity, Adult Obesity Facts, "Obesity Affects Some Groups More than Others," Centers for Disease Control and Prevention, *http://www.cdc.gov/obesity/data/adult.html* (JAMA. 2012; 307(5):491–97, doi:10.1001/jama.2012.39).

9. Overweight and Obesity, Data and Statistics, "Obesity and Extreme Obesity Rates Decline Among Low-Income Preschool Children," Centers for Disease Control and Prevention, *http://www.cdc.gov/obesity/data/childhood.html*.

10. Finkelstein, "Obesity: Forecasts through 2030," 563–70.

11. Richard Carmona, "Obesity Bigger Threat Than Terrorism?" AP (July 17, 2010), *http://www.cbsnews.com/2100-204_162-1361849.html*.

12. Fact Sheet, "Obesity and Cancer Risk," National Cancer Institute, (January 3, 2012), *http://www.cancer.gov/cancertopics/factsheet/Risk/obesity*.

13. Diabetes Programme, World Health Organization, *http://www.who.int/diabetes/en*.

14. National Diabetes Fact Sheet, Centers for Disease Control and Prevention, National Center for Chronic Disease Prevention and Health Promotion: Division of Diabetes Translation, released January 26, 2011.

15. Diabetes Basics, "Diabetes Statistics," American Diabetes Association (January 26, 2011), *http://www.diabetes.org/diabetes-basics/diabetes-statistics/*.

16. Diabetes Public Health Resource, 2011 National Diabetes Fact Sheet, "Diagnosed and Undiagnosed Diabetes among People Aged 20 Years or Older, United States, 2010," Centers for Disease Control and Prevention, *http://www.cdc.gov/diabetes/pubs/estimates11.htm#1*.

17. "Number of Americans with Diabetes Projected to Double or Triple by 2050," Centers for Disease Control and Prevention, CDC Newsroom, (October 22, 2010), *http://www.cdc.gov/media/pressrel/2010/r101022.html*.

18. Diabetes Basics, "Diabetes Statistics," American Diabetes Association, *http://www.diabetes.org/diabetes-basics/diabetes-statistics*.

19. Ross DeVol and Armen Bedroussian, *An Unhealthy America: The Economic Burden of Chronic Disease* (Santa Monica, CA: Milken Institute, 2007), 59, *http://www .milkeninstitute.org/healthreform/pdf/AnUnhealthyAmericaExecSumm.pdf.*

20. Fast Stats, "Leading Causes of Death," Centers for Disease Control and Prevention, *http://www.cdc.gov/nchs/fastats/lcod.htm.*

21. Diabetes Basics, Diabetes Statistics, American Diabetes Association (January 26, 2011), *http://www.diabetes.org/diabetes-basics/diabetes-statistics.*

22. Heart Disease, "Heart Disease Conditions," Centers for Disease Control and Prevention, *http://www.cdc.gov/heartdisease/conditions.htm.*

23. Centers for Disease Control and Prevention, "Heart Disease and Stroke: The Nation's Leading Killers," *http://www.cdc.gov/chronicdisease/resources/publications/AAG/dhdsp.htm.*

24. Kenneth D. Kochanek, Jiaquan Xu, Sherry L. Murphy, Arialdi M. Miniño, and Hsiang-Ching Kung, "Deaths: Final Data for 2009," *National Vital Statistics Reports* 60, no. 3 (Dec. 29, 2011).

25. Survey by Statin Usage, "Understanding Statin Use in America and Gaps in Education," *http://www.statinusage.com/Documents/usage-press-release.pdf.*

26. Mayo Clinic staff, "Cholesterol Levels: What Numbers Should You Aim For?" Mayo Clinic (September 21, 2012), *http://www.mayoclinic.com/health/cholesterol-levels/CL00001.*

27. Mayo Clinic staff, "Are These Cholesterol-Lowering Drugs Right for You?" Mayo Clinic (March 13, 2012), *http://www.mayoclinic.com/health/statins/CL00010.*

28. At a Glance 2011, "Heart Disease and Stroke Prevention: Addressing the Nation's Leading Killer, Centers for Disease Control and Prevention, *http://www.cdc.gov/ chronicdisease/resources/publications/AAG/dhdsp.htm.*

29. Yusuf et al., "Effect of Potentially Modifiable Risk Factors Associated with Myocardial Infarction in 52 Countries (INTERHEART Study): Case-Control Study," *Lancet* 364, no. 9438, (September 11–17, 2004): 937–52.

30. "Is Inflammation the Root of All Disease?" *Berkeley Wellness Letter* (January 2008), *http://www.wellnessletter.com/ucberkeley/feature/inflammation/#.*

31. Pereira et al., "Dietary Fiber and Risk of Coronary Heart Disease: A Pooled Analysis of Cohort Studies," *Archives of Internal Medicine* 164, no. 4 (February 23, 2004): 370–76.

32. Park et al., "Dietary Fiber Intake and Mortality in the NIH-AARP Diet and Health Study," *Archives of Internal Medicine* 171, no. 12 (June 27, 2011): 1061–68.

33. Yang Q., "Gain Weight by 'Going Diet?' Artificial Sweeteners and the Neurobiology of Sugar Cravings," *International Journal of Neuroscience* (2010), *Yale Journal of Biology and Medicine* 83, no. 2 (June 2010): 101–8.

34. Michael L. Dansinger et al., "Comparison of the Atkins, Ornish, Weight Watchers, and Zone Diets for Weight Loss and Heart Disease Risk Reduction: A Randomized Trial," *Journal of the American Medical Association* 293, no. 1 (January 5, 2005): 43–53.

about the authors

Susan Gregory started writing and teaching about the Daniel Fast in 2007. Since then she has come alongside hundreds of thousands of men, women, and teens throughout the world to support them toward a successful fasting experience. Her blog, website, and social media pages have become the leading resource centers for the Daniel Fast. Susan is the author of several books, including the best-selling *The Daniel Fast: Feed Your Soul, Strengthen Your Spirit, and Renew Your Body* and *Out of the Rat Race.* She spent many years working with nationally known ministries, leading her to work and serve in more than thirty-eight countries. Susan enjoys writing, quilt making, gardening, traveling, and learning. Her greatest passion is to help people lead the extraordinary life Jesus came to give them. She is a mother and grandmother and lives on a small farm in central Washington State.

Rick Bloomer received his PhD from the University of North Carolina at Greensboro and held prior positions at Duke University Medical Center and Wake Forest University. He is currently Department Chair of Health and Sport Sciences at the University of Memphis, where he holds the title of Professor and Director of the Cardiorespiratory/Metabolic Laboratory. He is an active researcher, having published well over 100 peer-reviewed scientific manuscripts and book chapters in the areas of oxidative stress, dietary intake, nutraceuticals, and exercise. He has been investigating the health-related effects of the Daniel Fast since 2009. He enjoys spending quality time with his family, weight lifting, playing hockey and baseball, bike riding, inline skating, engaging in a variety of outdoor activities, and listening to music. He lives outside of Memphis, Tennessee, with his wife and their two children.

general index

recipe index

Recipes are capitalized; ingredients are lowercase.

Share Your Thoughts

With the Author: Your comments will be forwarded to the author when you send them to *zauthor@zondervan.com*.

With Zondervan: Submit your review of this book by writing to *zreview@zondervan.com*.

Free Online Resources at
www.zondervan.com

Daily Bible Verses and Devotions: Enrich your life with daily Bible verses or devotions that help you start every morning focused on God. Visit www.zondervan.com/newsletters.

Free Email Publications: Sign up for newsletters on Christian living, academic resources, church ministry, fiction, children's resources, and more. Visit www.zondervan.com/newsletters.

Zondervan Bible Search: Find and compare Bible passages in a variety of translations at www.zondervanbiblesearch.com.

Other Benefits: Register to receive online benefits like coupons and special offers, or to participate in research.